SCOTLAND'S NEW WRITING THEATRE

The Slab Boys Trilogy

by John Byrne

The Traverse Theatre's
40th Anniversary Revival

The revival of
The Slab Boys
opened on Friday 14 November 2003
having premiered at the Traverse Theatre
on 6 April 1978

The revival of
Cuttin' a Rug
opened on 12 December 2003
having premiered at the Traverse Theatre
on 19 May 1979

The revival of
Still Life
opened on Tuesday 30 December 2003
having premiered at the Traverse Theatre
on 27 May 1982

TRAVERSE THEATRE

Powerhouse of new writing DAILY TELEGRAPH

Artistic Director Philip Howard

The Traverse is Scotland's new writing theatre. Founded in 1963 by a group of maverick artists and enthusiasts, it began as an imaginative attempt to capture the spirit of adventure and experimentation of the Edinburgh Festival all year round. Throughout the decades, the Traverse has evolved and grown in artistic output and ambition. It has refined its mission by strengthening its commitment to producing new plays by Scottish and international playwrights and actively nurturing them throughout their careers. Traverse productions have been seen world-wide and tour regularly throughout the UK and overseas.

The Traverse has produced over 600 new plays in its lifetime and, through a spirit of innovation and risk-taking, has launched the careers of many of the country's best known writers. From, among others, Stanley Eveling in the 1960s, John Byrne in the 1970s, Liz Lochhead in the 1980s, to David Greig and David Harrower in the 1990s, the Traverse is unique in Scotland in its dedication to new writing. It fulfils the crucial role of providing the infrastructure, professional support and expertise to ensure the development of a dynamic new writing culture for Scotland.

The Traverse's activities encompass every aspect of playwriting and production, providing and facilitating play reading panels, script development workshops, rehearsed readings, public playwriting workshops, writers groups, discussions and special events. The Traverse's work with young people is of supreme importance and takes the form of encouraging playwriting through its flagship education project, *Class Act*, as well as the Traverse Young Writers Group.

Edinburgh's Traverse Theatre is a mini-festival in itself THE TIMES

From its conception in the 1960s, the Traverse has remained a pivotal venue during the Edinburgh Festival. It receives enormous critical and audience acclaim for its programming, as well as regularly winning awards. In 2001 the Traverse won Fringe Firsts and Herald Angels for its productions *Gagarin Way* and *Wiping My Mother's Arse* and a Herald Archangel for overall artistic excellence. Again in 2002 the Traverse produced two award-winning shows, *Outlying Islands* by David Greig and *Iron* by Rona Munro, which both transferred to the Royal Court Theatre, London. In 2003, *The People Next Door* by Henry Adam picked up a Fringe First and a Herald Angel and transferred immediately to Theatre Royal, Stratford East. The Traverse has also reinforced its international profile and touring activities with performances in Toronto (World Stage Festival), Leipzig, the Salisbury Festival and throughout the Highlands and Islands with *Iron* and *Outlying Islands*. *The People Next Door* will go out on an international tour in 2004.

For further information on the Traverse Theatre's activities and history, an online resource is available at www.virtualtraverse.com. To find out about ways to support the Traverse, please contact Norman MacLeod, Development Manager on 0131 228 3223.

JOHN BYRNE

It is hard somehow to picture John Byrne aged seventeen in 1957, the year *The Slab Boys Trilogy* begins. No Victorian comic-book whiskers, in those days; the brooding look of an Old Testament prophet, which periodically crosses his features, well in the future. But I suspect the twinkle in the eyes, the hint of mischief temporarily held at bay, would have been the same.

He was a dandy then: drainpipe trousers, winkle-pickers and a great camel-haired overcoat from America, the mythically distant continent that was starting to exert such a grip on Scotland's imagination. He remains a dandy today. The artists' smocks wouldn't look out of place in Toulouse-Lautrec's Montmartre; the handmade shoes a flash of luxury amid the boho chic. Spanky and Phil would be proud of him.

If the young Byrne had got his way first time round, *The Slab Boys* would never have been. Paisley's La Scala cinema had first call on the imagination of the boy who had left school early and wanted to be an artist. There a Mr Brown painted each film poster by hand. 'I thought what a glamorous job that would be – like Bollywood for God's sake, not that we'd have known anything about that then. I'd put a portfolio together and I went to see him but he wasn't interested.'

Film posters' loss was theatre's gain. Instead, he sent Byrne to Stoddard's carpet manufacturers in Elderslie where for £2 10s 6d a week he mixed paint: crimson lake, cobalt blue, Persian red, raw sienna, cadmium yellow, French ultramarine and Hooker's green.

It was less sensual than it sounded. 'It was the most boring thing I could ever imagine in the whole wide world. It was bizarre. It was Dickensian. When I came to write about it in the seventies it was like writing about a blacking factory or Fagin's den, with the Artful Dodger and everyone else. It was an Aladdin's Cave full of surreal characters.' These characters, mixed and blended like paint on the slab, would one day become the boys.

Jim Rafferty, older brother of the singer Gerry, was the jumping off point for Spanky. Phil McCann owes most to Byrne himself and to his older brother Jim, 'who was always much more outgoing and gallus than I ever was'. Their mother, Alice, like Phil's, spent much of her life in and out of mental institutions. Her off-stage presence anchors the trilogy and gives it weight. As for Hector, poor, put-upon, bullied Hector. Hector was just Hector. He didn't even change the name . . .

But biography only explains so much. It certainly doesn't make sense of the plays' extraordinary success when they were first produced at the Traverse.

John was tickled in what he saw as the 'very particular and parochial' nature of his work. But that parochialness would not stop *The Slab Boys* being a success on Broadway in 1983, with Val Kilmer, Kevin Bacon and Sean Penn in the leads. What New Yorkers made of Spanky's 'gadgey' dinner suit and Sadie's sugary baps is anyone's guess.

Byrne's theatrical influences were eclectic, eccentric even. 'If I had a model at all it was George Bernard Shaw's *Man and Superman* – can you see the connection there? I can't – and the Whitehall farces. They used to do them on television live from the Whitehall Theatre and somebody always lost their trousers.' At one point, too, he had even decided to tell the story as a musical, with songs by Gerry Rafferty.

With this kind of bastard lineage, *The Slab Boys* had every right to fall flat on its face. Yet through rewrite after rewrite (under the watchful eye of the Traverse's then artistic director Chris Parr), the voice now instantly recognisable as John Byrne's emerged.

'I'd seen sentimental things about Scotland. I'd seen puerile comedies about Scotland. But I'd never seen plays about people like me. For a start, there were no plays written about Catholics: Catholic situations with Catholic protagonists. Everyone on the stage was Church of Scotland or whatever. And yet the Catholic Protestant divide has been a huge part of life on the West Coast of Scotland.

'*The Slab Boys* is not an after-dinner conversation about the fact that the characters are Catholic. That's just who they are – and it gives them a different sensibility. It was about seeing myself portrayed for the first time.'

This act of self-recognition clearly wasn't confined to any one side of the sectarian divide. Scots, the critic Edwin Muir once argued, are condemned to writing in one language and speaking in another. On seeing *The Slab Boys*, one of the more astute Scottish reviewers remarked that it had proved Muir wrong. A sense of inferiority had been shrugged off.

The funny thing is that – as in Irvine Welsh's novel *Trainspotting* – the language of the slab room at AF Stobo and Co Carpet Manufacturers is anything but naturalistic. Often it tends towards the baroque. Phil and Spanky's verbal acrobatics, their penchant for wordplay, verges on the obsessive. Yet it has the freshness of a joke overheard as you wait in line at the butcher's, and it's the perfect medium for Byrne's brand of tragicomedy.

'I wanted to make people laugh and cry at the same time. But in the serious stuff – the hard stuff, the true stuff, the painful stuff, the stuff about Phil's mother – there are even more jokes than in the rest. That's what makes It funny. You think you're watching a comedy, which you are, then you come out and go, hold on, I shouldn't have been laughing at that.' In *The Slab Boys* this dark core keeps sentiment at arm's length.

The carcass of the 1950s gets regularly picked over these days, often re imagined in the rosiest of hues (*Happy Days, Grease*). Not for Byrne. A moralist as well a humorist, his fascination with the decade transcends nostalgia. 'The Fifties never had that gloss for me. What appealed is that it was a much more restrictive time. I hated the Sixties and the Seventies, this alleged liberal time where nothing mattered. When 1960 arrived, it was the end of innocence. The start of the rot set in.'

Byrne's 1957 may be a hard place to grow up: poor, class-ridden and full of small-c conservatives. But in pushing against those boundaries, Phil, Lucille and the rest generate a tremendous anarchic, innocent energy that still seems unquenched 25 years after the first performance.

As Spanky says at the end of *Cuttin' a Rug*: 'Who cares? I'm 19 with a wardrobe full of clothes . . . I've got everything to live for!'

Adrian Turpin
Edinburgh, October 2003

John Byrne was born in Paisley in 1940. He worked as a 'slab boy' at A.F Stoddard, the carpet manufacturers, before going to Glasgow School of Art. There he won a scholarship in painting which enabled him to study in Italy. He then became a graphic artist at Scottish Television and later returned to A F Stoddard as a designer. He became a full time painter in 1968 following his first London exhibition.

John Byrne is also a distinguished theatre designer and playwright. Other plays include WRITER'S CRAMP, NORMAL SERVICE, CARA COCO, CANDY KISSES, COLQUHOUN AND MacBRYDE, and a version of Gogol's THE GOVERNMENT INSPECTOR. On television he is best known for his BAFTA Award-winning series TUTTI FRUTTI and YOUR CHEATIN' HEART. He has also designed for the Traverse Theatre, 7:84, Hampstead Theatre, The Bush Theatre and Scottish Opera. He also wrote and directed BOSWELL & JOHNSON'S TOUR OF THE WESTERN WORLD (BBC TV) and the film of THE SLAB BOYS (Skreba/Channel 4 Films).

THE ORIGINAL PRODUCTIONS

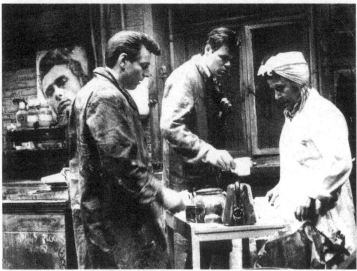

The Slab Boys
Freddie Boardley, Jim Byars, Elaine Collins, Robbie Coltrane, Pat Doyle, Billy McColl,
Ida Shuster, Carey Wilson. Directed by David Hayman. Designed by Grant Hicks.

Cuttin' a Rug
Freddie Boardley,
John Breck,
Elaine Collins,
Robbie Coltrane,
Pat Doyle,
Kay Gallie, Tony
Hollis,
Phyllis Logan,
Ida Schuster,
Carey Wilson.
Directed by
David Hayman.
Designed by
Grant Hicks.

Still Life
Elaine Collins, Andy Gray, Gerard Kelly, Billy McColl, Alexander Morton.
Directed by David Hayman. Designed by John Byrne.

COMPANY BIOGRAPHIES

Neil Alexander (Sound Designer) Neil Alexander's recent designs include: DEMOCRACY, POWER, ELMINA'S KITCHEN, HONOUR, SHE STOOPS TO CONQUER & A LAUGHING MATTER (co-productions with Out Of Joint); A PRAYER FOR OWEN MEANY, LIFE AFTER LIFE, VINCENT IN BRIXTON, MOTHER CLAP'S MOLLY HOUSE, MARRIAGE PLAY/ FINDING THE SUN, REMEMBRANCE OF THINGS PAST, THE WAITING ROOM, BLUE/ORANGE, SPARKLESHARK (National Theatre); THE LYING KIND, YARD GAL, BEEN SO LONG, FAIR GAME, BAILEGANGAIRE, HEREDITY, PENETRATOR (Royal Court); MACBETH (Sheffield Crucible); OBSERVE THE SONS OF ULSTER MARCHING TOWARDS THE SOMME (Pleasance). Other design credits include: TWO HORSEMEN (Gate/Bush); THE SNAKE HOUSE (Greenwich); THE YEAR OF THE FAMILY (Finborough).

Lorne Campbell (Assistant Director) Lorne's assistant directorship at the Traverse is funded by Channel 4 Theatre Director Scheme. For the Traverse: DARK EARTH, OUTLYING ISLANDS, MR PLACEBO, HOMERS, CLASS ACT. Before joining the Traverse he ran Forge Theatre Company for four years. His directing credits include: DEATH AND THE MAIDEN; THE CHEVIOT, THE STAG AND THE BLACK BLACK OIL; THE CHAIRS; THE DUMB WAITER; COMEDY OF ERRORS; OLEANNA. Trained: MA at RSAMD, BA at Liverpool John Moores.

Rick Fisher (Lighting Designer) Recent theatre work includes: A WOMAN OF NO IMPORTANCE (Theatre Royal, Haymarket); HAMLET (EIF, Barcelona, Birmingham); HONOUR (National Theatre); RED DEMON, PERIBANEZ (Young Vic). Other theatre includes FAR AWAY (New York); A NUMBER (Royal Court); A RUSSIAN IN THE WOODS (RSC); MOTHER CLAP'S MOLLY HOUSE (National Theatre); LOBBY HEROES, A BOSTON MARRIAGE (Donmar); BLUE/ORANGE (National Theatre and West End); THE HUNCHBACK OF NOTRE DAME (Disney, in Berlin); VIA DOLOROSA (Royal Court and Broadway). Winner of 1998 Olivier Award for Best Lighting Design for LADY IN THE DARK and CHIPS WITH EVERYTHING (both National Theatre). Previously won an Olivier Award for MOONLIGHT (Almeida and Comedy), MACHINAL (National Theatre), HYSTERIA (Royal Court); and a Tony Award for AN INSPECTOR CALLS on Broadway. Recent opera includes: JERRY SPRINGER THE OPERA (West End, National Theatre); MADAME MAO (Santa Fe); THE LITTLE PRINCE (Houston Grand Opera); WOZZEK (Royal Opera House); TURANDOT (Bolshoi, Moscow); TRAVIATA (Santa Fe); LA VESTALE (English National Opera). Dance includes the award-winning SWAN LAKE (London, Los Angeles and Broadway); CINDERELLA (London and Los Angeles) for Matthew Bourne's Adventures in Motion Pictures. Currently working on the new operas SNOW IN JUNE (Boston) and FIERY ANGEL (Bolshoi, Moscow). Rick is Chairman of the British Association of Lighting Designers, and is also Visiting Professor in Lighting Design at the Dramatisk Institut, Stockholm.

Paul Thomas Hickey (*Phil*)   Trained: RSAMD. For the Traverse: GAGARIN WAY, GREEN FIELD, OLGA, PASSING PLACES, THE ARCHITECT. Other theatre work includes: SAN DIEGO (EIF/Tron); THE ENTERTAINER (Citizens); THE BACKROOM (The Bush), SAILMAKER, TWELFTH NIGHT (TAG), A.D., MACBETH, ECSTASY, WASTED, MACBETH (Raindog), JUMP THE LIFE TO COME (7:84 Scotland), SHINING SOULS (Peter Hall Company at the Old Vic), MAINSTREAM, TIMELESS (Suspect Culture), CRAVE (Paines Plough/Royal Court). Television includes: TINSEL TOWN, NIGHTLIFE, CARDIAC ARREST, THE JACOBITES (BBC), TAGGART, HIGH ROAD, THE BRITOIL FRAUD (STV) THE SWEETEST FEELING (Starcatch). Radio work includes several plays for BBC Radio Scotland including: BATTLE OF THE AIRWAVES, BODIES OCCUPATION, THE BASEMENT TAPES, PASSING PLACES. Film work includes: WANTING AND GETTING, THE LUCKY SUIT, CALIFORNIA SUNSHINE, CHARMED, LAY OF THE LAND.

Philip Howard (Director – *Cuttin' A Rug*)   Trained under Max Stafford-Clark at the Royal Court Theatre, London, on the Regional Theatre Young Director Scheme from 1988-90. Associate Director at the Traverse from 1993-6, and Artistic Director since 1996. Productions at the Traverse include 16 world premieres of plays by David Greig, David Harrower, Catherine Czerkawska, Ronan O'Donnell, Nicola McCartney, Linda McLean, Sue Glover, Iain Heggie, Iain F MacLeod and the late Iain Crichton Smith. Fringe First awards for KILL THE OLD TORTURE THEIR YOUNG, WIPING MY MOTHER'S ARSE and OUTLYING ISLANDS. Other productions at the Traverse include FAITH HEALER by Brian Friel, THE TRESTLE AT POPE LICK CREEK by Naomi Wallace, and, as Co-Director, SOLEMN MASS FOR A FULL MOON IN SUMMER by Michel Tremblay (also Barbican Centre, London). Productions elsewhere include THE SPECULATOR by David Greig in Catalan (Grec Festival, Barcelona), ENTERTAINING MR SLOANE (Royal, Northampton) and SOMETHING ABOUT US (Lyric Hammersmith Studio). Radio: BEING NORWEGIAN by David Greig (BBC Scotland).

Molly Innes (*Lucille*)   For the Traverse: GREEN FIELD, SOLEMN MASS FOR A FULL MOON IN SUMMER, WIDOWS, SHINING SOULS, STONES AND ASHES. Other theatre work includes: WIT (Stellar Quines); THE GOOD WOMAN OF SETZUAN, ANTIGONE (TAG); PLASTICINE (Royal Court); BLOODED (Boilerhouse); A LISTENING HEAVEN, JEKYLL AND HYDE, TO KILL A MOCKING BIRD, THE PRIME OF MISS JEAN BRODIE (Royal Lyceum); TIMELESS (Suspect Culture); DOING BIRD (Cat 'A' Theatre & UK Tour); PLAYBOY OF THE WESTERN WORLD (Communicado); THE STINGING SEA (Citizens); TARTUFFE (Dundee Rep); JOLLY ROBERT/GLORIA GOODHEART (Theatre Workshop); HAMLET (National Theatre Workshop). Television work includes: TAGGART (STV), REBUS (Clerkenwell Films); PSYCHOS (Channel 4); LIFE SUPPORT, A MUG'S GAME, STRATHBLAIR, THE FERGUSON THEORY,

RAB C NESBITT, TAKIN' OVER THE ASYLUM, TREV AND SIMON (BBC); THE BILL (Thames). Film work includes: AFTERLIFE (Gabriel Films); RATCATCHER (Holy Cow Films); STELLA DOES TRICKS (Channel 4); KARMIC MOTHERS (Fresh Films). Awards: Ian Charleson Awards commendation for ELECTRA (Theatre Babel); The Stage Awards Best Actress nomination for MOVING (Brunton).

John Kazek (*Jack Hogg/Terry*) For the Traverse: SOLEMN MASS FOR A FULL MOON IN SUMMER (Traverse/Barbican), PERFECT DAYS (Traverse/Vaudeville), PASSING PLACES, THE CHIC NERDS, STONES AND ASHES, KING OF THE FIELDS, EUROPE. Other theatre includes: THEBANS, UNCLE VANYA, MACBETH, DOLLS HOUSE, 'TIS PITY SHE'S A WHORE (Babel); WORD FOR WORD (Magnetic North); PLEASURE AND PAIN, GLUE, A MIDSUMMER NIGHT'S DREAM, THE CARETAKER (Citizen Theatre); MARABOU STORK NIGHTMARES (Citizens/Leicester); VARIETY (Grid Iron); THE BIG FUNK (Arches); PENETRATOR (Tron); MARY QUEEN OF SCOTS, KIDNAPPED (Lyceum); NAE PROBLEM, GOVAN STORIES (7:84); TWILIGHT SHIFT (7:84/Edinburgh Festival); GREAT EXPECTATIONS (Lyric, Belfast); WUTHERING HEIGHTS, DRIVING MISS DAISY (Byre), KING LEAR, AS YOU LIKE IT (Oxford Stage Company); JUST FRANK (Stratford East). Film and television credits include: HOW D'YAE WANT TAE DIE (Dead Man's Shoes Ltd); NATURAL HISTORY (Scorpio Films); THE KEY (BBC/Little Bird); YOUNG ADAM (Recorded Picture Company); AUF WIEDERSEHEN PET, CITY CENTRAL, DOUBLE NOUGAT, RAB C NESBITT, PUNCH DRUNK, STRATHBLAIR, NERVOUS ENERGY, CASUALTY (BBC); TAGGART, HIGH ROAD (STV); RIFF RAFF (Parallax Pictures); SILENT SCREAM (Antonine Productions).

Struan Leslie (Movement Director) Training as dancer and choreographer: Royston Maldoon, London Contemporary Dance School, The Naropa Institute Colorado. Over the last fifteen years, Struan has been establishing a movement practice that develops the physical skills and abilities of actors, singers and educationalists both as facillitators and participants. This has resulted in Struan being involved in a wide area of movement application from Plays and Musical Theatre to Urban Design and Architecture. Movement direction includes for the Traverse: SOLEMN MASS FOR A FULL MOON IN SUMMER (also BITE at the Barbican). Other recent work includes: THE GIRL OF SAND (Almeida Opera); JEPHTHA, JENUFA (Welsh National Opera); IVANOV, ORESTEIA (National Theatre); ATTEMPTS ON HER LIFE (Teatro Piccolo, Milan); A MIDSUMMER NIGHT'S DREAM (Regent's Park); IPHIGENIA AT AULIS (Abbey Theatre); JULIUS CAESAR (Young Vic/Japanese tour also as actor); ENDGAME (Donmar Warehouse), ANTIGONE (TAG); AS YOU LIKE IT, MERCHANT OF VENICE, CYRANO DE BERGERAC (RSC). As a director his work includes six devised theatre pieces for his own ensemble The Water Company including THE HOLY WHORE and

SexyGenderBaby. Other direction includes: OPERA CUTS CARMEN (Welsh National Opera); MOURNING BECOMES ELECTRA, SERIOUS MONEY (ArtsEd London); 10,000 BROKEN MIRRORS, SPINNING (Oval House); KATYA KABANOVA (Geneva). His many Education posts include: Lecturer in Dance and Choreography, Physical Education and Primary Education, at University of Greenwich; Visiting Professor at University of Illinois as a director and deviser of new theatre. Future plans include OLIVER TWIST at the Lyric, Hammersmith London.

Una McLean (*Sadie*)   Born in Strathaven and trained at RSAMD. For the Traverse: FAMILY, THE ARCHITECT, SKY WOMAN FALLING, BLENDING IN, INES DE CASTRO. Other theatre includes: VAGINA MONOLGUES (EFT/Glasgow Theatre Royal); FIVE BLUE HAIRED LADIES SITTING ON A PARK BENCH (National tour, Brian Hewitt-Jones); OKLAHOMA (Perth); SHINING SOULS, BEAUTY QUEEN OF LEENANE (Tron); PERFECT DAYS (Borderline); ALBERTINE IN FIVE TIMES (Clyde Unity Theatre); LOVERS, THE STEAMIE (Royal Lyceum); MRS WARREN, A PASSIONATE WOMAN (Pitlochry); BOURGEOIS GENTILHOMME (Dundee Rep); COUPLES (Cacciatore Fabbro Prods, Edinburgh Festival); REVOLTING PEASANTS (7:84); PADDY'S MARKET (Tron); ANNIE (Perth); BEGGAR'S OPERA, FIDDLER ON THE ROOF (Scottish Opera). She has played pantomimes for 25 years uninterrupted including CINDERELLA, SNOW WHITE, ALADDIN and BABES IN THE WOOD. Television work includes her own shows DID YOU SEE UNA? and the children's series CAPTAIN BONNY. Scottish Television profiled Una in an hour long ARTERY special, NUMERO UNA. Film work includes: STRICTLY SINATRA (Universal Focus); NAN (Scottish Screen); THE DEBT COLLECTOR (Film Four/Pine Film); SMALL MOMENTS (The Short Film Factory). Una was awarded a Doctorate of Letters in 1995 from Edinburgh's Queen Margaret College.

Michael Mackenzie (*Willy Curry, Workman*)   Trained at Bristol Old Vic Theatre School. Started professionally at Worthing Rep in 1967, and performed widely in England before moving back to Scotland in 1975. For the Traverse: THE CASE OF DAVID ANDERSON, Q.C. He has appeared in over 30 productions at the Royal Lyceum and nine seasons in Pitlochry. Among many roles have been Robert Burns, Armstrong in ARMSTRONG'S LAST GOODNIGHT, Higgins in PYGMALION, Elyot in PRIVATE LIVES, Richard Greatham in HAY FEVER, Hobson in HOBSON'S CHOICE, Crichton in THE ADMIRABLE CRICHTON, Oliphant in LET WIVES TAK TENT, James Tyrone in LONG DAY'S JOURNEY INTO NIGHT, Walter in THE PRICE, Joe Gargery in GREAT EXPECTATIONS and Salieri in AMADEUS. Last season at the Lyceum he was in THE TAMING OF THE SHREW, was Merlin in MERLIN THE MAGNIFICENT, and Littlejohn in THE BREATHING HOUSE. He has just finshed playing Tulliver in a Nottingham Playhouse/Exeter Northcott co-production of THE MILL ON THE FLOSS. His TV work includes: Tarot in ACE OF

WANDS (Thames TV); Four IAGGARTs (STV); Ferdinand McLopez in HAMISH MACBETH, THE FOURTH ARM (BBC); two American mini-series PETER THE GREAT and MUSSOLINI; Dr Graham Turner in three series of CARDIAC ARREST (World Productions). Michael appears frequently in plays and readings on radio, and is proud to be the chair of West Lothian Youth Theatre.

Iain Robertson (*Spanky*)   Iain trained at the Sylvia Young Theatre School. Theatre credits include: THE GOOD HOPE, THE WINTER'S TALE, THE MYSTERIES (National Theatre); THE TEMPEST (Sheffield Crucible/The Old Vic); PASSING PLACES (Derby Playhouse/Greenwich); SUMMERTIME BLUES (Access All Areas TC); GIE'S PEACE (Govan TC); SPROGGS (Toonspeak TC). Television work includes: GUNPOWDER, TREASON AND PLOT (Box TV for BBC); KINGFISHER TAILOR ANIMATION; TAGGART, INSPECTOR REBUS (STV); BAND OF BROTHERS (Dreamworks); OLIVER TWIST (Diplomat Films); PSYCHOS (Kudos Prods); TRIAL BY JURY, SILENT WITNESS, A MUG'S GAME, RAB C NESBITT (BBC); THE BILL (Thames); KAVANAGH QC, BRAMWELL (Carlton). Film includes: ONE LAST CHANCE (Hero Films); WATCHMEN (Blue Glass Prods); FAT CHANCE (Wiggin O'Neill Films); THE MATCH (Football Match Films); THE DEBT COLLECTOR (Dragon Pictures); PLUNKETT & MACLEANE (Macleane Productions); SMALL FACES (Easterhouse/BBC Films); POACHED (Freshwaters Films); HOMESICK (Halo Prods). Radio includes: THE NATIVITY, THE PASSION (BBC Radio 4), ROMEO & JULIET, THE PRISONER OF PAPA STOUR (BBC World Service). Iain received a Scottish 'Best Performance' BAFTA for SMALL FACES, and was nominated twice for the Ian Charleson award receiving a commendation for THE MYSTERIES and third prize for THE TEMPEST.

Grant O'Rourke (*Alan*)   Will graduate from RSAMD in June 2004. For the Traverse: RENTS (rehearsed reading Anniversary Season 2003). Other theatre work includes: Richard III (RSAMD/Polish International Shakespeare Fetsival); THE COCK ARTIST (RSAMD/Tron); Teddy in FAITH HEALER (Hurrah Productions); Oedipus in OEDIPUS REX, THREE SISTERS, ROMEO & JULIET (RSAMD); LIKE LEAVES IN AUTUMN (Turin Historical Theatre); THE NORMAL HEART (Majick Men Theatre).

Roxana Silbert (Director – *The Slab Boys* and *Still Life*)   Currently Literary Director of the Traverse, previously Associate Director at Royal Court Theatre and West Yorkshire Playhouse. For the Traverse: THE PEOPLE NEXT DOOR (also Theatre Royal, Stratford East), 15 SECONDS, IRON (also Royal Court), GREEN FIELD, QUARTZ. For the Royal Court: BEEN SO LONG, FAIRGAME, BAZAAR, SWEETHEART, ESSEX GIRLS, MULES, WOUNDS TO HER FACE, VOICES FOR NINE (Barclays New Stages) and Artistic Director of COMING ON STRONG (Young Writers Festival 1994). Roxana has also directed THE FAST SHOW LIVE (Phil McIntyre Productions at the Apollo Hammersmith and National Tour),

PRECIOUS (West Yorkshire Playhouse), SPLASH HATCH ON THE E
GOING DOWN (Donmar Warehouse), CADILLAC RANCH (Soho Theatre),
A SERVANT OF TWO MASTERS (Crucible Theatre), TRANSLATIONS and
TOP GIRLS (New Vic), THE PRICE (Bolton Octagon), LOVE (London Opera
festival), TWO HORSEMEN (Bush Theatre/Gate Theatre), THE LOVERS
(Gate), THE TREATMENT (Intercity Festival, Florence), BACKSTROKE IN A
CROWDED POOL (National Theatre Pakistan/British Council). Television
includes: THE FAST SHOW LIVE (BBC); OPERA LOVERS, APHRODISIAC
(World Productions). Radio includes: A DAY IN THE LIFE OF A HUMBLE
BEE, THE TALL ONE (BBC R4); BRACE POSITION (BBC Radio Scotland).

Ros Steen (Voice/Dialect Coach)   Trained at RSAMD. Has worked
extensively in theatre, film and TV. For the Traverse: DARK EARTH,
HOMERS, OUTLYING ISLANDS, THE BALLAD OF CRAZY PAOLA, THE
TRESTLE AT POPE LICK CREEK, HERITAGE (2001 and 1998), AMONG
UNBROKEN HEARTS, SHETLAND SAGA, SOLEMN MASS FOR A FULL
MOON IN SUMMER (as co-director), KING OF THE FIELDS, HIGHLAND
SHORTS, FAMILY, KILL THE OLD TORTURE THEIR YOUNG, THE CHIC
NERDS, GRETA, LAZYBED, KNIVES IN HENS, PASSING PLACES,
BONDAGERS, ROAD TO NIRVANA, SHARP SHORTS, MARISOL, GRACE
IN AMERICA. Recent theatre work includes: DANCING AT LUGHNASA,
DUCHESS OF MALFI, (Dundee Rep); BASH, DAMN JACOBITE BITCHES,
OBSERVE THE SONS OF ULSTER MARCHING TOWARDS THE SOMME
(Citizens' Theatre); WORD FOR WORD (Magnetic North); CAVE
DWELLERS (7:84); EXILES (Jervis Young Directors/Young Vic); THE PRIME
OF MISS JEAN BRODIE, PLAYBOY OF THE WESTERN WORLD (Royal
Lyceum); SUNSET SONG (Prime Productions); THE BEAUTY QUEEN OF
LEENANE (Tron); SINGLES NIGHT, HOME (LookOUT); THE PRICE (Brunton);
TRAINSPOTTING (G & J Productions). Films include: SMALL LOVE,
GREGORY'S TWO GIRLS, TV includes: ROCKFACE, 2000 ACRES OF SKY.

Dawn Steele (*Bernadette*)   Theatre credits include ELECTRA and
MEDEA for Theatre Babel. Television work includes: Mary in THE KEY,
Lexie in MONARCH OF THE GLEN (5 series), Laura in SNODDY, TINSEL
TOWN, HAYWIRE, SPLIT SECOND, IN SEARCH OF THE UNICORNS,
RAIN DOG PILOT (BBC); HIGHLANDER – WAR AND PEACE (Raindog
for BBC); DREAMS AND RECOLLECTIONS (STV). Film includes: TABLOID
TV (Tabloid TV Prods); CLUB LE MONDE (Club Le Monde Films); THE
DEBT COLLECTOR (Dragon Pictures); GREGORY'S TWO GIRLS (Film
Four Ltd).

Alan Tripney (*Hector*)   Theatre includes: THE CHRYSALIDS (Complete
Productions); THE TWITS, SCROOGE (Citizens); U.N., SAVAGE, LORD
OF THE FLIES (Raindog). College appearances include: THE DON,
BRUTOPIA, THE HYPOCHONDRIAC, THE WAR OF THE ROSES,
PROMETEUS BOUND, THE MOUNTAIN GIANTS, ATTEMPTS ON HER
LIFE (RSAMD). Graduated 2003.

Anne Marie Timoney (*Miss Walkinshaw*)   For the Traverse: ANNA WEISS, WIDOWS, WORMWOOD, STONES AND ASHES. Other theatre includes: THE CUTTING ROOM, THE NUN, DIAL M FOR MURDER, THE TRIALS OF OSCAR WILDE, DAMN'D JACOBITE BITCHES, THE CHERRY ORCHARD (Citizens); THE BEAUTY QUEEN OF LEENANE, PADDY'S MARKET, MARLENE – FALLING IN LOVE AGAIN (Tron); THE MEETING, OTHELLO, DEATH OF A SALESMAN, THE MERCHANT OF VENICE, (Lyceum); CASANOVA (Suspect Culture); ASYLUM, ASYLUM, HUEY ON THE WIRE (Wiseguise); ROAD, LONG STORY SHORT (7:84). Television includes: VELVET SOUP, KARMIC MOTHERS, BAD BOYS, RUFFIAN HEARTS, ATLETICO PARTICK, FRAN'S PEOPLE (BBC); TAGGART, HIGH ROAD, DR FINLAY (STV); PSYCHOS (Channel 4). Film includes: NATURAL HISTORY (Scorpio Films); YOUNG ADAM (Recorded Picture Company); WILBUR WANTS TO KILL HIMSELF (Sigma Films); THE HOUSE OF MIRTH (Three Rivers); GREGORY'S TWO GIRLS (Young Lake); CARLA'S SONG, RIFF RAFF (Parallax).

Neil Warmington (Designer)   Graduated in Fine Art Painting at Maidstone College of Art before attending the post-graduate Theatre design Course at Motley, London. For The Traverse: HELMET (Traverse/ Paines Plough), WIPING MY MOTHER'S ARSE, GAGARIN WAY (also RNT and Arts Theatre and on tour), SOLEMN MASS FOR A FULL MOON IN SUMMER, KING OF THE FIELDS, FAMILY, PASSING PLACES (TMA Award for Best Design). Recent Theatre includes: THE STRAITS, DROWNED WORLD, SPLENDOUR, RIDDANCE (Paines Plough); THE BIRTHDAY PARTY (TAG); KING LEAR (Old Vic), LOVES LABOURS LOST, DON JUAN, TAMING OF THE SHREW (English Touring Theatre); DESIRE UNDER THE ELMS, JANE EYRE (Barclays Stage Award for Design – Shared Experience): THE DUCHESS OF MALFI (Bath Theatre Royal); LIFE OF STUFF (Donmar Warehouse); WOYZECK, COMEDIANS, GLASS MENAGERIE (Lyceum, Edinburgh); DISSENT, ANGELS IN AMERICA (7:84); HENRY V (RSC); MUCH ADO ABOUT NOTHING (Queen's London); THE TEMPEST (Contact); WAITING FOR GODOT (Liverpool Everyman); PLAYHOUSE CREATURES, FIDDLER ON THE ROOF, LIFE IS A DREAM -TMA award for best design (West Yorkshire Playhouse); LIFE OF STUFF (Donmar Warehouse);TROILUS AND CRESSIDA (Opera North); OEDIPUS REX (Connecticut State Opera); MARRIAGE OF FIGARO (Garsington Opera). Designed the launch of Glasgow 1999 Year of Architecture. He has also won the Linbury Prize for Stage Design and the Sir Alfred Munnings Florence Prize for Painting.

'SLAB FOR THE BOYS' SUPPORTERS

Our thanks go to the following people for supporting the restaging of
The Slab Boys Trilogy by buying a 'Slab for the Boys'

ADRIENNE CHALMERS
ALAN CAMERON
ALEX SUMMERS
ANDREW BURNET
CATHARINE WARD THOMPSON
CHRISTINE HAMILTON
CLARA, PAOLA & ROBERTA DOYLE
IN MEMORY OF JOHN DOYLE/BRECK
DAMIAN KILLEEN – THE POVERTY ALLIANCE
DOROTHY DEY OF MIAM-MIAN EDINBURGH
DR KENNETH C. B. WILKIE
EDINBURGH CITY LABOUR PARTY
FENELLA KERR
FELICITY THOMSON ('FLISS')
FIONA & JENNY McDONALD
GLENFINLAS LTD.
HALLA BELOFF
IAIN F. MACLEOD
IAIN MILLAR
JANET & JIM McCOLL
JOAN & JERRY MATTSON
LESLEY & JOHN STONE
LESLEY HINDS – LORD PROVOST OF EDINBURGH
MARILYN IMRIE
MICHAEL & JANE RIDINGS
MRS GLORIA HUGHES
MRS JOAN CLARK
PATRICIA D. STANIFORTH
REX & ANNE BIRCHENOUGH
RICHARD BUCKLAND
RICHARD BURTLES
ROBIN HARPER
SARA MACAULAY
SENAY BOZTAS
STEPHEN COTTON
STUART HEPBURN
AND ANONYMOUS DONORS

The above inscriptions will appear on their very own personalised,
colourful 'slab' in the Traverse Bar Café, to commemorate
the re-staging of this trilogy in our 40th Anniversary year.

Some 'slabs' are still available, to support this production. Please contact
either Norman McLeod or Graeme Davies on 0131 228 3223.

SPONSORSHIP

Sponsorship income enables the Traverse to commission and produce new plays and to offer audiences a diverse and exciting programme of events throughout the year

We would like to thank the following companies for their support throughout the year

CORPORATE SPONSORS

 (UK) LIMITED
www.acseurope.com

BANK OF SCOTLAND

LAURENCE SMITH & SON
(EDINBURGH) LTD
WINE AND SPIRIT SHIPPERS
Established 1883

 smg tv productions

 BAIRDS fine and country wines

 ESPC

 KPMG

B B C Scotland

Canon

 ARCAS Computing Ltd.

 pinnacle communications ltd

STEWARTS

NICHOLAS
GROVES
RAINES
ARCHITECTS

CHAMPAGNE
ALAIN THIENOT
REIMS · FRANCE

 Nomad

ANNIVERSARY ANGELS

A Burrell Company/EDI Group Joint Venture

edNET internetworkingsolutions

BENNETT & ROBERTSON LLP

 Priority Management Training
People & Projects

Jean McGhee
R E C R U I T M E N T

 BAILLIE GIFFORD

Whiteburn
projects limited

grey*friars*
chartered accountants

 New Horizons Computer Learning Centers
Scotland

This theatre has the support of the Pearson Playwright's Scheme sponsored by Pearson plc

The Traverse Trivia Quiz in association with Tennents

With thanks to Douglas Hall of IMPact Human Resourcing for management advice arranged through the Arts & Business Skills Bank.

Thanks to Claire Aitken of Royal Bank of Scotland for mentoring support arranged through the Arts & Business Mentoring Scheme.

Purchase of the Traverse Box Office, computer network and technical and training equipment has been made possible with money from The Scottish Arts Council National Lottery Fund.

Scottish **Arts** Council
LOTTERY FUNDED

The Traverse Theatre's work would not be possible without the support of

 Scottish **Arts** Council

 •EDINBVRGH•
THE CITY OF EDINBURGH COUNCIL

The Traverse Theatre receives financial assistance from

The Calouste Gulbenkian Foundation, The Peggy Ramsay Foundation, The Binks Trust, The Bulldog Prinsep Theatrical Fund, The Esmée Fairbairn Foundation, The Gordon Fraser Charitable Trust, The Garfield Weston Foundation, The Paul Hamlyn Foundation, The Craignish Trust, Lindsay's Charitable Trust, The Tay Charitable Trust, The Ernest Cook Trust, The Wellcome Trust, The Sir John Fisher Foundation, The Ruben and Elisabeth Rausing Trust, The Equity Trust Fund, The Cross Trust, N Smith Charitable Settlement, Douglas Heath Eves Charitable Trust, The Bill and Margaret Nicol Charitable Trust, The Emile Littler Foundation, Mrs M Guido's Charitable Trust, Gouvernement du Québec, The Canadian High Commission, The British Council

Charity No. SC002368

For their generous help on
THE SLAB BOYS TRILOGY
the Traverse would like to thank

George Grant at A.F Stoddard's Carpet Factory
Behar Carpets, Howe Street
Storrie's Home Bakery, Leith Walk
Royal Lyceum Theatre
Edinburgh City Council, Inverleith Workshop
Dundee Rep Theatre
Brian at Alpha Marble Importers
Mr Kersley at Edinburgh Pen Shop
Sarah Hepworth at Glasgow School of Art Archive
Deneon at Bonhams Auctioneers of London
Helen Redmond-Cooper at Bank of Scotland Archive
The Deepsea Fish Shop, Edinburgh
Kevin at Edinburgh School of Art College Shop
Anne at Manacraft, Leather & Highland Co.
Kylie Harper at Swedish Match
Kevin Ritchy at Fiber Star Drums
National Library
Scotsman Newspaper
Jonathan Russel at Paisley Daily Express
Mike Hunter
Cornellissen & Son Ltd, Artists' Colourman

Sets, props and costumes for *The Slab Boys Trilogy*
created by Traverse Workshops
(funded by the National Lottery)

Scottish
Arts Council
LOTTERY FUNDED

Production photography by Douglas Robertson
Print photography by Euan Myles

For their continued generous support
of Traverse productions the Traverse thanks

Habitat
Marks and Spencer, Princes Street
Camerabase
BHS

TRAVERSE THEATRE – THE COMPANY

The Slab Boys Trilogy

JOHN BYRNE

The Slab Boys Trilogy

THE SLAB BOYS
CUTTIN' A RUG
STILL LIFE

faber and faber

First published in 2003
by Faber and Faber Limited
Bloomsbury House
74-77 Great Russell Street
London, WC1B 3DA

Typeset by Country Setting, Kingsdown, Kent CT14 8ES
Printed and bound by CPI Group (UK) Ltd, Croydon, CR0 4YY

Earlier versions of these plays were first published
as *Threads* in *A Decade's Drama: Six Scottish Plays*
by Woodhouse Books in 1980
then as *The Slab Boys*, *Cuttin' a Rug* and *Still Life*
by The Salamander Press, Edinburgh, in 1982

The right of John Byrne to be identified as author
of this work has been asserted in accordance with Section 77
of the Copyright, Designs and Patents Act 1988

A CIP record for this book
is available from the British Library

ISBN 0-571-22345-1

Contents

THE SLAB BOYS

The Slab Boys was revived at the Traverse Theatre, Edinburgh, on 14 November 2003. The cast (in order of appearance) was as follows:

Spanky Iain Robertson
Hector Alan Tripney
Phil Paul Thomas Hickey
Willie Curry Michael Mackenzie
Jack Hogg John Kazek
Alan Grant O'Rourke
Sadie Una McLean
Lucille Molly Innes

Director Roxana Silbert
Designer Neil Warmington
Lighting Designer Rick Fisher
Sound Designer Neil Alexander
Assistant Director Lorne Campbell
Voice Coach Ros Steen
Stage Manager Dougie Wilson
Deputy Stage Manager Gemma Smith
Assistant Stage Manager Kenna Grant

The Slab Boys was first performed at the Traverse Theatre, Edinburgh, on 6 April 1978. The cast (in order of appearance) was as follows:

Spanky Jim Byars
Hector Pat Doyle
Phil Billy McColl
Willie Curry Carey Wilson
Jack Hogg Robbie Coltrane
Alan Freddie Boardley
Sadie Ida Schuster
Lucille Elaine Collins

Directed by David Hayman
Designed by Grant Hicks

This production was revived at the Royal Court Theatre, London, on 17 November 1982, with the folowing cast:

Spanky Gerard Kelly
Hector Iain Andrew
Phil Billy McColl
Willie Curry Alexander Morton
Jack Hogg Andrew Gray
Alan Nicholas Sherry
Sadie Jan Wilson
Lucille Elaine Collins

Directed by David Hayman
Designed by John Byrne
Lighting designed by Colin Scott

Characters

Phil McCann
A Slab Boy. Nineteen. An artist with
great natural talent, as yet uncelebrated.
Working class, from Ferguslie Park (Feegie)

George 'Spanky' Farrell
A Slab Boy. Nineteen.
From the same background as Phil

Hector McKenzie
Slab Boy and 'runt of the litter'.
Nineteen, but small for his age

Jack Hogg
A Designer. Early twenties.
Very bad skin and hand-crafted lumberjackets

Lucille Bentley
Sketcher. Every Slab Boy's dream

Alan Downie
A new boy

Willie Curry
The Gaffer. Mid-fifties. Scourge of the Slab Room

Sadie
The tea lady. Middle-aged. Bad feet

Scene

The Slab Room is a small paint-spattered room adjacent to the Design Studio at A. F. Stobo & Co., Carpet Manufacturers. It is here that the powder colour used by the designers in the preparation of the paper patterns is ground and dished. The colour is kept in large cardboard drums. It is heaped onto marble slabs by the Slab Boys (apprentice designers), water and gum arabic is added, and it is ground with large palette knives till deemed fit to be dished. A window overlooks the factory sheds from where the distant hum of looms drifts up. Beneath the window is a sink. Beside the sink are stacks of small pottery dishes (some of them very dirty). There is a broom cupboard in one corner of the room. Rolls of drafting paper, rug samples, paint rags etc. litter the shelves and floor. A large poster of James Dean (unidentified) hangs on the wall. The action takes place during the morning and afternoon of a Friday in the winter of 1957.

Act One

The Slab Room. Enter George 'Spanky' Farrell in dust-coat, drainpipe trousers, Tony Curtis hair-do, crepe-soled shoes. He crosses to his slab and starts working. Enter Hector McKenzie, similarly attired in dustcoat. He is shorter and weedier than Spanky. He wears spectacles and carries a portable radio.

Spanky Hey, where'd you get the wireless, Heck? Never seen you with that this morning . . .

Hector Had it planked down the bog . . . didn't want 'you-know-who' to see it.

Spanky Does it work? Give's a shot . . . (*Grabs radio.*) Where's Luxembourg?

Hector Watch it, Spanky . . . you'll break it! You can't get Luxembourg . . . it's not dark enough.

Spanky Aw . . . d'you need a dark wireless? I never knew that. Mebbe if we pull the aerial out a bit . . . (*He does so. It comes away in his hand.*)

Hector You swine, look what you've done!

Spanky Ach, that's easy fixed . . .

Hector Give us it. (*Twiddles knobs. Gets Terry Dene singing 'A White Sport Coat'.*)

Spanky Good God, could you not've brung in a more modern wireless? That's donkey's out of date.

Hector I like it.

Spanky That's 'cos you're a tube, Hector.

Enter Phil McCann in street clothes and carrying a portfolio under his arm. He sets folio down behind the door.

Morning, Phil. You're early the day . . . (*Consults wristwatch painted on wrist.*) 'S only half-eleven.

Phil Anybody been looking for us?

Spanky Willie Curry was in ten minutes ago looking for that lemon-yellow you promised, but I told him you had diarrhoea and you'd take a big dish of it down to him later on.

Phil (*changing into dustcoat*) Who belongs to the juke-box?

Hector 'S mines . . .

Enter Willie Curry.

Curry Ha . . . there you are, McCann. Where've you been this morning? Farrell there said you were unwell.

Phil Er . . . um . . . yes . . .

Curry C'mon, what was up with you?

Phil Er . . . touch of the . . . er . . . drawhaw.

Curry The what?

Phil Dee-oh-raw-ho . . . the skitters . . . it was very bad.

Curry Why didn't you come to me earlier? I could've got Nurse to have a look at you . . .

Phil No . . . it's not what you'd cry a 'spectator sport', Mr Curly . . .

Curry In future you report all illnesses to me . . . first thing. How I am I supposed to keep tabs on you lot if I don't know where the devil you are?

Phil I was down the lavvies . . .

Curry You wouldn't get much done down there . . .

Phil Oh, I wouldn't say that, Mr Corrie.

Curry Godstruth, I don't know . . . If I'd had you chaps out in Burma. Diarrhoea? There were men in my platoon fighting the Japanese with dysentry.

Spanky How did they fire it – from chip baskets?

Curry Less of your damned cheek, Farrell. A couple of years in the Forces would smarten your ideas up a bit . . . they'd soon have those silly duck's-arse haircuts off you. And what've I told you about bringing that bloody contraption in, eh?

Spanky What contraption?

Curry How d'you expect to get any work done with that racket going on?

Spanky Pardon?

Curry Whoever owns this gadget can ask Mr Barton for it back.

Protests from boys.

I'll be calling back in five minutes and if you bunch are still lounging about you're for the high jump, understand? Now, get on with it . . . (*Exits.*)

Phil Chirpy this morning, eh?

Curry (*popping head round the door*) Five minutes! (*Exits.*)

Hector My bloody wireless! That was for my maw's Christmas present.

Phil Bless my boater, did you catch that, Cherry? A yuletide cadeau for the squirt's mater and blow me if old Quelch ain't went and confiscated the blighter!

Spanky Christ, Nugent, that's torn it.

Phil Buck up, Pygmy Minimus . . . Cherry and I'll think of something. Any ideas, Cherry, old chap?

Spanky How about a set of cufflinks?

Phil I'll wager that beast Bunter had a fat finger in this . . .

Enter Jack Hogg with Alan Downie.

Phil Yaroo!

Spanky Yeugh . . .

Jack Morning, you chaps. Just showing the new lad round the Design Room. This is our last stop . . .

Phil Natch. When're you off, Jacky Boy?

Jack Alan Downie . . . George Farrell . . . known to the riff-raff as Spanky.

Spanky Watch it, Jack. Howdy, Archie?

Jack And this is Phil McCann . . .

Phil Hi, Andy . . .

Jack And last but by all means least . . . Hector.

Hector McKenzie . . . hello.

Jack This is the Slab Room, Alan . . . where the colours are ground and dished for the Designers . . . you saw the patterns out there. What the lads do, basically, is dole out a quantity of dry colour from those drums over there . . . Persian red, rose pink . . .

Phil . . . bile green . . .

Spanky . . . acne yellow . . .

Jack . . . dump it onto one of these marble slabs, add some gum arabic to prevent it flaking off the paper . . . do we have some gum arabic? Then it's just a matter of grinding . . . (*Demonstrates.*) Bit of a diff from the studio, eh?

Spanky Why don't you vamoose, Jacky Boy?

Phil Yeh, Plooky Chops . . . them boils of yours is highly smittal.

Jack I'm warning you, McCann . . .

Phil Keep away from me! Hector, fling us over the Dettol!

Jack Jealousy will get you nowhere, McCann . . . just because I'm on a desk.

Spanky It's a bloody operating table you want to be on, Jack. That face . . . yeugh.

Phil You can put in for plastic surgery, you know . . . on the National Health.

Spanky Or a 'pimplectomy'. . .

Phil It would only take about six months . . .

Spanky . . . and a team of surgeons . . .

Phil . . . with pliers.

Jack (*to Alan*) I've just got to dodge down the factory . . . have a look at a couple of 'trials' . . . shouldn't be too long. (*to Spanky and Phil*) The boss would like you to show Alan what goes on in here . . . in the way of work. (*to Alan*) Don't worry, you haven't been condemned to spend the rest of the day here . . . I'll have a word with

Bobby Sinclair the colour consultant. He could take you through the dyeing process. . .

Spanky collapses into Phil's arms.

See you shortly . . . (*Exits.*)

Phil Get a brush and some red paint, Heck.

Hector What for?

Spanky To paint a cross on the door, stupid. To warn the villagers . . .

Hector What villagers?

Phil (*to Alan*) Okay, son, what did you say your name was again?

Alan Alan . . . Alan Downie.

Phil Right, Eamonn . . . let's show you some of the mysteries of the Slab Room. Mr Farrell . . .

Spanky Mr Mac?

Phil I'm just showing young Dowdalls here some of the intricacies of our work. If you and the boy would care to stand to the one side . . .

Spanky Certainly. Hector . . .

Phil Many thanks. Right, Alec . . . this here is what we call a sink . . . s–i–n–k. Now I don't expect you to pick up all these terms immediately but you'll soon get the hang of it. And this – (*Grabs Hector.*) – is what we cry a Slab Boy . . .

Spanky You say it . . . Slab Boy . . .

Phil Note the keen eye . . . the firm set of the jaw . . .

Spanky They're forced up under cucumber frames . . .

Phil Note too the arse hanging out of the trousers . . . this last because the Slab Boy, for all he is a special breed . . .

Spanky Trained to a hair . . .

Phil . . . is expected to put in a full eight hours sweated labour a fortnight for a few measly shillings . . .

Spanky . . . and all the gum crystals he can eat . . .

Phil Hence the firm set of the jaw. Thank you, Mr Farrell.

Spanky Don't mention it.

Phil Don't you wish you was one of this happy band, Archie? Grinding out those spanking shades for our designer chappies, so that they in their turn can churn out those gay little rugs one sees in our more select stores?

Hector Yeh, you don't know what you're missing.

Spanky Neither you do, you lucky bastard.

Alan I wouldn't mind working in here but they're putting me in with Bobby Sinclair.

Phil 'Much are you getting?

Alan Er . . . three pounds a week . . .

Spanky Three pound a week!

Alan Round about that . . .

Spanky That's more than the three of us put together.

Phil Is Waldorf Bathroom your uncle or what?

Hector Old Barton . . . the boss.

Alan What d'you mean? Of course he isn't . . .

Spanky Must be some kind of blood relation to start you off at three quid.

Alan It doesn't seem an awful lot to me. I've got a kid brother who's earning that and he's only sixteen.

Phil What is he, a brain surgeon? Three quid!

Spanky 'Much d'you get in your last job?

Alan I haven't had a job before. I'm at the Uni. University. I've only just left school.

Phil Eh? What age are you?

Alan Nineteen.

Phil Did you get kept back a lot?

Alan Stayed on to get my Highers . . .

Spanky What school did you go to?

Alan The John Nielston.

Spanky Aw, another one!

Alan Oh, did you go there too?

Phil No, Albert . . . what Spanky means is you're another one of 'them' . . . a mason . . . or your old man is. Place is crawling with masons.

Hector Don't listen to them. They're always going on about masons. 'Jimmy Robertson's a mason . . . Bobby Sinclair's a mason . . . Willie Curry's a bloody mason . . .'

Spanky He's a bloody mutant.

Hector How come if everybody's a mason you and Phil's working here, eh? Tell us that . . .

Spanky I lied about my age and Phil there swore to Waldo Bathtaps he'd flush his Nine Fridays down the pan if only we could get to be Slab Boys. Aw, no . . . when Mr Bathtub took me into his office, grasped my hand . . . strangely but firmly . . . and offered me one pound two-and-nine a week. I went straight home and set fire to my scapulas.

Phil And don't think it wasn't sore. I was there when he done it. Soon as Father Durkin heard we were working here . . .

Spanky Phil's Auntie Fay got beat up by the Children of Mary . . .

Phil Gave her a right doing . . .

Spanky She had to go to Lourdes . . .

Phil And the entire family were refused entry to Carfin Grotto . . .

Spanky And that really hurt. They were out there every Holiday of Obligation . . . down on their knees . . .

Phil Dragging the ponds for money . . .

Spanky Having a quick burst on the beads . . .

Phil Heh, that's an idea. You ready?

Together In the Name of the Father, and of the Son . . .

Hector Cut it out, you pair. Don't pay any heed to them loonies. Alan.

Alan But I'm not a mason, honestly. I don't know what you're talking about . . .

Phil Aw, no? Tell us this then . . . When you were in at Barton's office this morning you shook hands, didn't you?

Spanky And did it feel like you were in the grip of a man that was throwing a mild epileptic fit?

Alan I don't really . . .

Phil And did he give your bahookey a pat as you went out?

Spanky And said you'd be working with Bobby Sinclair?

Phil At three pounds a week?

Alan Yes, but . . .

Spanky Told you he was a mason!

Phil Definitely! First day us poor sods were handed a packet of peanuts and told to report to the Slab Room . . .

Spanky Not even a pat on the bum . . .

Phil Look at that boy there . . . (*Grabs Hector.*) He was going to be a Capucci monk . . . look at him now.

Hector Hang off! I went to Johnstone High . . . I'm not a bloody pape!

Phil No sense denying it, Heck . . . how else would you be in the Slab? Show the boy your knees. (*to Alan*) They're all caved in from praying to St Wilton for a desk.

Hector Don't listen to them bums, Alan . . . they're always going on about getting out of the Slab Room and onto a desk. Some hope. Jack Hogg was four years in here before he even got a sniff of a desk.

Spanky There was a lot more designers in Jack's day. Look at it now . . . Gavin's away to Australia . . . Billy Sproul's in Kidderminster . . . and Hughie Maxwell's got TB. There's hundreds of desks out there. I'm asking Willie Curry for one . . .

Phil Ask him for two . . .

Hector What about three?

Spanky Hector, you might as well resign yourself . . . you're in the Slab Room till Miss McDonald down the canteen gets a rise out of her suet soufflés.

Hector I was only . . .

Spanky I can see you now . . . unemployable. . . scoffing Indian ink with the down-and-outs . . .

Phil Going round the doors with clothes pegs . . . choking weans for their sweetie money . . .

Spanky So don't go getting any big ideas about asking for a desk, kiddo. You're lucky to be in a job.

Phil (*with newspaper*) Lend us a pencil, Spanks . . .

Spanky What would I be doing with a pencil?

Phil 'S that a pen there, Adam? (*Plucks it from Alan's pocket.*)

Alan Hey . . .

Phil Gee . . . a Parker Fifty-One! What's a slip of a boy like you doing with a pen like this?

Alan Just be careful with . . .

Phil Aaargh, the nib's fell off!

Alan Jesus Christ! That belongs to my dad!

Phil I was only kidding. And less of the bad language, sonny boy . . . a bit of decorum, if you please.

Spanky That's right, Phil . . . you tell the young turk. Don't think you can let rip with that kind of talk in the Slab Room. We fought two world wars for the likes of you. That lad there lost a couple of legs at Wipers so the world would be a cleaner and better place . . .

Phil Where a man could walk tall . . .

Spanky Legs or no legs . . .

Alan Can I have my pen back?

Phil Ach, I'm not in the prizewinners this week either. Hey, know what the first prize is?

Spanky No, what?

Phil 'First Prize . . . Two Matching Hampsters.'

Spanky Hamsters? They allowed to give away livestock like that?

Phil What're you talking about? 'Two Matching Picnic Hampsters . . . Handy for the Beach and Country Walks.' No mention of livestock.

Alan Pen . . .

Phil Here's one . . . twenty-three across . . . says it's an 'anagram'. What's an anagram?

Spanky 'S like a radiogram but not as high off the ground. Give the boy his pen, Phil, you're never going to win it . . .

Phil Came pretty close last time . . . three out of forty-eight. I'll win them hampsters yet.

Spanky And what're you going to do with them when you do?

Phil Cross-breed them with ferrets and send them out hunting for Sadie and her tea trolley . . . I'm starving. Anybody got the time?

Reaches over and tugs Alan's cuff. Alan takes his pen back.

You'll give yourself a hernia lugging that about, son. (*referring to Alan's wristwatch*)

Spanky You going to the canteen the day, Phil?

Phil No option . . . no pieces.

Hector (*to Alan*) D'you fancy the canteen? Sometimes quite good . . .

Alan Depends what's on the menu . . .

Spanky No . . . they don't have a menu, kid. 'S all chalked up on a big blackboard. There's your Forfar Bridie . . .

Phil Hawaiian-style . . .

Spanky Your Links Over-Easy . . .

Phil Scotch Pie Thermidor . . .

Spanky Or if you're really hungry, Ostrich in a Hamper.

Alan I might give that a try . . .

Alan looks away.

Spanky Healthy appetite, the boy.

Phil Aha. (*following Alan's gaze*) Thought those might catch your eye, Albert. (*Crosses to shelf and takes down jar.*) This one here contains the mortal remains of one Joe McBride, the oldest Slab Boy in the long history of this illustrious company. Going on for eighty-four was Joe when he got word he was to start on a desk . . . He'd been in the Slab Room man and beast for nigh on sixty year.

Spanky That's his withered scrotum drying over the radiator there . . .

Phil As I was saying, Alma, they eventually put the poor old bugger onto a desk . . . made him a Designer. Of course, the shock was too much for the elderly chap . . . when the cleaners arrived on the Monday morning they found the veteran Slab Boy slumped over his newly acquired and greatly prized desk . . . stone dead . . .

his hoary old pate in a jar . . . a jar of freshly ground indigo . . . and you know what they say, Arthur?

Alan What's that?

All When you indigo . . . you indigo!

Enter Jack Hogg.

Jack Sorry I took so long, Alan . . . bit of bother with one of the jute backings. How're we doing? Lads filling you in all right?

Alan Oh, yeah . . .

Jack Good . . . good. Ready for a recce round the rug works, are we?

Alan Sure . . .

Phil Mind you don't get lost down there, kid. If you don't get in and out quick the herries eat you alive. . .

Spanky Like pirhana.

Phil You'll be okay with Jacky Boy though. Soon as they see his kisser all the lassies dive under the looms.

Spanky Yeh . . . Big Jinty says it's like somebody smacked him with a bag of hundreds and thousands.

Jack Just you keep that up, Farrell . . . (*Beckons to Alan.*) Just you keep that up. Alan . . . (*to Spanky*) Don't imagine I'm going to stand here and bandy words with the likes of you.

Exeunt.

Spanky And don't imagine we're going to stand here and bandy legs with the likes of you, Torn Face!

Pause.

Phil Hey, Spanks.

Spanky What?

Phil D'you think going off your head's catching?

Spanky Eh? You mean like crabs or Jack's plooks?

Phil No, I'm serious . . . d'you think it is?

Spanky How . . . who do you know that's off their head apart from everybody in . . . 'S not your maw again, is it?

Phil Yeh . . . they took her away last night.

Spanky Christ . . .

Phil She wasn't all that bad either . . . not for her, that is. All she done was run up the street with her hair on fire and dive through the Co-operative windows . . .

Spanky Thought that was normal down your way?

Phil Yeh . . . but that's mostly the drink.

Spanky How long'll she be in this time?

Phil Usual six weeks, I expect. First week tied to a rubber mattress, next five wired up to a generator.

Spanky That's shocking.

Phil That's when we get in to see her. Never knew us the last time. Kept looking at my old man and saying, 'Bless me, Father, for I have sinned.' Course, he's hopeless . . . thinks it's like diphtheria or something. 'The doctors is doing their best, Annie . . . you'll be home soon. You taking that medicine they give you?' Medicine? Forty bennies crushed up in their cornflakes before they frog-march them down to the 'relaxation classes', then it's back up to Cell Block Eleven for a kitbagful of capsules that gets them bleary-eyed enough for a chat with the consultant psychiatrist.

Spanky Not much of a holiday, is it?

Phil Did I ever tell you about that convalescent home my maw and me went to? At the seaside . . . West Kilbride?

Spanky Don't think so.

Phil I was about eleven at the time. Got took out of school to go with her . . . on the train. Some holiday. Place was chock-a-block with invalids . . . headcases soaking up the Clyde breeze before getting pitched back into the hurly-burly of everyday life . . . Old-age pensioners, their skulls full of mush . . . single guys in their forties in too-short trousers and intellects to match . . . Middle-aged women in ankle socks roaming about looking for a letter box to stick their postcards through. Abject bloody misery, it was. Dark brown waxcloth you could see your face in . . . bathroom mirrors you couldn't. Lights out at half-seven . . . no wireless, no comics, no nothing. Compulsory hymn-singing for everybody including the bedridden. Towels that tore the skin off your bum when you had a bath. Steamed fish on Sundays for a special treat . . .

Spanky Bleagh . . .

Phil The one highlight was a doll of about nineteen or twenty . . . There we all were sitting in our deck chairs in the sun lounge . . . curtains drawn . . . listening for the starch wearing out on the matron's top lip . . . when this doll appears at the door, takes a coupla hops into the room, then turns this cartwheel right down the middle of the two rows of deckchairs . . . lands on her pins . . . daraaaaa! Brilliant! I started to laugh and got a skelp on the nut. The matron was beeling . . .

Spanky About the skelp?

Phil About the doll's cartwheel, stupid. Two old dears had to get carried up to their rooms with palpitations and a guy with a lavvy-brush moustache wet himself. It was the high spot of the holiday.

Spanky What was it got into her?

Phil Who knows? Maybe she woke up that morning and seen her face in the waxcloth . . . remembered something . . . 'Christ, I'm alive!' Everybody hated her after that.

Spanky Did you have much bother when they took your maw away last night?

Phil No . . . they gave her a jag to knock her out.

Spanky Eh?

Phil So they could sign her in as a 'voluntary patient'.

Enter Curry carrying a paper pattern.

Curry Who is responsible for this? Eh? What one of you geniuses is responsible for this mess?

Spanky 'S not us that do them, Mr Cardew . . . 's them out there with the collars an' tie . . . we only grind the colour.

Curry That is precisely what you don't do, Farrell . . . and don't try and get smart with me . . . young upstart. Look at this paper . . . just look at it. Feel that . . . go on . . . feel it! 'S like bloody roughcast. Who ground these shades? Or should I say who didn't grind them? This colour's just been thrown onto a slab willy-nilly, whisked round a couple of times and dished . . . no damned gum, nothing! It's a disgrace, that's what it is. Mr Barton's just blown his top out there. What do you bunch get up to in here, eh? It's more like a rest home for retired beatniks than a Slab Room. Things were a damned sight different in my day, I can tell you. If we'd tried to get away with shoddy work like that we'd've been horsewhipped. Too well off, you lot. Twelve and six a fortnight and we thought ourselves lucky to be learning a trade . . .

Phil Oh . . . what trade was that, Mr Curry?

Curry Any more lip from you, McCann, and you'll be up in front of Mr Barton's desk before you can say 'Axminster broadloom'.

Phil Oh . . .

Curry And that doesn't just apply to you. I want to see some solid work being done in this department from now on . . . d'you hear? I've had nothing but complaints from that Design Room all week. Those people out there are getting pretty cheesed off with the abysmal standard of paint coming off those slabs. And what have I told you about smoking! (*Takes out small pair of scissors and snips off the end of Phil's cigarette.*) Miss Walkinshaw came across two dog-ends in the rose pink yesterday . . . not just one . . . two! What've you got to say to that? Eh?

Spanky (*sotto voce*) They were meant to be in the emerald green.

Curry When Jack Hogg was in here this Slab Room used to be my pride and joy . . . never a word of complaint from the Design staff . . . place was like a new pin. Now what've we got? Bloody mayhem! Jimmy Robertson . . . out there . . . Jimmy Robertson showing Mr Barton a paper . . . contract Persian for Canada . . . held up the pattern . . . his bloody scrolls dropped off. No bloody gum! I want to see a very definite improvement. Okay? Now, get on with it . . . that colour cabinet outside's half-empty . . .

Spanky It was half-full this morning . . .

Curry I want to see those slabs glowing red hot! Or there'll be trouble . . . Big trouble. (*Exits.*)

Spanky D'you think that might've been a good moment to ask him for a desk, Phil?

Phil Yeh, you might've been lucky and got your jotters.

Enter Curry.

Curry What did you say was wrong with you this morning, McCann?

Phil Er . . . Christ . . . emm . . . severe diarrhoea . . . of the bot.

Curry If you think I'm swallowing that you're very much mistaken, friend. You were spotted making your way through the gates at quarter past ten. Well?

Phil I had to . . . er . . . run down to the factory toilets. Ours were full up.

Spanky That's right . . . Miss MacDonald made a mutton curry yesterday . . . even I had a touch of it . . .

Curry I'm putting in a report to Mr Barton and you, McCann, are at the top of my list. What little time you condescend to spend on these premises is not being utilised to the full . . . in other words you're a shyster, laddie . . . get me? And you can wipe that smile off your face, Farrell, you're on the report too . . .

Spanky What for . . . what've I done?

Curry Like your pal there, as little as you think you can get away with. Well, I'm not standing for it. That cabinet out there speaks for itself.

Phil Christ . . . talking furniture.

Spanky I'm not supposed to fill it myself . . . what about them? What about Hector? You've never said nothing to him.

Curry Yes, McKenzie . . . I'll see you later . . . in my office. (*Exits.*)

Hector Thanks a bloody lot, Spanky! What'd you go and say that for? You're a rotten big bastard, so you are.

Phil God, I wouldn't like to be in your shoes, Heck . . . must be real serious. Yeh, Spanks, you must admit . . .

Spanky Shut your face. I'm buggered if I'm going to carry the can for the colour cabinet being empty.

Phil Half-empty . . . don't exaggerate.

Spanky Half-empty, well . . . 'S not my job.

Phil But you didn't have to . . .

Spanky Shut up, okay? That's the last time I make excuses up for you.

Phil Nobody asked you to make excuses . . . I can look after myself.

Spanky What was up, you were late anyhow?

Phil I already told you!

Spanky Aw, yeh . . . your maw . . .

Phil Wasn't just that. She hit the cop with the alarm clock.

Spanky They were there and all?

Phil They had a phone call from the manager of the Co about his windows. They knew where to come. 'S the third time.

Spanky She not like the Co-operative then?

Hector We get all our clothes from there.

Phil Something about a lovat suit our Jim got. When they got it home it had only one leg on the trousers . . . bastards wouldn't exchange it. Said it was something to do with the nap of the cloth.

Spanky What did you do . . . amputate?

Phil Jimmucks just had to force both legs down the one trouser . . . gave him a kind of funny mince, that was the only thing . . .

Spanky Aw . . . I used to wonder about your Jim . . . that's what it was?

Phil He would arrive home from the jigging . . . forty sailors in his wake . . .

Hector I had an Uncle Bertie that was in the Navy . . .

Spanky Here we go again. We know . . . he went down with his boat.

Hector Ship . . . the *Royal Oak*. He was only nineteen.

Spanky Nobody mentioned your Uncle Bertie, Heck.

Hector His photo's on our mantelpiece . . .

Spanky We know, we know . . . he was your mother's only brother . . . you've got his medals in the wardrobe and his clothes are on the wall, we know!

Hector It's his clothes that're in the wardrobe and his medals that're . . .

Spanky In the bunker, we know . . . we weren't implying nothing.

Hector Just don't . . . he was my uncle.

Spanky For God's sake . . .

33

Hector And he died for his country!

Spanky Aw, Christ.

Phil Okay, Hector . . . okay . . . I was only kidding about the sailors . . . honest . . . honest. (*Slight pause.*) It was forty Sea Scouts!

Hector You pair of stinking bastards! You've no regard for nothing! My uncle went straight onto battleships from the Sea Scouts . . .

Enter Sadie with tea trolley.

Sadie Tea's up.

Hector . . . and he was wounded twice before he got killed.

Sadie Some nice wee fairy cakes the day. What's up with yous? 'S that not terrible? Behave yourselves! Come on . . . tea's up. And where's my wean? Here, son, come and look what your mammy's brung you. (*Produces cream cookie.*) That's for being a good boy.

Howls from Phil and Spanky.

There's only the one . . . the rest's for the Board Room. I got Miss McDonald to put on an extra one for my baby. D'you like that, son?

Spanky Give's a bit, Heck . . .

Hector Get off!

Phil You rotten sod . . .

Sadie Leave my beautiful wean alone, you pair of hooligans! You enjoying that, flower? That's the stuff. Now . . . what're yous two wanting . . . tea or coffee?

Spanky How come he gets special treatment, Sadie?

Phil Yeah, how come? Can me and Spanky not have one of them cookies?

Sadie I told you . . . they're for the Board Room. There's fairy cakes for yous.

Phil (*taking fairy cake and banging it off side of trolley*) Fairies been putting cement in them again? Give us a coffee.

Sadie Please. Where's your manners? Your mothers would be ashamed of yous, so they would . . .

Enter Alan.

Spanky Ah . . . just in time for the chuck wagon, cow-boy . . . slip out of them wet chaps and lasso yourself a wee fairy cake . . . mmm, mmm.

Alan I'll take a tea, please.

Sadie See that? There's a showing-up for yous . . . there's what you cry manners. Help yourself to milk and sugar, son. Here, I haven't seen you before . . . you in beside these boys?

Alan Er . . . just for the day, I think . . . Jack Hogg mentioned something about Bobby Sinclair . . .

Sadie Ha . . . you'll be lucky . . . nobody's seen him since VJ Night . . . (*quietly*) Try one of them wee scones and butter . . . there's a knife next to your hand . . .

Phil Haw, Sadie, you never told us there was butter!

Spanky That's not fair . . .

Sadie Shut it, yous. And you never put your monies in the tin . . . come on, threeha'pence for tea . . . fourpence for coffee . . . (*to Phil*) Fourpence, I said.

Phil I've only got a tanner.

Sadie I've got plenty of coppers . . . (*to Alan*) When did you start, son?

Alan This morning.

Sadie Very nice. And what do they cry you?

Phil Agnes . . .

Alan Alan . . .

Spanky Dowdy . . .

Alan Downie . . . Alan Downie.

Sadie Ignore them, son. Look, I'll try and keep you something nice for after dinnertime . . . wee Chelsea bun or that? I've got some cream cookies on this morning but they're for the directors . . . couldn't let you have one of them . . . 's more than my life's worth . . .

Alan No, I'm fine, thanks . . .

Sadie That boy could learn you savages a thing or two. You stick in, son . . . you'll go places. Now . . . (*Takes out book of tickets and purse.*) . . . have yous all got your tickets for the Staff Dance the night?

Phil Christ, is it tonight? I thought it was next Friday.

Sadie (*to Alan*) He thought it was next Friday . . . Course it's the night, glaikit . . . don't you try that on with me, Phil McCann . . . I don't see your name down here as paid . . . c'mon, stump up.

Phil Have a heart, Sadie, I gave you my last tanner. I'll pay you next month. How's that?

Sadie You'll pay me after dinnertime or you'll hand your ticket back. Yous boys get plenty. I'll mark you down for this afternoon.

Spanky You still going, Phil?

Phil Yeh . . . how would I not be?

Sadie You've got yours, Spanky . . . aye. What about you, Hector son? I don't see your name down here. You giving it a miss this year?

Spanky Course he is . . . his legs would never reach the floor. (*Places empty cup on trolley. Pinches cream cookies.*)

Sadie D'you not want a ticket, darling?

Hector 'Much are they again?

Sadie Fifteen shillings single . . . twenty-five double . . .

Spanky passes a cookie to Phil.

Hector I'll take a double.

Phil and Spanky freeze, cookies poised.

Sadie What?

Hector I said, I'll take a double.

Sadie That's what I thought you said, sweetheart . . . D'you want to pay me now or leave it till after?

Hector I've got the money here. (*Brings out two one-pound notes.*)

Sadie Did your mammy come up on the horses? Thanks, son . . . That's your change. See and the both of yous have a lovely time. What about you, flower?

Alan Oh . . . I hadn't thought about it . . .

Sadie Well. you always know who's got the tickets. Is that all your cups? I better get a move on . . . them directors'll be greeting if they don't get their cream cookies. That's just your money to get, Phil McCann . . . right? See yous after . . .

Alan holds door open.

Aw, thanks, son . . . you're a gent.

Exits.

Phil Aw, Hector . . . you didn't need to go that far. I know we were giving you the needle but you didn't need to go and throw away twenty-five bob on a ticket just to get your own back. We never said your Uncle Bertie was like that . . . Doesn't run in families anyhow . . .

Hector Not like lunacy . . .

Phil What?

Spanky He said he knows that. (*to Hector*) Watch it!

Hector Yous started it.

Phil Who're you going with, anyhow? Anybody we know?

Spanky Yeh, c'mon, give us a clue, Heck. Is it a dame?

Phil Or is it her from the Post Desk with the face like a walnut?

Spanky C'mon, tell us . . .

Phil Yeh . . . who's Miss X?

Hector Mind your own business.

Phil It's Miss McDonald from the Canteen . . . right?

Spanky Yeh, you're fond of her big cookies, aren't you, kiddo?

Hector Shut your mug.

Phil Well, if it isn't the lovely Miss Walnut . . .

Spanky And it isn't Miss McDonald with the big cookies . . .

Phil Doesn't leave much to choose from, does it? I think it's a kid-on, what d'you say, Spanks? The Big KO?

Spanky Tell us, Hector . . . please. (*Gets down on knees.*) Please . . . (*Grabs Hector's coat tails.*) We're begging you.

He is joined by Phil.

Phil Put us out of our misery.

Hector Ach, stop acting the goat, will you? If you must know . . .

Phil *and* **Spanky** (*together*) Yes? Yes?

Hector It's . . .

Phil *and* **Spanky** (*together*) Yes??

Hector (*blurts out*) It's Lucille Bentley.

Spanky What??

Phil Who??

Spanky I don't believe . . . Lucille . . . Lucille Bentley??

Phil Lucille would never consider going to the Staffie with you, Hector . . . you're havering.

Spanky Lucille and . . .? Never! He's flipped. Have you seen her, Alfie?

Phil She's every Slab Boy's dream . . .

Spanky And she wears these . . .

Phil Yeah . . .

Spanky When did you ask her, Heck?

Hector Well, er . . . I . . . er . . .

Phil Where did you get the patter, kiddo?

Spanky Yeh, all of a sudden?

39

Phil And she said, yeh . . . just like that?

Hector Well, I haven't actually . . . er . . .

Spanky God, our Hector and Lucille . . . phew . . .

Phil Our Hector . . .

Spanky And Lucille . . .

Hector God, I'm bursting! (*Exits.*)

Phil Wasn't half hiding his light, eh, Spanks?

Spanky Couldn't've been all he was hiding . . .

Phil Shhhhhh . . .

Lucille (*sings off*)
Once I had a secret love . . .
That lived within the heart of me . . .
All too soon that secret love . . .
Became impatient to be free . . . (*Enters.*)

What one of you greedy gannets's been in at Miss
Walkinshaw's lunchpail? Her sandwiches are covered
in yellow ochre and her orange is glued to her tomato.
(*to Alan*) Hi. You know she's got a caliper . . . (*Crosses
to sink with water jug.*)

Spanky Looking forward to the dance, Lucille?

Lucille 'S there any of them dishrags about? Not the
clatty ones . . .

Phil (*producing rag*) Ecco.

Spanky You've . . . er . . . just missed him.

Phil Lover boy.

Lucille Eh?

Spanky The pocket-size Casanova . . . he just went out.

Phil Wee guy. . . about this height. Give us a look at your shoe. (*Lifts Lucille's foot.*) No . . . just wondering if you'd stood on him . . .

Lucille What're yous talking about now? (*to Alan*) Honest to God, see when you come in here it's like trying to find your way through the middle of Gene Vincent's wardrobe with a glow-worm on the end of a stick. (*to Phil*) Quit talking in riddles. If you've something to say, spit it out. Who is it you're on about?

Phil Hector.

Lucille So?

Spanky So . . . you've just missed him. Just letting you know.

Lucille Yeh, thanks. Is that supposed to be significant or am I just being thick?

Phil Thought you might've wanted to brush up your foxtrot . . .

Spanky Fan down your dangoes . . .

Lucille (*to Alan*) Can you translate all that?

Alan I think they're meaning about you and Hector going to the Staff Dance.

Lucille What? Me and who?

Alan Hector.

Lucille Hector?? Going to the what?? Who's been giving you that guff? What would I be doing going to the . . .

Phil You mean he hasn't . . .

Spanky The little . . .

Lucille It's the Staff Dance, not the Teddy Bears' Picnic! You mean, somebody actually said I was going with . . .

Spanky Hector. Yeh . . . somebody actually said.

Lucille What a bloody insult! I've seen better hanging from a Christmas tree! Hector! Don't make me laugh! (*to Alan*) Mind and circulate. Sketching Department's straight through . . . you can't miss it. (*Exits.*)

Phil A right pair of chookies we looked!

Spanky Wait till I get a hold of that wee . . .

Phil He's for it!

Spanky I'll strangle him!

Enter Hector.

Aw, here it comes . . . Prince Charming.

Phil You shall go to the ball, Lucille.

Spanky What was all that mouthwash about you asking her to the Staffie, you little toley?

Phil You had him and me believing you, you . . . She's just been in here.

Hector You never gave us a chance to explain . . .

Spanky What's to explain? You led us to believe that you and her were cutting a rug tonight . . .

Phil Tripping the light fantastic . . .

Hector I only meant I was going to ask her . . .

Phil He was going to ask her . . .

Alan That's what I thought he meant . . . that he was going to ask her . . .

Spanky Who cares what you thought, sonny boy? You just stand there, and model that blazer!

Hector I didn't actually say I had asked her . . .

Phil You certainly gave me and Spanks the impression that you had . . .

Spanky And that she was champing at the bit to go.

Phil She had to ask Fancypants there what one of us was Hector . . .

Hector That doesn't say much for yous either.

Spanky It struck a wrong chord with me at the time . . . that a doll like Lucille would want to partner you to the dance. . . I mean to say, look at you.

Hector What's wrong with me!

Phil Everything's wrong with you. Look at the state of the clothes for a start.

Hector There's nothing up with my clothes.

Spanky There's nothing up with my clothes. You must be joking. I've seen more up-to-date clothes on a garden gnome. You're a mess, Heck.

Phil Them duds of yours is twenty years behind the times, kid. You never stood a chance of getting Lucille to the Staffie.

Spanky Dames like her only go for a guy with style . . . style, that's what counts . . .

Alan Don't let them bully you. Your clothes are perfectly all right.

Spanky You throwing your voice, Phil?

Spanky and Phil start searching in pockets, cupboards, etc.

Alan Okay, you've had your joke . . .

Phil Aha . . . I've found where the voice is coming from, Spanks . . .

43

Spanky Aw . . . Creepybreeks here. And what d'you know about clothes, eh? Look at the trousers . . .

Phil And take a gander at the footwear . . .

Spanky Aaaargh! What's that on your feet, kid?

Alan What's wrong with brogues?

Phil You don't really want me to tell you, do you?

Alan Go ahead.

Phil Well, they're full of holes for a start.

Spanky And they look stupid.

Alan They're better than those efforts you're wearing . . .

Spanky D'you hear that, Phil?

Phil Good Christ, man, that's the very boot that conquered Everest.

Spanky I thought the sole was wearing a bit thin . . .

Phil The Dermot Walsh All-British Bubble Boot endorsed by medical men the world over has to be one of the most stylish items of manly footgear on the market and you're comparing them to a stupid-looking pair of brogues?

Spanky You and Hector's just the same . . . a pair of tubes.

Phil Take it from us, you guys . . . yous'll never get a lumber . . .

Spanky . . . without this gadgey number . . .

Phil It's the finest little boot in all the land . . . What is it?

Spanky *and* **Phil** The Finest Little Boot In All The Land – taraaaa!

Enter Jack Hogg.

Jack Would you lot care to put a cork in the glee club? Miss Walkinshaw's migraine. Thanks. Sorry, Alan, must've taken a wrong turning at the spindle shed . . . find your way back up all right? Listen, I think I've tracked down Bobby Sindair . . . he's in the Lab, if you'd like to . . .

Alan Yeh, I would . . .

Jack Good. You two clowns better watch out. The boss's on the prowl. I've just seen him have a shufti in the colour cabinet . . . bloody thing's empty . . .

Spanky Half-empty . . . don't exaggerate.

Jack Half-empty, then. Jimmy Robertson's going to be yelling for some crimson lake shortly. Miss Walkinshaw's just upended an entire dish of it over that Alpine Floral she's been working on. (*to Alan*) You want to see it . . . what a mess. Six months' work down the toilet. You can have a swatch on the way past. (*to Spanky and Phil*) So, that's crimson lake, magenta, olive, cobalt blue, Persian red, raw sienna, cadmium yellow, rose pink, French ultramarine, violet and Hooker's green . . . okay? This way, Alan . . .

Exeunt.

Phil Did you get all that, Hector?

Hector What came after magenta?

Spanky Have you got your dinner suit for tonight, Phil?

Phil No . . . I thought I'd go in my old man's dungarees and muffler. Course I've got my dinner suit. Jackson's. Want to get a load of this. White jacket . . . Yankee . . . fingertip drape . . . roll collar . . . swivel button . . . full back . . . sharkskin. Black strides . . . fourteens . . . flying seams . . . razor press . . . half-inch turnups . . .

Hector He did say say Persian red, didn't he?

Spanky 'Much is that setting you back?

Phil Twenty-five and six. Option to buy. Jacket's two quid . . . trousers, five bob. What're you doing, Heck?

Spanky Five bob?

Phil Yeh . . . guy knocked a half-note off them. You can still see the stitches where the truncheon pocket was. You'll do yourself a mischief, Hecky boy . . .

Spanky I'm getting mine from Caledonian Tailors . . . 'Executive Rental'. Pick it up at six. Guy's waiting on three dozen return from the Orange Lodge in Castle Street. Hoping he's got something to fit me . . . it's my arms, you see. They're three and a half inches longer than my legs . . . or so the Caledonian Tailor guy says. It was him that measured us up. Hard to believe, isn't it?

Phil Not really.

Hector Hey, did you really mean that about . . . style? Clothes and all that stuff. No . . . come on . . . kidding aside . . .

Phil Course we meant it, kid. You'll never get nowhere with those who wear the lumpy jerseys unless you're up to scratch sartorially . . . style-wise. I mean, what doll's going to take a guy seriously in that outfit and with a head like that, Heck?

Hector I can't help the way my hair grows . . .

Spanky That's where you're wrong, son. Mr McCann . . . (*Produces large pair of carpet shears.*) And don't worry about the clobber . . . we'll organise the alterations . . .

46

Hector What alterations? No, I only meant . . .

Phil You want to go to the Staffie with Lucille, don't you?

Hector I wouldn't mind, but . . .

Spanky Then leave it to me and Phil. The togs is no problem. His Auntie Fay was a tailoress . . .

Phil . . . in the Dolls' Hospital. This way, Hector. (*Throws Hector over his shoulder.*)

Hector Hey, wait a minute!

Spanky (*holding door open*) If you need to give him a friction, Jimmy Robertson's got a lighter . . .

Hector You bastard!

Phil To the lavvies!

> *Exeunt. Hector's pleas fade off down the corridor. Spanky stands for a moment . . . then starts going over the list of colours in his head.*

Spanky Crimson lake, magenta, olive, cobalt blue, Persian red, raw sienna, cadmium yellow, rose pink, French ultramarine, violet and Hooker's green . . .

> *Starts working quickly and methodically. Pause.*

Jack (*off*) Sorry about that bum steer, Alan . . . thought I had him pinned down for sure that time . . . Trouble is that nobody else knows as much about the bloody biz as he does . . .

> *He and Alan enter.*

Jack Aha . . . all on your ownio, Georgie? What . . . nobody pulling the strings? Thought Alan here might come back and do another spot in the Slab . . .

47

Spanky The floor's just been mopped.

Jack I'll leave you to it, Alan. Don't take any snash from these guys. (*to Spanky*) Look, why don't you go through the entire process from the top, Farrell?

Spanky I'm busy, Jack.

Jack Source materials . . . pigmentation . . . texture . . . density . . . all that sort of guff . . . fugitive colours . . . wrist technique. See the way he's handling that knife, Alan? Strain some gum . . . that's always gripping. (*to Alan*) I'd love to show you myself but the boss has just hit me with a half-drop for Holland. Any problems give me a shout . . . okay? Okay, Farrell? Ciao. (*Exits.*)

Spanky works on. Alan watches. Silence.

Spanky Okay, okay . . . you get the stuff, pap it on the slab, water, gum, bingo . . . you grind away till you feel like a smoke.

Alan And that's it?

Spanky That is it.

Alan Fugitive colours . . . all that stuff?

Spanky Listen, kiddo, the only fugitive colours we've ever had in here was Coronation Year . . . nineteen fifty-three. Six drums of red, white and blue went missing. There . . . you can use Phil's slab . . .

Alan What about texture . . .? Density . . .?

Spanky Texture . . . seldom varies. Rough . . . that goes for the lot. Smoothest colour we ever had delivered was a poke of mahogany lake . . . lumps the size of Jacky Boy's plooks. Hughie Maxwell broke a wrist grinding a pot this big for Bobby Sinclair . . . him and his wife were going to the Baptists' Christmas Ball as Amos 'n' Andy.

Alan Density?

Spanky Doesn't matter a bugger as long as it doesn't run off the paper onto their cavalry twills. Best to err this side of the concrete scale. Fling us up that daud of muslin . . . I'll strain some more gum.

Alan works away while Spanky prepares the gum.

Alan Phew . . . goes for the wrists . . .

Spanky Don't worry, kiddo . . . by the time five o'clock comes you'll have arms like Popeye. No, no . . . too high up the shank . . . (*Adjusts Alan's grip.*) That's better . . .

Alan Yeh . . . How long have you been in here?

Spanky Too long, kiddo. Be three years this Christmas.

Alan That's quite normal, is it?

Spanky Nothing's normal in this joint, son. If you mean is that average . . . ? (*Shrugs.*) Jack Hogg was four . . . Gavin Dyer, two . . . Hughie Maxwell, six months . . . who knows? Depends if they take to your features . . . how many desks are free . . . how the boss is feeling . . . what the Berlin situation's like . . .

Alan How long's your pal done?

Spanky Phil? Year and a bit. Stayed on at school . . . to get his Highers . . .

Alan And did he?

Spanky No . . . jacked it in. Got sent down for smacking the French teacher in the mouth with a German biscuit.

Alan What'd he do that for?

Spanky What does Phil do anything for? Laughs, of course.

Alan You mean he's nuts . . .

Spanky We're all nuts, kiddo.

Alan Look, going to cut calling me 'kiddo'? It gets really annoying . . .

Spanky Sure, sure . . . anything you say . . . kiddo.

Alan Is this about ready to dish, d'you think?

Spanky What d'you think?

Alan I'm asking you . . .

Spanky That's one thing you'll learn in here, Archie . . . don't ask nobody nothing. It's up to you.

Alan I think I'll dish it . . . or maybe I'll give it a bit more . . . no, I'll dish it, I reckon. (*He does so.*)

Spanky (*waiting till he's finished*) Enough gum in it?

Alan Gum? Oh, Christ . . .

Pours it back onto slab. Accepts dish of gum from Spanky. Keeps an eye on Spanky as he adds it to paint.

I thought you might be able to add it once it was dished . . .

Spanky You can.

Enter Curry.

Curry Where's McKenzie?

Spanky Oh . . . er . . . Phil had another attack and Hector had to go with him.

Curry An attack of what, for God's sake? Not bloody conscience, I trust . . . Oh, no . . . not the loose stools again?

Spanky No . . . diarrhoea. Hector had to give him a coalie-back down the stairs.

Curry Yes, very good, Farrell. You're not too big for a clip round the ear, you know. Give me out a large sheet of paper . . .

Spanky produces a tatty, crumpled sheet.

Is this what you call a large sheet?

Spanky 'S all we've got.

Curry Alan, nip out and ask Mr Robertson for a large sheet of drafting paper . . . oh, and some willow charcoal and a chamois . . . on you go, look sharp.

Alan Which one's Mr Robertson?

Curry Nylon overall, briar pipe . . .

Spanky 'S that not Miss Walkinshaw? Sorry.

Exit Alan.

Curry Have we got any tracing paper in here?

Spanky Tracing paper?

Curry Tracing paper.

Spanky For tracing?

Curry Just so.

Spanky No.

Curry What happened to that roll Mr Barton left?

Spanky There's no trace of it.

Curry Steady, Curry. How's that gum coming along, Farrell? I take it that is gum you're making?

Spanky Yeh . . . there was an awful lot of straw in that last lot of crystals so . . .

Curry Probably camel chips . . .

Spanky Eh?

Curry Dung . . . camel droppings . . . let's have a look . . . Yes . . . we used to burn a lot of this stuff under our billies out East . . .

Spanky Billies?

Curry Billy cans. You were never in the Scouts, were you? No . . . Yes, many's the night we sat hunkered over the old camel-dung bonfire after a hard day's trek across the dunes . . .

Spanky In the Scouts?

Curry In the desert, Farrell. A fountain of bright sparks winging into the velvet sky. . . Some of the lads would hitch up their kilts and get their ukeleles out . . .

Spanky Dirty pigs.

Curry . . . we'd have a sing-song. Yes, those were days. (*Hums 'We'll Meet Again'.*) Here, what's all this business about McCann's mother? D'you know anything about it, Farrell? Miss Walkinshaw's got a brother-in-law . . . shop manager in some housing scheme . . . and he was telling her about a carry-on last night. McCann's mother was involved, seemingly. Darkwood Crescent, they stay, isn't it?

Spanky Er . . . no . . . I think they've moved from there now. They live in Foxbar 's far as I know. (*inadvertently giving the game away*) Couldn't've been Phil's maw that broke the windows . . . must've been some other . . .

Curry Thank you, Farrell.

Spanky . . . loony.

Enter Alan with sheet of paper.

Curry Well done, lad. Have we got something to lean on?

Alan looks around, spots Phil's folio, hands it to Curry.

Thanks. Now, let's run over some pointers with you. You too, Farrell . . . you might learn something.

Spanky I'm trying to mix up some gum.

Curry Leave the gum for the time being and gather round.

Spanky You've showed us all that before.

Curry You're never too long in the tooth to learn how to execute a floral, Farrell. I'll show you again, won't I? Charcoal . . . ?

Alan holds out a tiny stick.

Is that all he had?

Alan No, he was going to give me the whole box but when I said who it was for . . . and a chamois.

Holds out tattered rag.

Curry (*taking rag between finger and thumb*) I find it difficult to picture this ever making its way sure-footedly up the treacherous slopes of the Matterhorn, but still . . .

Lucille pops her head round the door.

Lucille Telephone, Mr Curry.

Curry Hell!

Lucille Trunk call from Troon. (*Exits.*)

Curry Don't go away, Alan, I'll be right back. Who is it, Lucille? (*Exits.*)

Alan turns over the folio . . . idly looks inside.

Alan (*taking out drawings*) Hey, these aren't yours, are they?

Spanky No, they must be Phil's . . . ho, put them back. If he catches you going through his stuff he'll break your jaw.

Alan I'm not touching them. Hey, some of these are not bad . . . look at this one . . .

Spanky I'm telling you, Alec . . . (*Crosses to have a look.*) God, they are good, aren't they? There's one of Elvis . . . 's dead like him, isn't it? Right . . . shut the folder or I'll get the blame. I get the blame for everything round here . . .

Alan Hey . . . how about that red chalk drawing?

Spanky That's his old man . . . I recognise the ears . . . like Dumbo. And there's one of his maw. Christ, you can tell, can't you?

Alan Tell what?

Spanky Nothing . . . tell it's his mother. Shut that folder, I said.

Alan Look at the way he's done those hands. Whenever I have a bash at hands they turn out looking like fankled pipe-cleaners . . .

Spanky Which is exactly how your features are going to look if Phil comes back. Get that shut . . . I'm not telling you again.

Alan I wonder how he got that effect?

Spanky What effect?

Alan There – the way he's got the nose coming forward from the head . . .

Spanky Mines comes forward . . .

Alan Some of these are quite accomplished . . .

Spanky Aw . . . quite accomplished, are they? And what d'you know about it?

Alan Not a great deal, but anyone can see they're rather good. He's wasting his time in here . . .

Spanky Yeh, you have a word with him, kiddo . . . I'm sure he'll appreciate it. Now for the last time, are you going to shut that folder or . . .

Enter Curry.

Curry I've just been having a natter with your dad, Alan . . .

Alan Oh . . . (*Tries to gather up drawings.*)

Curry On the phone. You never let on Bob Downie was your father . . . eh? Godstruth, see you young fellows . . . Chief Designer at Templars . . .? I'd've been as proud as punch . . . Hello, what's this? Some of your artwork? Let's have a butcher's . . .

Alan No, these aren't . . .

Curry Tch, tch, tch, tch . . . a chip off the old block, eh?

Alan I'm afraid they aren't.

Curry A right talented pair of buggers . . . I remember when Bob Downie used to work here he was always . . .

Alan These aren't mine, Mr Curry.

Curry What?

Spanky Yeh, they're not his.

Alan I was just . . .

Curry Who belongs to them, then? They aren't yours Farrell, that's for sure. You've got trouble trying to draw water from that tap over there . . .

Alan They were just lying around . . .

Curry And they can't be Hector's. Too bold for him . . .

Alan I think they must be . . .

Curry (*interrupting him*) You're not going to tell me they're McCann's. What's this. . . (*Turns drawing over.*) That's the Art School stamp, isn't it? Jimmy Robertson and I used to go up to Saturday morning classes together . . . (*Reads.*) 'Glasgow School of Art . . . First-Year Entrance Exam . . . Nineteen Fifty-Sev . . .' What??

Spanky Eh?

Curry Whose are these?? Come on . . .

Spanky How should I know?

Curry (*finding label on front of folder*) 'P. J. McCann, 19 Darkwood Crescent, Ferguslie Park . . .' So that's what the loafer's been up to. A flyman, eh? Well, we'll soon see about this . . . Farrell!

Spanky What?

Curry Away down to the ablutions and fetch that crony of yours up here.

Spanky I'll need to wash my hands first.

Curry Get a move on! Tell him to drag that miserable carcase of his up those flaming stairs. You and McKenzie can take an arm and a leg each if he can't manage.

Spanky And just leave the rest of his body down there?

Curry Get those mitts washed! Bloody corner boy. Now, Alan, where were we? Ah, yes . . . now, I'm going to rough in a few roses here. I dare say your dad's covered some of this ground with you . . . still, no harm in seeing it again, eh? I showed Bob Downie a few tricks while he was with us. Expect he told you, eh? Now, what's the first . . . Farrell, will you gee yourself up a bit! You'd think it was a damned bath you were having! Right, Alan . . . what's the first thing we do when we're starting a charcoal sketch?

Spanky Get a bit of charcoal.

Curry That's right . . . get the old wrist moving. Make sure it's good and supple before committing yourself to paper. Put those two fingers just there and you'll see what I mean. (*Places Alan's fingers in his wrist, waggles his hand to and fro.*) Feel?

Alan Yes . . .

Enter Phil. He is carrying a bundle of clothing which he hurriedly throws into a corner.

Phil Sorry, I can see you're busy . . . call again tomorrow.

Curry Get you in here, McCann. Bowels back to normal, are they?

Phil Eh? Oh . . . er . . . yeh . . .

Curry Good. Perhaps you can enlighten us a little? (*Produces portfolio.*)

Phil Hey, what're you doing with them drawings? That's private!

Curry There's nothing 'private' in here, chum. 'Glasgow School of Art Entrance Exam . . .' Well?

Phil You've no right . . .

Curry Aha . . . not so . . . not so, lad. By the terms of your indentures . .

Phil My what?

Curry Your indentures . . . that's what you signed when you started here . . .

Phil I never signed nothing! And even if I had that doesn't give you the right to go through my stuff. That portfolio's mine, I collected it this morning.

Curry So that's why you were more than an hour late. That diarrhoea business was just a red herring . . .

Phil Wasn't me that told you about the diarrhoea . . . it was him.

Spanky You bastard!

Curry But you went along with it, McCann . . . oh, yes, you certainly went along with it. Thought you had me fooled, eh? Oh, no . . . I smelled a rat right away. So you were up collecting this little lot, were you? Now, don't for a moment think I'm accusing you of being in the least underhand but don't you think it might have been prudent to seek permission before . . .

Phil You must be joking! Whose permission do I need? Yours?

Curry Or Mr Barton's.

Phil Away to . . .

Curry Watch it, boy, remember who you're speaking to! Any more of that and . . .

Enter Jack Hogg.

Jack 'Scuse me interrupting, Mr Curry, but you're wanted in Mr Barton's office.

Curry What?

Jack Right away.

Curry Right. (*Heads for door. Stops.*) Right! (*Exits.*)

Phil The little . . .! Did you hear it? His permission? His bloody . . .?

Spanky You didn't need to shop us like that, did you?

Phil What?

Spanky I was only trying to stop you getting into trouble. Some thanks I get.

Phil What're you talking about?

Spanky The dia-bloody-rrhoea. 'It was him.' Thanks a bloody lot!

Phil That isn't important. Did you hear what that little keech was saying about me going to Art School?

Jack So that's what all the racket was about?

Phil Yeh . . . Curry was making out I was being devious 'cos I wanted to get out of here . . .

Spanky Well, I never knew nothing about it either.

Phil I don't have to tell you everything, do I?

Spanky You told us about your maw . . . (*Pause.*)

Jack It's a pretty tough entrance exam, you know. I've tried it . . .

Phil Who asked you? You can't even get the tin trunks off a chocolate soldier, Jack.

Jack Hey . . . wait a minute . . .

Spanky Yeh, the boy was only saying . . .

Phil I knew you'd turn on us, ya whore! I bet you it was you showed Hitler my folio.

Spanky It was not!

Alan It was me, if you must know, and I didn't do it deliberately . . .

Spanky I warned him to leave it alone . . . didn't I, Archie?

Jack I don't see what all the fuss is about anyway. Time enough when the results come out. I've got a friend sat the exam and she says you don't hear till next month . . . you get notified by post . . .

Phil Bully for her. Well, I'll be hearing sooner than that, Jacky Boy . . . in fact, I'll know by this afternoon . . . so there.

Spanky How come? If Jack's china doesn't get word till . . .

Phil Doll in the Art School said she'd give us a ring . . . gave her the number . . .

Spanky This number?

Phil Used a bit of the old charm . . .

Spanky Don't see Willie passing on any messages. Doesn't let any of us get personal calls unless it's a matter of life and death . . .

Phil Told her to say it was the hospital . . .

Jack That's a bit off. Other people have to wait on their letters . . .

Phil I'm not other people, Jack.

Jack How about that, Alan?

Phil (*to Alan*) You open your mouth and your head's going down it!

Jack Hey . . . hey . . .

Phil Piss off, Pimple Chops . . . away back to your desk and fester.

Alan It's all right, Jack . . .

Jack It's just as well for you I'm on a rush job, McCann. (*Exits.*)

Alan All he was saying was it's a difficult exam . . .

Spanky There's that voice again . . .

Phil Difficult? It was a cakewalk, kiddo. All this dame has to do is pick up the phone . . . give us the nod.

Alan I hope you're right . . . (*Exits.*)

Phil Of course I'm right!

Spanky It'll blow over, Phil . . . you know what Curry's like . . .

   Enter Curry.

Curry Did McKenzie come up with you, McCann? (*to Spanky*) Did McKenzie come up with him?

   Spanky shrugs.

Well, tell him to come to my office the moment he appears. (*Exits.*)

Spanky See? It's Hector he's got it in for . . . not you. You and me gets off light compared to Heck. That's the second time he's asked to see him today.

Phil What d'you think? His cards?

Spanky What d'you think?

Phil Where is he, anyhow?

Spanky Who?

Phil Hector.

Spanky Thought he was down the bog along with you?

Phil Yeh . . . but he managed to get free.

Spanky Free?

Phil I had him tied to a radiator but he must've chewed through the ropes while I was having a . . .

Spanky You mean he's wandering about without a stitch?

Phil He's got his simmit on . . . that didn't need restyling.

Spanky He'll get bloody frostbite, ya swine. How could you do that to him?

Phil It was your idea and all, don't forget.

Spanky How're we going to find him?

Phil Easy. Follow the trail of blood.

Spanky Blood? You never beat him up as well, ya pig!

Phil I gave his ear a nick with the shears while I was trimming his hair . . .

Spanky You're a bloody sadist, Phil.

Phil I was trying to get the boy a date with Lucille.

Spanky Yeh . . . some chance he's got now. Who'd want to go to the Staffie with a one-eared, baldy-headed midget in a blood-stained simmit! No, come on, Phil . . . we better do something.

Phil We'll do what we were going to do in the first place . . . get his clothes restyled.

Spanky D'you think that's wise?

Phil Listen, you know how much this means to Heck . . . getting a date with Lucille. I mean, to you and me she's just a bit of stuff . . .

Spanky Some bit of stuff . . .

Phil Yeh, but to Hector she is 'It' . . . the Real Thing . . . the Empire State . . . Niagara Falls . . .

Spanky The thruppenny in the dumpling.

Phil Exactly. It's the least we can do. What're you laughing at, ya dog? You don't reckon Heck's sophisticated enough to get his loins in a fankle over a dame? (*Holds up Hector's shirt.*) What d'you think . . . a Billy Eckstein . . . or a Dennis Lotis?

Spanky What about an Eve Boswell?

Phil It would mean a pretty drastic job with the shears.

Spanky Yeh, best just stick to altering the togs.

Enter Alan. Lunchtime hooter sounds.

Spanky Hurrraaaaaaaaaaaaaaay!

Phil Last one down the canteen's a Designer!

Exeunt. Alan is left standing in the middle of the room. Then he too exits.

Curtain.

Act Two

The afternoon. Enter Phil. He crosses to folio, starts sorting out his drawings. Enter Spanky.

Spanky God, that dinner was revolting . . .

Phil I told you not to have the salmonella on toast.

Spanky I think I'm going to be sick.

Phil Well, don't hang over the shades . . . there's gum in them already. (*He lights up cigarette.*)

Enter Alan.

Alan Quite a nice lunch they do.

Silence.

Bobby Sinclair's tied up with some problem hanks at the moment so I thought I might come and do some grinding.

Silence.

What's wrong with that? Mr Curry certainly thought I could do a bit.

Silence.

I don't mind . . . I'll just go and let Mr Curry know I'm not needed . . . (*Heads for door.*)

Spanky Hold on, Archie. Here . . . (*Indicates slab.*)

Alan I want to learn as much as possible while I'm here. (*Takes up palette knife.*)

Phil You haven't been drinking, have you?

Spanky Look at this, Phil . . . boy's a natural. Look at the way the calf muscles are bulging out on the back of his neck. When you've finished that there's some Hunting Stewart there . . .

Alan Thanks . . .

Spanky Me and Phil'll lie over here and watch you for a bit . . . okay?

Phil Ask him if he wants a drag . . . ?

Alan I don't smoke.

Enter Curry quietly.

Phil *and* **Spanky** (*together*) Surprise, surprise!

Curry Surprise, surprise! Young Downie working away and you two teddy boys lounging back having a puff. On your pins! Douse them smokes and let's be having you! Come on, jump to it! Finding it difficult to get up, McCann? What do they do . . . spray those trousers on? Or don't you take them off, is that the secret? Give him a hand, Farrell, for God's sake, or we'll be here all day. I don't know . . . if you'd seen those POWs breaking their backs on the Burma Road . . . young chaps . . . age of yourselves . . . dropping like flies . . . beri-beri . . . cholera . . . you name it . . .

Phil Windypops?

Curry Not a peep out of them. Scabbing away like billy-o rather than give in. Get those palette knives in your mitts, quick as you like, Farrell. You too, McCann . . . at the double! Alan, drag yourself away for a mo. Right, you pair, see if you can't do half as well as this young fellow. Come on, Farrell, don't just stand there like GI Joe looking for the soft option . . . get on with it. This way, Alan . . . Mr Barton's laid out some pre-war pattern books for us . . .

Exeunt.

Phil 'My Forty Years Giving the Japs Merry Gyp.' The memoirs of Jungle Jim.

Spanky Japs, my arse. Jimmy Robertson told me Willie was a typist in the Pay Corps. Nearest he ever got to Burma was the Bamboo Tea Lounge in Incle Street.

Phil He's a wee blowhard . . . he doesn't scare me.

Spanky Look out!

Enter Jack Hogg. He has a bundle of mags.

Jack Alan around?

Phil Tall fat guy with scarlet fever and his nose in a sling?

Jack Just tell him I've got those mags he asked about . . .

Spanky What mags are these, Jacky Boy?

Phil Yeh . . . how come we never get to see them?

Spanky Yeh . . . how come?

Jack They're about design . . . I shouldn't think you'd be remotely interested. . .

Phil Oh, is that right? Tell him, Spanks . . . are we interested?

Spanky Not really.

Phil So you think twice before lurching in here and accusing the brother and me of not giving a monkey's. The designing of carpets for the hoi polloi may mean nothing to you, Hogg, but it means a damn sight less to us. Right, Spanky?

Spanky Roger.

Phil Sorry . . . Roger.

Jack You're so smart, aren't you? So bloody smart, the pair of you. You're just pea green if anyone takes an interest in things . . .

Spanky Pea green? That's a new one . . .

Jack You nobbled Hector when he first started, didn't you? He used to come out to my desk, we'd go through some carpet mags together . . . but, oh no, you soon put a stop to that . . . called him for everything . . . made his life a misery. A pair of bullyboys, that's what you are. Hector could've been a pretty good designer by now . . . yes, he could! Better than either of you, anyway. When was the last time you were down the showroom, eh? Neither of you takes the least interest in any trials that come up. In fact, I bet you don't even know what any of us is working on out there . . .

Phil (*producing tatty piece of carpet*) Fourteen and eleven the square furlong.

Jack That's right . . . go on, make a fool of things. Some of us take a pride in what we do!

Phil Ach, pish, Jack! Some of us take a pride in what we do . . . You? You lot! You're a bunch of no-talent no-hopers, arse-licking your way up the turkey runner to Barton's office, a fistful of brushes in this hand and the other one tugging at the forelock . . . 'Good morning, Sir Wallace, by Christ but that's a snazzy Canaletto print up there on the wall next to that big clock that says a quarter to eight . . . Suffering Jesus, is that the time already? My, but how time flies when you're enjoying yourself. Pardon me, while I flick this shite off my boot . . . Just after stepping on one of Jimmy Robertson's sketches . . . it'll wash off, I'm sure. What? No, no, not at all, Sir Wallace . . . of course I don't mind putting in a bit of unpaid overtime . . . it's results that count, isn't it?' Jack, you wouldn't know a good design from a plate of canteen mince. Interest? As soon as Barton starts revving up his Jag you're the first one out the door and the leg over the bike before Miss Walkinshaw's even got her teeth out of her waterjug!

Jack Yeh . . . yeh . . . very noble . . . very smart. Listen, you ned, I went to night school for three and a half years . . . I've got a Diploma in Wool Technology!

Phil So, what does that mean?

Spanky He's haun-knitted.

Jack One day you're going to go too far, Farrell. When you do . . . watch out. That's all I'm saying . . . watch out. As for you, McCann . . . grow up. There's a real world out there. Some of us have to live in it. (*Exits.*)

Spanky It's hard to believe he was ever a Slab Boy, isn't it? You don't suppose there's any truth in the rumour that he's really the love-child of Miss Walkinshaw and Plastic Man? No? Well, I think I'll stroll down the showroom and have a look at the new rugs . . .

Phil Eh?

Spanky I'm going for a smoke . . . hold the fort. D'you want me to have a skite for Hector?

Phil Christ, I forgot all about him . . .

Exit Spanky. Pause. Enter Lucille.

Lucille What've yous been saying to Jack Hogg? He's sitting out there with his face like a half-chewed Penny Dainty.

Phil Aw, it's clearing up, is it?

Lucille Bernadette Rooney's boyfriend's going to come up here and give you and your pal a doing if you don't hang off.

Phil Hang off what?

Lucille Jack Hogg. They went to school together.

Phil Tremble . . . tremble . . .

Lucille It's only Bernadette that's holding him back from coming.

Phil Ah, she's a Catholic?

Lucille Eh?

Phil Nothing. (*Pause.*) Er . . . tell me something, Lucille . . .

Lucille God, is there never any dishes washed in this Slab?

Phil See the new guy . . .

Lucille What new guy? Aw . . . him . . . yeh, what about him?

Phil Nothing, nothing . . . Just wondered what you thought about him, that's all.

Lucille He's all right. How?

Phil Just asking . . .

Lucille What're you asking for?

Phil You know he's got scruffula, don't you?

Lucille He's got what?

Phil Scruffula. Like very bad impetigo . . . only worse.

Lucille Who told you that rubbish??

Phil He caught it off Jack. Tough eh?

Lucille Quit acting it, you.

Phil I'm serious. Of course, it's dormant at the moment but any minute his face could just erupt. Him and Jack's been pally for years . . . Used to live next door to each other . . .

Lucille I never knew that . . .

Phil I mean, Jack's as upset about it as everybody else . . . Arthur included . . .

Lucille I thought his name was Alan?

Phil Arthur . . . Alan . . . makes no odds. Another couple of weeks and nobody's going to recognise him anyhow. Face'll be eaten away totally . . . just like Jacky Boy's.

Lucille I thought what Jack had wasn't infectious? He told Miss Walkinshaw he's getting treatment for it . . .

Phil He would say that, sweetheart. He's what you call a 'carrier', you see. Like some people are carriers for infantile paralysis . . . some are carriers for smallpox . . . Jack's a carrier for plooks. Course, you're okay if you've got 'natural immunity' like I've got . . . Look at that . . . clear as a baby's . . . (*Shoves his face up next to Lucille.*)

Lucille Gerroff!

Phil Not young Aldo, I'm afraid . . . D'you ever see that movie where the guy gets buried up to his chin in quicksands and they put this cardboard box full of soldier ants over his noggin and pour treacle through a pin-hole in the top?

Lucille Stop that, you!

Phil That's how his features'll be in about three weeks. There's no known cure for it . . .

Lucille Give us that dish. (*Snatches dish and crosses to sink. Starts washing it.*)

Phil Er . . . Lucille . . .

Lucille What?

70

Phil I was . . . er, wondering . . .

Lucille Wondering what? Don't start on about folk with half-eaten-away faces, I'm warning you.

Phil No . . . I was wondering if you'd, er . . .

Lucille Wondering if I'd what?

Phil If you'd like to . . . er . . .

Just then a face appears at the dirty window. It is Hector half-visible through the dirty glass. He has a bloodstained rag knotted round his head. He is in his underwear.

Lucille Like to what?

Phil (*in a rush*) If you'd like to go to the Staffie with me?

Lucille (*sees face at window*) Aaaaaaaaaaaaaaaaaaargh! (*Exits.*)

Phil What the . . .? I know I'm not exactly Monty Clift but . . . (*Sees Hector.*) God Almighty!!

Hector Let me in, ya bastard! I'm freezing to death out here!

Phil (*throwing window open and dragging Hector in*) What the hell are you playing at!! We're three floors up!

Hector I climbed up the wrone pipe! Ahyah! (*Holds ear.*) I've lost a lot of blood from this. Where's my clothes!

Phil Making a lovely job of them, son.

Hector Where's my trousers? Are they going to be much longer?

Phil No. . . I got Spanky to cut a big daud off them . . . they'll probably come up to about here . . . (*Indicates his kneecap.*)

Hector What??

Phil Don't be stupid . . . I had a skite at them at dinnertime.

Hector Is it the afternoon already? I must've passed out in the Bobbin Shed . . . ahyah! (*Holds ear.*)

Phil Shut up and pull yourself together. Look at the state of you.

Hector That's your fault!! Where's my stuff!!

Phil Keep your voice down! I'll go and see if it's ready. Just quit whining, okay! You stay here . . . (*Exits, only to reappear immediately.*) Willie Curry! . . . Hide!

Hector Waaaaaahhhh!

Phil In the cupboard . . . quick!

> *Bundles Hector into cupboard and stands with his back against the door. Enter Curry.*

Curry (*pointing at cupboard*) That's his little hidey-hole, isn't it?

Phil Eh?

Curry Didn't Farrell put it there this morning?

Phil Eh?

Curry The fresh batch of gum . . . where is it?

Phil Er . . . there?

Curry (*turning to look*) Where?

> *Hector's hand appears from cupboard with gumpot. Phil grabs it.*

Phil There.

Curry Good God! . . . (*Takes gumpot and moves to door. Stops.*) About this morning, McCann . . .

Phil What about this morning?

Curry I was only going to say that if you're prepared to pull your socks up . . . toe the line . . . then I'm prepared to forget the whole episode.

Phil Yeah?

Curry Just show you're willing, McCann . . . that's all I'm asking. These things don't go unnoticed, you know. Mr Barton keeps a weather eye open for lads like yourself . . . ones that buckle down and get on with it. Right? (*Looks at gumpot in hand.*) Good God . . . (*Exits.*)

Phil Thanks, Heck . . .

Hector (*muffled*) Can I come out now?

Phil No . . . you'll only start to annoy me again. I'm not in the mood.

Hector Let me out, ya pig!

Phil See what I mean? Shut your face.

Hector What about my clothes!

Phil (*grabbing palette knife*) Shut it! You're getting your clothes. (*Thrusts knife through edge of door.*) One more sound and I swear before the Virgin Mary I'll come in there and slice your beans off!

Hector Ahyah!

Exit Phil. Pause. Enter Spanky.

Spanky I couldn't find the wee fella . . .

Hector (*muffled, from inside cupboard*) 'S that you, Phil?

Spanky (*looking around*) Eh?

Hector Is the coast clear?

Spanky Who is that?

Hector It's me . . . Hector . . .

Spanky (*looking up*) Aw, yeah . . . are you dead?

Hector (*tumbling out*) Ahyah!

Spanky Waaaaaaah! God Almighty . . . your head!

Hector What's up . . . is it bad!!

Spanky No, no . . . it's . . . er . . . 's really stunning.

Hector I had to dive out the lavvy window. Look at my knees . . . they're all skint.

Spanky They go nice with your head.

Hector If Willie catches me like this I've had it.

Spanky You're not forgetting you've to go and see him?

Hector How could I forget? I can't do nothing till my clothes arrive!

Spanky Ach, stop your moaning, Heck. You'll just have to be patient.

Hector Patient? Patient?? I'm standing here freezing to death . . . blood running out my ear . . . head nipping with the cold . . . Willie's after me . . . my hands are like two bunches of frozen bananas . . . and you've got the cheek to say be patient!! Look at my nut! Go on, look! Maybe it is stunning but Christ Almighty it isn't half gouping! Mammmmmmmy!

Spanky (*alarmed*) Keep your voice down, Hector! And don't keep blaming yourself . . . it was that swine Phil.

Hector And you, ya pig! Where's my clothes??

Spanky Shhhhhhhhhh . . . there's somebody coming! Back in your hole, Heck . . . hurry!

Bundles Hector back into cupboard. Enter Jack Hogg with Lucille at his back,

Lucille I'm telling you, Jack, I definitely saw something . . . outside the window . . . Mother's life . . . a horrible face, like one of them gargoyles . . . a dirty rag round here and great big staring eyes . . .

Jack (*looking out of window*) There certainly doesn't seem to be anything there now, Lucille. You're positive about this 'face'?

Lucille I swear to God. I nearly shit a brick.

Spanky and Jack look at her in disbelief.

Well, I did . . . I got the fright of my life.

Jack But we're three floors up . . .

Lucille He'll tell you . . . he seen it and all.

Spanky Me? I never seen nothing. I've only just came in.

Lucille Were you not here? You were going on about 'soldier ants' and 'treacle'. . .

Spanky What is it . . . a recipe?

Jack Well, there's certainly nothing there now, Lucille . . . so if I could get back to my desk . . .?

Lucille What? Yeh . . . okay . . . thanks for having a look, Jack . . . but I definitely seen something . . .

Jack As if I didn't have enough on my plate. Women . . . (*Exits.*)

Lucille Are you absolutely positive?

75

Spanky How could I if I wasn't here?

Lucille Yeh, right enough . . .

Spanky Er . . . Lucille . . . while you're here. . .

Lucille (*preoccupied*) What . . .?

Spanky While you're here I thought I might have a word . . . about the Staffie . . .

Lucille Eh?

Spanky The Staff Dance. If you fancied . . . you know . . .?

Hector's face appears from the cupboard. Lucille can see it, Spanky can't. Lucille screams . . .

Lucille Aaaaaaaaaaaaaargh! (*Exits.*)

Spanky What was up with her? Honest to God, you ask a civil question . . . (*Sees Hector.*) Aw, it was you, ya wee shite! You went and gave that doll a helluva fright!

Hector I couldn't help it . . . I was trying to hear what you were saying to her.

Spanky I was trying to soften her up for you, ya wee pig!

Hector How was I to know? I'm sorry . . . Oh, my ear.

Enter Phil.

Phil Ho!

Spanky *and* **Hector** (*together*) Ahyah!!

Phil I thought I told you to stay in there? I could've been Willy Curry there.

Spanky Not without a series of very painful operations, Phil.

Hector Where's my clothes? You promised to get my clothes!

Phil Sadie's putting a hem up on the blouse.

Hector almost has a seizure.

Look, you better make yourself scarce . . . Willie's hovering about like a king cobra waiting to strike. Give us a hand, Spanks.

Hector Ahyah! Ahyah!

They bundle Hector back into the cupboard. Enter Alan in brand new white dustcoat. Spanky and Phil start humming Dr Kildare *theme. They pick up their palette knives.*

Spanky Who's under the knife today, Kildare?

Phil It's that young kid that lost both his playpieces in the bus smash, Gillespie.

Spanky What group is he, Kildare?

Phil Fourteenth Sahara Boy Scouts.

Spanky This is gonna be tricky, Doc, there's none in the Frigidaire . . . whadda we gonna do?

Phil I'll give him one of my kidneys . . . see if that'll pull him through . . . poor li'l guy.

Spanky Is that what was on the pieces?

Phil No . . . but I gave my potted heid to the nun we operated on last night.

Spanky And how's she doing, Kildare? Did the graft take?

Phil I'm afraid not, Doctor . . . it was a Friday. (*Makes a lunge at Alan.*)

Alan Hey, watch out! That was a stupid thing to do . . . these things are bloody sharp!

Phil Which is more than can be said for you at this precise moment, kiddo. Look at you . . . you're like one

of the chorus from *The Desert Song*! What're you
wearing that for?

Alan I should've thought that was obvious.

Phil Yes, it's certainly that, pal. Don't try sneaking out
for a fly smoke unless it's snowing.

Enter Curry.

Curry Fit all right, Alan?

Alan Like a glove, Mr Curry.

Spanky Is that the thumb hanging out the back?

Alan (*craning round*) Where?

Phil snatches his Parker pen.

Curry There's magenta and rose pink needed in the
Design Room right away. Jack's on a rush job. McCann,
Farrell . . . in the cabinet in twenty minutes . . . two
large dishes . . . or Mr Barton's going to hear. Okay?
Twenty minutes . . . and I don't want to see either of you
poking your nose out that door till those shades are
ready . . . capeesh? (*Exits.*)

Spanky Plooky Jack and his plooky rush jobs . . .

Phil Better do as he says, Spanks . . . he wasn't kidding.
(*Combs his hair.*) The young intern'll give you a hand . . .

Spanky What about you?

Phil I'm waiting on a phone call.

Alan I don't mind helping . . .

Spanky No . . . leave it to the pros, kid. You've got
something more important to do.

Alan Oh?

Spanky Yeh . . . pop down to the lavvies and bring up Heck's clobber . . .

Alan What?

Spanky Togs . . . clothes . . . clobber. Is there something up with you?

Alan I don't see that that's more imp . . .

Spanky grabs him by the lapels.

Okay, okay . . . I think I can manage . . . (*Exits.*)

Spanky (*crossing to cupboard*) Keep breathing, Heck . . . we've sent Snow White for the threads. We'll soon have you out of there . . .

Phil And looking a million . . .

Spanky Half a million . . . don't exaggerate. Lucille'll be a pushover . . .

Phil A cinch . . .

Spanky Putty in your hands . . .

Phil Don't be dirty, you.

Hector Let me out of here . . . I'm choking!

Phil Choke away . . . you're not bothering us, kid.

Hector Help!

Phil (*shoving knife through crack*) What was that?

Silence.

Spanky You might've brung his togs up . . .

Phil Don't you start. It was difficult enough getting somebody to tackle the bloody things.

Spanky Where d'you find the sewing machine?

Phil Down the Finishing Department. Promised the doll I'd take her out sometime if she done them for us.

Spanky Did she make a nice job of them?

Phil Need you ask?

Spanky Yeh . . . did she make a nice job of them?

Phil I don't know yet, do I? They were wrapped up . . .

Spanky She did know what was expected of her?

Phil I done a drawing, stupid.

Spanky That's all right then. Here . . . d'you want to pulverise some rose pink? (*Dumps a heap of colour onto Phil's slab.*) Heh . . . it wasn't the wee doll with the beer-bottle specs you gave the togs to, was it?

Phil Look, I'm not really going out with her. I only said that so she'd . . .

Enter Alan, out of breath and carrying a parcel.

Alan God, that was a close shave . . .

Spanky (*grabbing parcel*) Give us a gander. (*Unwraps parcel and holds trousers up. They look like jodhpurs.*) Jeesus . . . who did you draw . . . Lester Piggott? And look at the shirt! (*Holds shirt up.*) What size is Heck?

Phil Thirteen and a half.

Spanky Not his chest, stupid . . . his neck?

Phil Three and five-eighths with a muffler on.

Spanky Heh, Alfie, you'll need to take these down to the Finishing . . . there's a wee herrie with X-ray goggles . . .

Phil Don't be stupid . . . he can hardly find his way to the sink.

Spanky Heck's going to look a right palooka in this get-up!

Phil Sssssssshhhhh, he'll hear you.

Alan How can Hector hear?

Hector (*stumbling from cupboard*) Hello?

Alan Christ Almighty!

Phil You'll go to the Bad Fire.

Spanky Look out!! Somebody's coming!

They bundle Hector back into his cupboard and chuck in his togs behind him. Enter Curry.

Curry McKenzie still AWOL?

Spanky You just missed him, Mr Curfew.

Curry Where's he hiding himself now, I wonder?

Spanky Yeh, that's the question, isn't it?

Curry How's that magenta coming along?

Spanky (*grinding furiously*) Aw, not bad . . . just about ready.

Curry That's umber, Farrell . . .

Spanky Eh?

Curry . . . burnt umber.

Spanky 'S not my fault . . . I never burnt it!

Curry Get some magenta on there toot sweet and no more shenanigans! How's the rose pink, McCann?

Phil dollops a lump on Curry's hand.

Still very lumpy! Put some elbow grease into it. You've got another ten minutes or . . . (*Draws finger across throat.*) Comprendez? (*Exits.*)

Phil What is this . . . the bloody Berlitz Academy? Comprendez! Capeeshez . . . cahoochey . . . capucci . . .

Phil *and* **Sparky** (*together as they chop and grind at their slabs*) Comprendez? Capeeshez? Cahoochy? Capucci? Comprendez? Capeeshez? Cahoochy? Capucci? . . .

Alan (*having cleared and dished the burnt umber from Spanky's slab*) Will I put this out in the cabinet?

Phil and Spanky look at each other.

Phil Comprendez? Capeeshez?

Spanky Cahoochey? Capucci?

Exit Alan.

Phil Once I get that phone call . . .

Spanky Some mess you made of the boy's napper . . .

Phil Eh?

Spanky Hector.

Phil That's the thanks you get. I spent an hour trying to get him to look like Lucille's dreamboat, Van Johnson . . .

Spanky More like Van Gogh the way you went through his ear.

Phil 'S not easy cutting hair . . . Try it sometime.

Re-enter Alan.

Alan Hey, is it any good – the Staff Dance?

Spanky What?

Alan The Staffie. Is it good fun?

Spanky What you wanting to know for? You're not thinking of buying a ticket, are you?

Alan No . . . Curry's just given me his – a double. He won't be going. His wife's attending the Foot Clinic . . .

Phil That's handy. You don't need to try a leg, do you?

Alan I'll probably bump into you there . . .

Phil How . . . can you not dance right?

Spanky If you fancy a few pints of green wine before you get there let us know . . .

Alan I'll think about it.

Spanky You do that, son . . . so we can tell you where to meet up.

There is a moaning sound.

What'd you say??

Alan I didn't say anything.

Another moan . . .

Spanky Christ . . . Hector!

Hector promptly falls face-first out of the cupboard. He is wearing the restyled clothing. Phil and Spanky rush over . . .

Phil He's shamming . . . I saw one of his eyelids flicker.

Spanky Wake up, ya wee rat!

Alan Give him air, for God's sake . . .

Hector (*being hauled to his feet*) I think I must've blacked out . . . it got very warm in there . . . Well? What d'you think?

Spanky Er . . . 's incredible, Heck . . . just incredible . . . Never seen nothing like it. Right, Phil?

Phil That's for sure . . .

Hector (*to Phil*) What d'you think?

Phil Are they comfy? (*He is referring to Hector's trousers, which he has managed to put on back to front.*)

Hector Yeh. (*Looks down at trouser front.*) There's just one thing . . .

Phil Ah, you noticed. 'S the very latest . . .

Hector Yeh, but how do I go for a . . .?

Phil You don't, son. They run a pipe down your leg into a special ten-gallon rubber boot.

Alan You've got them on back to front.

Spanky Buttons are up the back . . .

Phil Just like Uncle Bertie's.

Hector (*rounding quickly*) What??

Phil Just like they had in the thirties. You must've seen them musicals. Fred Astaire dancing with Roy Rogers. They both had their trousers buttoned up the back . . .

Hector Eh?

Phil Course you wouldn't've noticed, kid. That's 'cos Fred wore these long tailcoats and Roy . . .

Spanky Roy was sitting down . . .

Phil On Trigger.

Spanky How does the shirt feel? (*referring to Hector's restyled 'off-the-shoulder' shirt*)

Hector 'S nice and easy on my throat.

Spanky Special design . . .

Hector Looks all right then, Spanky?

Spanky It's a knockout, kid.

Phil A knockout.

Hector So you think Lucille'll bite?

Phil Your maw'll be asking you whose the teethmarks are when she gives you your bath tonight. Lucille is going to flip.

Hector No kidding, Phil?

Alan Hector . . .

Phil holds up Parker pen out of Hector's line of vision but so that Alan can see it.

Hector D'you like it, Alan?

Alan It's . . . er . . .

Phil threatens to snap pen.

. . . really gadgey, Heck.

Hector Will I go now and ask her? Will I? (*Heads for door.*)

Spanky (*cutting him off*) Not just yet, Hector . . . Remember you've still got to go and see Willie.

Hector Yeh, but I can do that after I've asked Lucille . . .

Phil No, Spanky's right, kiddo . . . better go and see Willie first. It's important. Lucille'll not go off the boil. Here, I'll give you my coat to put on . . . (*Takes off coat.*)

Hector What do I want that for? I don't mind doing a bit of swanking now that my clothes are up to date.

Phil Yeh, but you don't want anybody else to get a preview, do you? Lessen the impact . . . know what I mean? Get the coat on. (*Forces Hector's arms into sleeves.*)

85

Spanky (*pulling balaclava helmet from cupboard*) You better put this on and all . . . it's draughty in Willie's room. (*Pulls helmet over Hector's head.*) Cosy, eh?

Hector (*slightly bamboozled*) Yeh, but will he not think I'm a bit happed up?

Phil That's just it. You've been down at Nurse. Influenza verging on pleurisy. She ordered you home but you decided to soldier on. He'll like that. Maybe not give you your . . . (*Stops.*)

Spanky (*quickly*) Wireless back.

Hector I'm not expecting my wireless back. You know what he's like.

Spanky Well, you can't expect it back just 'cos you've got the flu, Heck . . .

Phil Triple pneumonia, Spanks.

Hector I'm all mixed up . . . what've I got again?

Spanky Triple pneumonia . . .

Phil Double rupture . . .

Hector I'll away along, then.

Spanky Good man. All the best.

Phil Good luck, son . . .

They shove Hector out the door.

You'll need it.

They hold on to each other, laughing.

Alan Well, I hope you're proud of yourselves . . . that was a pretty lousy trick to play!

Spanky Oh, was it, by jove?

Phil A trick, you cad! Take that! (*Bops Alan's head a smack.*)

Alan Hey, watch it! That was sore . . . Chuck it! Okay, so I'm speaking out of turn but that poor little bastard's gone off to Willie Curry's office thinking underneath that dustcoat and helmet he really does cut a dash . . . and he'll probably stop off on the way back to have a word with Lucille . . . doff the coat and hat and you know what'll happen then . . . she'll wet herself. Which will probably give you and your crummy friend a big laugh, won't it?

Phil Gosh and All Serene, the Fifth Form at St Dominic's. Listen, Steerforth Minor, if it wasn't for me and Spanks there that 'poor little bastard' wouldn't have any pals. Yeh, that's right. So, we do take the piss . . . set him up a bit . . .

Alan More than a bit.

Phil Shut it! Know what he done last summer?

Spanky I don't think he wants to. hear, Phil . . .

Phil He's talking about us playing dirty tricks? He's going to hear. Know what the mug done? Just 'cos some stupid lassie wouldn't look the road he was on? Took the string out of his pyjama trousers, tied it round his throat and strung himself up from the kitchen pulley.

Spanky His old dear had to get the man next door to cut him down with the bread knife. You can still see the rope burns.

Phil Touch and go, it was . . .

Spanky He still can't swallow a whole chip . . .

Phil What me and him's done is give Hector the courage to go and ask Lucille straight out for a date instead of wishing his life away. Okay, so she's going to crease herself but you think twice before you start applying your stupid counterfeit *Boys' Own Paper* code of 'fair play' in here. You don't know you're living, sweetheart! (*Heads for door. Stops.*) And if Willie Curry wants to know where I am, I'm down the bog smoking . . . two fags at once!

Exits. Pause.

Alan Is that true about Hector?

Spanky Yeh . . . only I think it was his old dear that strung him up from the pulley . . . he can be a right pain at times. How's the rose pink coming along?

Alan (*moves to door*) I'm going to stop him before he makes a complete fool of himself . . .

Spanky I wouldn't do that, Alfie . . . you don't know what Phil's like.

Alan hesitates.

He's got some temper. Come on . . . The rose pink's waiting . . .

Alan returns to slab.

Wise boy. Get us they dishes over there . . . the clean ones.

Enter Jack Hogg with wages tray.

Jack I don't know what I'm doing this for. Lucille should be taking these round. (*Leafs through wage packets.*) Farrell . . . G. There you go . . .

Spanky Thanks, Jacko. I'll take Phil's and all, he's away to the cludgie.

Jack McCann . . . McCann . . . Two N's, am I right? McAllister, McBain, McCourtney, McDonald,

McFarlane . . . nope, doesn't seem to be anything for him . . .

Spanky Stop messing about, Jacky Boy.

Jack There's nothing for him . . . look.

Spanky Bloody hell. Give us Hector's, then.

Jack McFarlane, McInnes, McLaughlan, McManus . . . Nothing for Hector either . . . sorry.

Spanky Eh?

Jack There'll be something for you next time, Alan. Won't be a lot, you understand . . . just enough to invest in a gas mask for the occasional sortie into this crap hole. The boss is trying to fix you up with something a trifle more salubrious for next week. Must dash . . . got a big job on. Oh, I've got these mags you wanted to see. Some of your dad's stuff in one of them. Very nifty. See you.

Exits.

Spanky Bloody funny that . . . I was only half-surprised at Hector's pay-poke being missing, but Phil's and all?

Alan Could've been a discrepancy . . .

Spanky Eh?

Alan An oversight. They might not've put his in with the rest.

Spanky Yeh . . . I can see how you got into a university, son. I'll sprint along and have a word with the Cashier. If Phil comes back just say I'm away mending a fuse in Miss Walkinshaw's glass eye . . . okay? (*Exits.*)

Alan carries on grinding. Enter Lucille, very warily. She goes to cupboard door and nervously inches it open.

Alan The gum's over there if you want some.

Lucille No . . . it's not that . . .

Alan Oh . . .

Lucille You haven't seen . . .? (*Opens cupboard. Finds it empty.*)

Alan Yes?

Lucille What?

Alan You were about to ask if I'd seen something . . .

Lucille Was I?

Alan Yes . . . you said, 'You haven't seen . . .?'

Lucille Oh, yeh . . . er . . . (*Points to poster of James Dean.*) *Rebel Without a Cause* . . . you haven't seen *Rebel Without a Cause. . .*?

Alan That's true. Must've missed it when it came round our way . . .

Lucille What? You've never seen it? Where've you been hiding? (*Offers Alan some chewing gum.*) D'you want a Chiclet?

Alan Thanks . . . (*Takes a Chiclet.*)

Lucille Tell us if you think that tastes like ointment. I usually get Juicy Fruit . . . Yeh, it was really brilliant. Me and Bernadette sat through it twice. It was on a double-bill with *East of Eden* . . . Me and her cried our eyes out when his Porsche turned over and he got killed.

Alan Ah . . . it was a racing picture?

Lucille What?

Alan *East of Eden* – it was a racing . . .?

Lucille I don't find that amusing!

Alan Sorry?

Lucille It didn't take you long to get into bad habits, did it!

Alan No, you don't understand . . . wasn't . . .

Lucille Ach, yous are all the same! I hope it's terminal, whatever you got off Jack!

Alan Hang on . . . I don't think you . . .

Exit Lucille.

Christ, I love Terry Dene. Lucille . . .

Enter Phil.

Phil (*looking after Lucille*) We'll need to get you a cake of Lifebuoy, Arthur . . .

Enter Spanky.

Spanky Aw . . . er . . . hi, Phil . . .

Alan (*pointing at poster*) That is whatdyoucallim, isn't it?

Phil Miles Malleson . . . ? Yeah. Tragic, eh? There they were . . . Miles . . . Lesley Howard . . . the entire Glen Miller Orchestra . . .

Spanky Flying down to Rio . . .

Phil When their plane crashed . . .

Spanky In the mountains . . .

Phil The Urinals . . .

Spanky Pilot was pissed.

Enter Sadie with tea trolley.

Sadie Tea's up. There's your dainties . . .

Spanky *and* **Phil** Aha!

Sadie Roobert tarts . . .

Spanky Hello!

Sadie Chocolate horns . . .

Phil Hooray!

Sadie Penny baps . . .

Spanky Whoopee!

Sadie And your macaroni turnovers . . .

Spanky *and* **Phil** Wow!

Sadie Don't all rush us . . . I know you've just been paid.

Phil Hey . . . you never told us the wages was round, Spanks . . . make with the green jobs . . . I'm starving.

Spanky I can lend you a couple of bob . . .

Phil Quit the kidding . . . I'm ravenous.

Alan There wasn't anything for you. Jack Hogg looked twice. Two, please, Sadie, and I'll have one of those . . .

Phil What??

Spanky That's right, Phil. I've just been along to check with the Cashier. They said you and Heck's was being made up special . . .

Phil Suffering Christ . . .

Sadie Tch, tch, tch, tch . . . (*to Alan*) You hold your ears, son.

Spanky At least you've got the Art Academy to look forward to. Heck's got sweet damn all . . . absolute piss nothing.

Sadie Language. Language. That's bloody hellish.

Phil What about me? The Art School's still six months away . . .

Sadie Are you wanting tea, yous two? I'm taking this trolley away in a minute . . .

Spanky The lassie'll be phoning soon. It's Hector that's the problem . . . there's only his wages coming into that house. What about his maw . . . what's he going to tell her?

Sadie For the last time, are yous two wanting something?

Spanky Yeh . . . give us two teas. Want one, Phil?

Sadie What's up with him?

Spanky You want a macaroni cake?

Phil You know I've no money, what're you asking us for?

Spanky I'll get it. How's about a chocolate horn? You can play 'Old Man River' on it.

Phil I'm not wanting nothing!

Sadie Aw, stick, bubblyjock. (*Pours tea for Spanky.*)

Spanky Give us a bap.

Sadie Thruppence ha'penny.

Spanky How come? It's three ha'pence for tea and the baps are a penny.

Sadie You spent that long making up your mind they've went up. Thruppence ha'penny.

Spanky proffers a ten-shilling note.

You not got any change? How'm I expected to change a ten-shilling note? They're all giving me notes today. Look. . . not a bit of silver in my box. You'll need to get change.

Spanky I'll give you it tomorrow, Sadie . . .

Sadie Tomorrow's Saturday and fine you know it. D'you think I came up the Clyde on this trolley? Get change . . . I'll wait.

Spanky You got any, Arthur?

Alan I'm not sure . . . (*Takes out gent's purse.*)

Phil Christ, where d'you keep that, kid . . . up the leg of your brassiere?

Sadie I've had enough out of you. One more bit of language and I'll draw my hand across your jaw. Just give that boy there peace. . . what harm has he done you, you bloody . . .

Alan No, I don't seem to have that much . . . I can give you a loan of something . . .

Spanky No, it's all right . . . I'll do without. (*Bangs bap and tea onto trolley.*)

Sadie You not want these, then? The penny bap . . . or the tea?

Spanky The tea's cold and the bap's foosty.

Sadie That's because you're standing there trying to coax Dirty Gub out of his huff . . .

Phil Aw, piss off, you old trollop.

Sadie I heard that . . . I heard that, ya hooligan! (*Smacks Phil on head.*) If one of my boys was here he'd stoat you off that wall, so he would.

Phil Ahyah! Ohyah! (*Clutches head.*) You hit us with your ring! Owwww.

Sadie Aye, you're the big cheese in here, Philip McCann, but just you wait . . . somebody's going to sort you out before you're much older. Talk to me like that, would you! Just you wait . . .

Alan holds door open.

Thanks, son . . . you're a gentleman.

Phil Ow . . . that was some skelp . . .

Spanky Here . . . put that on it. (*Hands Phil an éclair that he's pinched.*)

Phil Ta . . . What'd she go and hit us for?

Spanky She's at a funny age. My maw's the same . . . lashes out at the bree and me for nothing. The *Sunday Post* Doctor says it's nothing to worry about . . . they all go like that. These are good, aren't they?

Alan That is Terry Dene, isn't it?

Spanky Where? (*Looks inside éclair.*)

Alan Come on . . . is it . . . Terry Dene?

Spanky You ignorant or something?

Alan The one that was in *Rebel Without a Cause* and *East of Aden* . . .?

Spanky Suez . . . *East of Suez.*

Alan About motor racing . . .?

Spanky That's the one . . . only it was camels. Him and Frankie Laine raced round the Sphinx for Audrey Murphy's hand. Frankie won by a nose so they gave him Audrey's hand. Terry got the rest of her . . . right?

Phil Think I'll take a walk, Spanks . . .

Spanky You not want to hang about in case that phone call comes?

Phil No . . . don't think I'm going to hear anyhow . . . it's that kind of day. If the doll phones, you take it . . . say you're me . . . okay?

Spanky Okay . . . if you're sure.

Exit Phil.

Alan That's the rest of the pink dished . . . will I put it out in the cabinet . . .?

Spanky What do you think?

Exit Alan. Pause. Enter Jack Hogg.

Jack I'm looking for your chum.

Spanky What're you wanting him for?

Jack There's a phone call in Mr Barton's office . . . sounded rather urgent. Girl said it was the hospital.

Spanky That's all right, I'll take it.

Jack No, no . . . she was most insistent she speak to McCann himself . . .

Spanky I'll take it, I said . . .

Jack No, I don't think . . .

Spanky I'm authorised! (*Exits.*)

Jack Hey . . . (*Exits.*)

Pause. Enter Sadie.

Sadie Too bloody soft, that's my trouble . . . He's not getting off with it, this time. Fifteen shillings? Not on your nelly . . . (*Sits down. Eases shoes off.*) Oooooohhhhh . . . I should trade these in for a set of casters . . .

Enter Lucille. Crosses to sink.

Any Epsom salts, hen?

Lucille Waaahh! God, it's you! What're you playing at, Sadie!

Sadie Have you seen that shy boy McCann on your travels?

Lucille Shy?

Sadie Aye . . . fifteen bob shy. He still owes us for that dance ticket he got.

Lucille Not again? When're you going to wise up? You'll just need to wait and grab him at the Town Hall . . .

Sadie Oh, no . . . I'll not be seeing any Town Hall the night, sweetheart. If I thought these had to burl me round a dance floor . . . (*Cradles feet.*)

Lucille Are you not going? Aw, Sadie, it was a right scream last year.

Sadie I know, flower . . .

Lucille That man of yours was a howl.

Sadie Aye . . . hysterical. Who else would sprint the length of the hall with a pint of Younger's in their fist and try leapfrogging over the top of Miss Walkinshaw with that beehive hairdo of hers . . . eh? Only that stupid scunner I've got . . .

Lucille How long was he off his work with the leg?

Sadie Too long, sweetheart. He had my heart roasted, so he did. Sitting there with the bloody leg up on the fender shouting at me to put his line on at the bookie's for him. 'See that?' I says. 'If you're not up and back to your work tomorrow I'll draw this across your back!' I had the poker in my hand . . . and I would've done it and all. Had me up to high doh. Couldn't get the stookie down the dungarees quick enough. Men? I wouldn't waste my time, hen.

Lucille Come off it, Sadie . . .

Sadie I'd to take the first one that came along. I'd've been better off with a lucky bag.

Lucille They're not all like that, for God's sake.

Sadie You'll learn, flower . . . you're young yet. You can afford to sift through the dross . . . till you come to the real rubbish at the bottom.

Lucille Not this cookie. Lucille Bentley . . . Woman of the World . . . Fling Out Your Men!

Sadie Wait till you get to my age and all you've got to show's bad feet and a display cabinet . . .

Lucille Who wants to get to your age?

Sadie Here, what time is it? I promised 'Leapfrog' I'd get him a nice bit of fish for his tea. Well, it's Friday . . . with any luck he'll be home with half his paypoke still on him . . .

Lucille Yeh, and it'll be his own half, by the sounds of it. You wouldn't get me putting up with that.

Sadie I'm biding my time, sweetheart. Soon as I've a good wee bankbook I'm showing that swine the door. See that? (*Indicates breast.*) I lost that over the head of him.

Lucille My God, what did he do??

Sadie Flang it in the midden.

Lucille Eh?

Sadie Thought it was one of our James's old footballs that got bursted.

Lucille What?

Sadie No, no . . . I had that off long before I got in tow with that sod. Up the Western . . .

Enter Spanky. He is preoccupied.

Hey, you, where's your pal?

Spanky Eh?

Sadie Fifteen bob for a dance ticket I'm after . . .

Spanky Aw, yeh . . . (*Reaches in pocket for money.*)

Sadie Mr Anderson . . . big strapping man . . . head surgeon up there . . . (*taking money from Spanky*) Thanks, son. (*to Lucille*) 'That'll have to come away, Miss Jowett, otherwise it'll go right through your whole system.' (*to Spanky*) Thanks, son, you can get it back easier than what I can. (*to Lucille*) Couldn't argue with that, flower . . .

Spanky Hey . . . (*Checks money.*)

Sadie Felt a bit lopsided at first but I kept my trolley money in this pocket till I got my balance back.

Spanky Hey, Sadie . . .

Sadie They've went away up as well. Nineteen and eleven for a replacement.

Lucille (*to Spanky*) I hope you and your pal catch it off Jack and all . . .

Spanky Eh?

Exit Lucille.

Sadie Nineteen and eleven . . . for a single . . .

Spanky Used to be only fifteen bob . . .

Sadie Aye, but they're made of foam rubber now, son. (*Exits.*)

Spanky Eh? Hey, Sadie. . . (*Crosses to door.*)

Enter Phil at the gallop.

Phil Well?

Spanky What way did the old bag go?

Phil You took a phone call . . . Jack says . . .

Spanky Oh, yeh . . . from the . . . er . . . hospital . . .

Phil And?

Spanky The doll thought I was you. You told me to say
I was you . . .

Phil I know that! Hurry up!

Spanky It was the hospital.

Phil I know! Tell us the worst.

Spanky Your maw's vanished.

Phil What??

Spanky Shot the crow . . . skedaddled.

Phil You mean it really was the hospital?

Spanky That's what I was trying to tell you, Phil . . .

Phil Christ.

Spanky They were phoning to see if she'd been in touch
with me . . . you, I mean. They said not to be alarmed . . .

Phil Not to be alarmed?? What if she turns up here?
She'll probably put a hatchet through old Walkinshaw's
head just to give me a showing up.

Enter Alan.

Spanky They've sent some people out to look for her.

Phil She can be real vicious, you know. She once took a bite out of a guy's nose up at the Out Patients . . .

Spanky Eh?

Phil It was only the Occupational Therapist. Jeeesus Christ, how come I couldn't have a sensible maw like you guys . . . eh?

Spanky You don't know that our maws is any more sensibler than yours, Phil . . .

Phil All my stupid maw ever done was worry. Worry about money . . . about schools . . . going to Mass . . . missing confessions . . . going out with lassies . . . getting our hole. Some bloody hope! All we ever knew about dames was their arms stuck out sideyways when they ran.

Spanky Most of our maws is a bit like that . . .

Phil I bet you his isn't!

Spanky Leave him alone, Phil . . . he doesn't know what you're talking about.

Phil I bet you he doesn't. (to Alan) What do you know about getting up in the middle of the night in your shirt tail to say five decades of the rosary over your maw's open wrists? What do you know about screaming fits and your old man's nut getting bopped off the Pope's calendar? What do you know about razor blades and public wards and row upon row of gumsy cadavers all sitting up watching you stumble in with your Lucozade and excuses? Christ, what one's mine? Is that you, Maw? What do you know about living in a rabbit hutch with concrete floors and your old man's never in and you're left trying to have a conversation with a TV set and a maw that thinks you're St Thomas Aquinas? What do you know about standing there day in, day out in the

Factor's office asking for a move and the guy with the shiny arse on his trousers shakes his head and treats your old dear like dirt??

Alan All right . . . you've had your say, but I don't see where I come in . . .

Phil Well, it certainly isn't the Tradesman's Entrance, petal. Straight up to the front door for you . . . 'This way, sir. Let me take your problems, sir . . . they must be cutting into your shoulder.' I know where I'd like to cut into you! (*Makes a lunge at Alan.*)

Spanky (*intervening*) Steady on, Phil! I don't think Archie's any idea what . . .

Phil That's right, Spanky old sport, you stick with his lot. You always did know what side your madeira cake was buttered!

Spanky That's not fair. I was only . . .

Phil I'm away to join the Hunt. I'll send my maw's head back for your dad's Trophy Room . . . Alan! (*using his right name for the first time with derisive emphasis*)

Spanky What about your wages?

Phil Stuff them up Curry's jaxie . . . I'm off. (*Exits. Off*) Tally-hooooooooooooo . . .

   Pause.

Spanky You don't want to pay too much attention to Phil, son . . . he reads a lot.

Alan I think he's off his chump. (*Pause.*) Was that true, all that . . . about his mother trying to . . . you know . . .?

Spanky Do away with herself? 'S true all right. Last time it happened was at a boarding house in Dunoon. His old man found the suicide note tucked into her beach bag. She'd went and swallowed a hundred and fifty aspirins . . . washed down with a bottle of Domestos . . .

Alan I thought he mentioned razor blades . . . ?

Spanky C'mon, Arthur . . . she'd need to be a real looney to swallow a hundred and fifty razor blades . . . No . . . they made her be sick down the toilet . . . phoned for the ambulance. Landlady was quite sympathetic . . . till Phil's maw brung up the bleach and took the flowers off her wallpaper. Did you say the rest of the rose pink was ready?

Alan It's in the cabinet . . .

Spanky Here . . . you can have a 'nice time' with the Hooker's green, honey . . .

Enter Jack Hogg.

Jack That's McCann's wages. Has he got a bonus or what? Right hefty wage packet. Hector not about? I've got his too. God, feel the weight of that. Have they been putting in a bit of overtime?

Spanky I'll take that, Jacky Boy. (*Takes Phil's wage packet.*)

Jack Would you see that Heck gets that one, Alan? I think we can trust you.

Spanky And what's that supposed to mean, Plooky Appearance?

Jack Why don't you dry up?

Spanky Like you, Jacky Boy? Not bloody likely. You know you can get stuff for that? You rub it all over your phizog. It's cried emery paper.

Jack Ho bloody ho. Look what's talking. Look at the arms. It's like somebody's put a dustcoat on a chimp.

Spanky There's nothing up with my arms!

Jack They're about seven inches longer than your legs.

Spanky Three and a half – don't exaggerate!

Enter Phil.

I thought you were away?

Phil I went along for my wages . . . doll said she gave them to Jack.

Jack The monkey's got them . . .

Spanky Catch. (*Flings packet to Phil.*) 'S that you off, Jackknife? Not fancy a hot poultice before you go?

Jack If you need a lift home, Alan, let me know . . . I'll try and arrange something . . .

Alan Thanks.

Exit Jack.

Spanky (*to Phil, who is opening his wage packet*) Your books?

Phil Yeh . . . P45, the lot . . . (*Reads document.*) 'Non-Contributory Pension Scheme' . . . what's that?

Alan It means you haven't paid directly into . . .

Phil Shut it, you! I'm talking to my friend. Well?

Spanky How should I know? I've got all these dishes to wash!! Can you not give us a hand? There's hundreds of them.

Phil You're forgetting something, Spanky. I don't work here any more.

Spanky You never did, Phil.

Phil Less of the sarcasm . . . (*sarcastically*) Slab Boy.

Spanky At least I still am one.

Phil Yeh . . . how come? Me and Hector get the heave and you're still here washing dishes safe and secure. How d'you manage it, eh?

Spanky Going to get out of my road? I've got work to do . . .

Phil Work? Has Noddy there been getting to you?

Spanky Why don't you can it, Phil? Me and the boy wants to get cleared up.

Phil Aw . . . it's 'me and the boy' now, is it?

Spanky Yeh . . . what of it?

Phil I think I'm going to be sick.

Spanky Well, don't hang over the shades, there's gum in them al –

Phil grabs him. They confront one another. Enter Curry.

Curry Still here, McCann? You can go any time, you know.

Phil I'm waiting for a phone call.

Curry Only urgent personal calls allowed . . .

Phil This is urgent. I'm waiting for word from the hospital.

Curry What's up . . . someone in the family ill?

Phil It's my maw.

Curry Oh, yes, of course. Were the lacerations severe? It can do a great deal of damage, plate glass . . .

Phil What?

Curry Plate glass . . . the stuff they have in shop windows.

Phil What d'you know about shop windows? Who told you about it?

Curry There was a bit in today's *Paisley Express* . . . 'Ferguslie Park Woman in Store Window Accident'. . .

Phil It wasn't an accident. She meant to do it.

Curry Eh? But the paper said your mother was thrown through the window by a passing car . . .

Phil Well, they got it wrong, didn't they? There was a car there but it wasn't passing . . . it was parked. What she done was take a header off the roof . . . straight through the Co window . . . simple.

Curry From the roof of a car? She must've been badly injured.

Phil Not a scratch. They say it was the angle she jumped off the roof of the motor.

Curry Good God, it must've been a miracle.

Phil Nope . . . a Ford Prefect.

Curry You're a callow bastard, McCann. As soon as that phone call comes through you can sling your hook, okay? Alan . . . my office.

Exeunt Curry and Alan.

Spanky I say, Nugent, d'you think I should've leapt into the scrum just then and chinned old Quelch about getting into Upper School? Hmmm?

Phil Yes, you might've been lucky and got the bag like me, old chap.

Spanky Some hope . . . I'm here for the duration.

Phil Well, if you play your cards right . . . don't give the screws too much cheek . . . time off for good behaviour . . . who knows, you might get it down to 'life'.

Spanky What about Pygmy Minimus? He thought he was here for life.

Phil So?

Spanky D'you not think we should put round the hat? Help tide him over till he gets his Broo money?

Phil What about tiding me over till I get mine?

Spanky You've got the Art College to look forward to.

Phil And my nearest and dearest wandering the fields and hedgerows eating worms.

Spanky C'mon, what d'you say? Just to see the boy's mammy over the hump . . .

Phil (*looking in wage packet*) Over the hump? There's hardly enough in here to buy Quasimodo a half of Bell's.

Spanky Ten bob'll do . . . look, I'll match it.

Phil Make it five. Don't say I'm not generous . . .

Spanky Ten. Come on . . .

Phil (*hands over ten-shilling note*) Stupid, but not ungenerous.

Spanky Heck'll not forget this, Phil.

Phil Nor will I . . . that's half my bloody wages.

Spanky May the sausage of true contentment sizzle in your sandwich.

Phil Confucius?

Spanky Tex Ritter . . . he sang it in a movie once. Right, I'll get this in an envelope, will I?

Phil Not be better with an armour-plated truck?

Spanky Let's have a celebration. Here's two bob . . . race down the canteen and bring us back a thousand Woodbine.

Phil Terrific. Open, Sesame.

Spanky *Voilà!*

Phil Back 'n a tricycle. (*Exits.*)

Spanky (*writing on wage packet containing Hector's 'presentation'*) Hector 'Threads' McKenzie . . . Slab Boy . . . Retired. Farewell, small chum . . . it has been fun, but now your days are numbered . . . We've had our laughs . . . we've shared our tears . . . You've left me effing lumbered.

   Enter Lucille. She crosses to sink.

Spanky Hi, Lucille. Replenishing the old 'jooga di aqua', I see.

Lucille You trying to be filthy again?

Spanky It's Italian . . .

Lucille Where'd you get it . . . off a chip poke?

Spanky D'you hear about Hector?

Lucille Hear what?

Spanky He's going to be leaving us . . .

Lucille Am I supposed to pass out or something? You should all be leaving. You're a bunch of good-for-nothing foul-mouthed pigs . . . in a foul-smelling pigsty. Take a look at this joint . . . what d'you see?

Spanky We're waiting for the decorators . . .

Lucille It's an absolute cowp. You're frightened to come in here in case you get something contagious. And by the way that isn't true what you said about the new guy . . . I checked with Jack. What Jack's got is described as 'parched skin' . . . and it is not smittal, so there.

Spanky Ah . . . that's good news.

Lucille You're a bunch of lying dogs. And you're bone idle . . . look at all them manky dishes.

Spanky Let lying dogs sleep, I always say. Er . . . Lucille, I was wondering . . .

Lucille Here we go again. Yes?

Spanky I was wondering if you . . . er . . . caught my drift earlier on?

Lucille And what drift was that?

Spanky The Staffie . . . ?

Lucille The Staffie?

Spanky Staff Dance.

Lucille Aw . . . that's what you call it? How childish.

Spanky If you fancied going with . . . ?

Lucille Fancied going with who? Not you?

Spanky Yeh . . . what's up with me? I know you aren't booked . . .

Lucille Oh, do you?

Spanky I checked with Miss Walkinshaw. How about it, eh? I'm getting a gadgey dinner suit from Caled . . . from Jackson's . . . real honey . . . roll collar . . . swivel button . . . fingertip drape. . . Yeh, I know my arms look a bit on the long side, but the guy in the shop said that was no problem . . . He's going to break them off at the elbow for us. What d'you say? Eh? What're you staring at?

Lucille I can't believe the cheek of you guys. Have you looked in a mirror lately?

Spanky Course I have . . . every morning when I'm shaving. I've got a very heavy growth, you know. Feel.

Lucille Don't come near me.

Spanky C'mon, cut the capers, Lucille . . . are you going to the dance or are you not going to the dance?

Lucille Oh, I'm going okay . . .

Spanky Terrific. What time d'you want me to . . .?

Lucille But not with you, sonny boy. I'm booked.

Spanky What? Who're you going with? I never heard nothing.

Lucille That's because your listeners are run up from the same material as your rompers . . .

Spanky C'mon, who is it? Who are you going with?

Lucille Excuse me . . .

Spanky Don't be lousy . . . tell me who it is.

Lucille All I'm saying is . . .

Spanky Yeh?

Lucille . . . it's someone from the Slab Room. Now, shift.

Spanky Eh?

Lucille Shift, I said. Move the torso.

Spanky Sure . . .

Enter Phil.

Phil Ah . . . Lucille . . . help yourself to a cork-tipped Woodbine . . . Don't scar the chest, throat or lungs . . . just tear the skin off your lips. On you go, I've got hundreds . . .

Jack Hogg looks round the door.

Jack Farrell . . . Boss wants to see you. I mean now.

Phil Oho. Put this behind your ear, kiddo. (*Places Woodbine behind Spanky's ear.*) When he offers you the desk . . . light up . . . that'll impress him.

Spanky Thanks . . .

Jack And you better quit spreading lies, McCann. This is non-transmittable. Serious but non-transmittable. Right, Farrell, follow me . . .

Exeunt.

Lucille Let me out as well.

Phil Hold your horses, sweetheart.

Lucille Let me past, I said.

Phil Wait a second . . . this is important.

Lucille Aw, yeh? What is it? I'm dying to know . . .

Phil Shhhh . . . listen . . . you're going to the dance tonight, right?

Lucille If this is a mind-reading act it's pathetic.

Phil I know it's asking a lot but . . . you don't have a date . . . right? (*Pause.*) Have you or have you not got a date?

Lucille I might have . . .

Phil When did this happen?

Lucille Couple of minutes ago . . .

Phil Bloody hell. You can break it, can't you? C'mon, doll, you can break it.

Lucille All right . . . yeh . . . maybe. Depends who asks.

Phil I'm asking.

Lucille Then I'll think about it . . .

Phil Yes or no?

Lucille Quit pressing me . . . I said I'd think about it . . . okay, yeh.

Phil Terrific. You're a doll.

Lucille What time are you picking us up at?

Phil No, no . . . you don't understand, sweetheart. Not me . . . Hector.

Lucille What!

Phil Look, I know me and Spanks take the piss out of him but underneath he's . . .

Lucille This is another one of your jokes, isn't it!

Phil Course it isn't . . . I'm dead serious. What would I want to . . .

Lucille Hector! I'd rather play Postman's Knock with Jack Hogg!

Phil You don't have to dance every dance with the wee shite . . . just come in the door with him . . .

Lucille Not on your life! Move!

Phil He's crazy about you, for Christ's sake!

Lucille So what!!

Phil It's all he ever thinks about . . . the Big Date . . . the Staffie . . . The guy's in love with you, Lucille.

Lucille Don't talk romantic. I wouldn't be seen dead with that smout at a dance. You're off your head, Phil McCann. I'd be laughed out of the Design Room.

Phil Listen . . . you only have to give the boy the impression you're with him . . . flash him the occasional smile . . . the odd nibble at his ear . . . not this one . . . me and Spanks'll do the rest . . . get him that pissed he'll never notice you're not around for the rest of the night . . .

Lucille Thanks a bunch.

Phil You know what I mean. As long as he thinks you've went with him.

Lucille No, I said . . . what do I have to do? Carve it in letters this size on my forehead? N–O! I've never heard anything so ridiculous. He's a dwarf, for God's sake!

Phil Even dwarves have feelings, doll. Christ, don't you have any? Where's your compassion . . . your sensitivity . . . your eye to the main chance? Alexander Pope was a dwarf . . . so was Lautrec . . . so was Turner . . . and what were they? Giants. That's what they were . . . giants. Jesus God Almighty . . . he's nuts about you . . . can't you see that?

Lucille He's a mess! Get out of my road! Get out of my life!

Phil Lucille . . .

Exit Lucille.

Aaaaaaahhhh . . . fuck it!

Pause. Enter Spanky.

What'd Barton want?

Silence.

You don't have to spare my feelings, kiddo . . . I'm off to pastures new. Where's it to be . . . next to Jimmy Robertson's?

Silence.

Miss Walkinshaw's?

Silence.

Aw, no . . . not beside Jack Hogg?

Spanky He told us to wire in and I just might get one in about eighteen month's time . . .

Phil Jeesus . . . I hope you told him where to stick it?

Spanky Not in so many words, no. (*Pause.*) You been talking to Lucille?

Phil Eh? What's it to you?

Spanky About the dance? Yeh, she said . . . (*Pause.*) Give us one of them Woodies, will you?

Phil You can have the lot. They keep them stacked up beside the kippers down there.

They light up. Enter Hector.

Hector I've seen him . . .

Spanky Seen who? Bela Lagoosey? You're as white as a sheet . . .

Hector Willie . . . I've just came from his office . . .

Spanky Get the boy a seat, Phil . . .

They sit Hector down.

Hector I had to be sick down the toilet . . .

Spanky So you know then?

Hector Yeh . . . I know. I came back to clear out my stuff. What's that funny smell?

Phil Fishbine. D'you want a drag? It'll clean out what's left in your stomach, kid.

Spanky Heh – the Presentation, Phil . . .

Phil I don't think I'm up to it, Spanks . . .

Spanky Nor me . . . we'll just have to force ourselves . . . look at the pale he is.

Phil Still in a state of shock, the boy . . .

Spanky Er . . . Hecky . . .

Hector (*getting up weakly*) Any of you guys seen my sables?

Spanky We'd like to present this little . . . er . . . this token of . . . er . . .

Hector There was five of them . . . plus a squared-off fitch with my name on it . . .

Spanky Are you going to shut your face and listen, Shorty? Me and Phil's trying to make a presentation here.

Phil It's a quid.

Spanky Shut up.

Hector Sorry, what were you saying?

Spanky We know it's come as a bit of a surprise to you, Hector . . . you having to leave the Slab Room . . .

Hector It's a bombshell . . . no kidding . . .

Spanky (*to Phil*) Doesn't make it easy, does he? Er . . . so what me and Phil's done is . . . er . . . well, we put round the hat and . . . er . . .

Phil Carry on, you're doing fine.

Spanky It's not a lot, you understand . . .

Phil It's a quid, son.

Spanky Shut up, will you!

Phil Give us it. (*Snatches 'presentation'*.) What Spanky was trying to say, Hector, is . . . er . . . och, here.

Spanky It's a quid.

They clap.

Hector What's this for?

Phil Not even a 'Thank you, boys, I'm really touched.' You are leaving the Slab Room, right?

Hector Yeh, but . . . .

Spanky Then that'll tide you over . . . you and your maw . . .

Phil Till you get another job.

Hector Eh?

Spanky He said, till you get another job.

Hector Eh?

Spanky *and* **Phil** (*together*) Till you get another job!

Hector I've already got another job.

Phil Christ, that was quick. Is there a mobile Broo outside?

Hector That's what I was along seeing Willie about . . . my new job . . . I start on a desk on Monday.

Spanky *and* **Phil** (*together*) What????

Hector I'm a Designer now. Seven quid a week back-dated a fortnight, rising in annual increments to twelve pounds fifteen and eleven after tax at the end of four years. God, I don't think I feel too well . . .

Spanky Me too . . .

Hector It's the excitement.

Enter Alan.

Alan Hey . . . guess what? Since two of you guys are vacating the Slab, Curry thought I should step in and fill the breach . . . how about that? Where are the gum crystals kept again? (*Hunts around.*) Oh . . . there was a phone call came through to Willie's office . . . I said I'd pass the message on . . .

Phil Eh? Is my maw safe??

Alan You didn't get in.

Phil What?

Alan Exceptionally high number of applicants this year . . . something like that . . .

Phil Christ . . .

Alan Hey . . . well done, Heck . . . Jack's just told me . . .

Enter Lucille, dressed for home.

Lucille Burton's Corner . . . quarter to . . . okay?

Phil and Spanky look towards each other.

Alan Yeh . . . right, Lucille.

Phil *and* **Spanky** (*together*) Eh?

Lucille Are you sure you can get your dad's MG?

Alan No problem . . .

Lucille And put some cream on that pimple . . . I swear it's twice the size it was this morning.

Alan For God's sake . . .

Lucille (*to Phil*) Sorry . . . couldn't've went through with it even if I had said yeh . . . you can see that, can't you? I mean to say . . . look at him . . . he's a skelf.

Phil You're looking at a skelf that's branching out, doll . . .

Lucille Aw, go to hell. And if I was you I wouldn't go home via Storey Street . . . that's where Bernadette's boyfriend's got his jew-jipsey parlour. He eats smouts like you for his breakfast! (*to Alan*) If you're not there on the dot I'm going in by myself so be warned! (*Exits.*)

Alan Listen, Heck . . .

Hector (*bravely*) Don't worry about it, Alan . . . I'm taking Willie Curry on my ticket. Well, you guys, I better shoot off . . . Willie's giving us a lift down the road. You can keep that fitch if you find it, anybody. (*Changes into overcoat.*)

Spanky Heh . . . hold on, Hector . . . you can't go just like that. What about that money we gave you?

Hector Aw, yeh . . . a quid, wasn't it? No . . . I'll just hold on to that, if yous don't mind. Help towards a skin graft for my ear and the down payment on a nylon overall like Jimmy Robertson's got. 'Night, all . . . (*Exits.*)

Spanky The cocky little . . .

Hector re-enters.

Hector And I'll be expecting some smart grinding from this department in the future. No palming me off with sub-standard shades, Farrell. Oh . . . sorry to hear you lost your job, Phil. Not to worry . . . you'll not find much difference now you're 'officially' out of work. (*Takes Parker pen from Phil's pocket and hands it to Alan.*) See yous at the Staffie. (*Exits.*)

Alan I better push off, too . . . heavy night ahead. (*Changes for home.*)

Spanky Christ, I even let him into the secrets of gum making . . . what happens? He strolls off into the sunset with the dame hanging from his top lip. Yeh, I think you better push off, Archie . . . go on . . . beat it.

Alan crosses to door . . . stops.

Alan (*to Phil*) There's always next year, you know . . .

Phil You heard : . . beat it!

Alan Fine. I was going to say 'sorry' but I can see you're doing a pretty good job of that on your own. See you at the dance. . . buy you a small beer, perhaps? And I'll be seeing you on Monday . . . Sparky . . . so take it easy on the floor . . . watch out nobody steps on your fingers . . . there's quite a bit of grinding to get through . . . That cabinet out there's an embarrassment . . .

Phil and Spanky pick up missiles. Exit Alan very smartly. The door gets the brunt of it. Enter Jack Hogg with note.

Jack Alan not around? Tch . . . he never said whether he was going on this trainspotters' outing on Sunday . . . This was left at the Gatehouse for you, McCann. Ambulance men said to give it to you straight away. I don't know what I'm delivering bloody messages for.

I'm supposed to be on a Top Priority rush job. Cheer up, Farrell, you'll feel at home once you're in your monkey suit tonight . . . owwwww! (*Exits.*)

Spanky One of these days I'm really going to give that guy a doing. (*Pause.*) Your maw?

Phil (*reads*) 'Got your mum in the back of the wagon. The boys in blue managed to fish her out of the river without too much difficulty. The grappling hooks did not break the skin. Regards to your dad and tell him Sammy Cairns will see him at Shawfield tonight as usual. Loopy Looloo, Trap Five, is a cert, tell him. All the best. S. Cairns. Driver. St Andrew's Ambulance Service.'

Spanky At least you know she's back in captivity . . . in safe hands, I mean. You can go to the Staffie and enjoy yourself now . . .

Phil Yeh . . .

Spanky Wonder what she was doing in the river?

Phil Water therapy. (*Screws up note and pops it in gumpot.*)

    Enter Curry, dressed for going home.

Curry Hector not here? Expect he's waiting at the car. Here, is there enough gum for Jack? (*Picks up gumpot.*) I'll take this out to him . . . Wait a mo . . . there's a foreign body in here . . .

Phil What is it . . . a Jap?

Curry (*pouring contents out*) You'll just have to make up some fresh stuff, Farrell . . . Mr Barton's waiting on that job Jack's doing, so . . .

Spanky I'm getting ready to go home, Mr Curry . . . it's the Staffie tonight.

Curry Never you mind about that . . . the Staff Dance can wait . . . Mr Barton can't. Get that overall back on and get weaving. And you can give him a hand, McCann . . . the muslin's down there. Come on, look alert. I often wonder how a pair of greasy-quiffed nancy boys like you would've fared in the tropics. By God, you had to be on your toes out there . . . Slant-eyed snipers up every second palm tree, drawing a bead on us jocks as we cut and hacked a path through the dense under-growth. Is this what Wingate gave up his last gasp for? So that louts like you could get yourselves a cushy little number? Get into those crystals.

Phil (*stops what he's doing*) Hey . . . wait a minute. What am I doing here? Wingate . . . snipers . . .? You're forgetting something, Curry . . . I don't work here any more, remember? And while we're at it, you can drop all that gibbon-shit about the jungle. Jimmy Robertson blew the gaff. The only stuff you've ever hacked your way through is a battalion's pay slips. You . . . fighting the Japs? You couldn't punch your way out of an origami toilet bag!

Curry You . . . you . . .

Phil And just what did you give me the boot for, anyhow? Wasn't for the cheek I gave you . . . we've all done that. And it couldn't've been for loafing about either . . . that's de rigeur in this joint. No . . . what got you by the short and curlies was the thought of me . . . scruff . . . going to the Art School, wasn't it? That I just might have the savvy to realise there was more to life than giving myself housemaid's fucking knee on them slabs!

Curry Shut it! Shut it, you miserable young upstart! How dare you shoot your mouth off like that?? How dare you! Since the day and hour you walked through that door you've tried to caw the legs from under me. Yes, I wish it had been me that gave you your cards but Mr Barton beat me to the punch. 'Get that lazy young bastard out of here, Curry, or I'll have those gaffer's stripes off you quicker than you can say "Super Saxe Three-Quarter Square".' Yes . . . that's knocked you back, McCann. Muggins here even asked for a second chance for you. Me! For you! So you go to your Art School and I hope it's a damn sight easier for you there . . . right?? And for your information Jimmy Robertson's got hammer toes. He couldn't even 'Dig For Victory'! (*Exits.*)

Spanky Plooky Jack and his plooky rush jobs. Wait till I get my desk . . . just wait!

Phil I wonder what the guv'nor's got for one's tea t'night? Plate of jolly fine mince, perhaps? Or a shoulder of lamb to cry on? Best fling the leg over the trike and zip back to Fairyland . . . find out, eh? Confront the old duffer . . . break the news about the scribblin' school, the sack, and . . . oh, yes, the old dear's impromptu dip, what? Might stop off en route and chuck a bottle of bubbly in the boot . . . cheer the little tike up. (*Picks up dustcoat.*) Would you mind stuffing that down Quelch's throat as you leave, old bean? Thanks. Oh, and do pop a few of Bunter's boils for me, there's a good chap. Think I've got everything . . .? Yes. Gosh and All Serene, what a bally day. Started off pleasantly enough . . . one's mater off for a few days in the country . . . but, fuck me, if it ain't gone downhill since then. Fuck me, if it ain't! (*Pause.*) Christ, I've just remembered something . . . (*Takes a couple of steps and executes a cartwheel.*) Giotto was a Slab Boy!

Curtain.

The End.

CUTTIN' A RUG

Cuttin' a Rug was revived at the Traverse Theatre, Edinburgh, on 12 December 2003. The cast (in order of appearance) was as follows:

Bernadette Dawn Steele
Terry John Kazek
Lucille Molly Innes
Alan Grant O'Rourke
Hector Alan Tripney
Miss Walkinshaw Anne Marie Timoney
Phil Paul Thomas Hickey
Spanky Iain Robertson
Sadie Una McLean
Willie Curry Michael Mackenzie

Director Philip Howard
Designer Neil Warmington
Lighting Designer Rick Fisher
Sound Designer Neil Alexander
Movement Director Struan Leslie
Assistant Director Lorne Campbell
Voice Coach Ros Steen
Stage Manager Dougie Wilson
Deputy Stage Manager Becky Duncan
Assistant Stage Manager Scu Moncur

The original version of *Cuttin' a Rug* was *The Loveliest Night of the Year*, first performed at the Traverse Theatre, Edinburgh, on 19 May 1979. The cast (in order of appearance) was as follows:

Spanky Robbie Coltrane
Phil John Breck
Hector Pat Doyle
Terry Freddie Boardley
Alan Tony Hollis
Curry Carey Wilson
Sadie Ida Schuster
Lucille Elaine Collins
Bernadette Phyllis Logan
Miss Walkinshaw Kay Gallie

Directed by David Hayman
Designed by Grant Hicks
Saxophonist Mark Goldringer

A rewritten version, *Threads,* was first performed at the Hampstead Theatre Club on 13 March 1980, with Mark Windsor as Alan, Claire Nelson as Miss Walkinshaw, and the rest of the cast as above.

As *Cuttin' a Rug*, the play was performed by the
Traverse Theatre Company at the Royal Court Theatre,
London, on 19 November 1982, with the following cast:

Bernadette Stella Gonet
Terry Freddie Boardley
Alan Nicholas Sherry
Lucille Elaine Collins
Hector Iain Andrew
Miss Walkinshaw Kay Gallie
Spanky Gerard Kelly
Phil Billy McColl
Sadie Jan Wilson
Willie Curry Alexander Morton
Jack Hogg Andrew Gray

Directed by David Hayman
Designed by John Byrne
Lighting designed by Colin Scott

Characters

Phil McCann
A Slab Boy. Nineteen. Dapper dresser, non-dancer.
Just been sacked that afternoon and been
turned down for Art School

George 'Spanky' Farrell
Another Slab Boy. Nineteen. Phil's pal

Hector McKenzie
A 'weed'. Nineteen. Newly promoted from
the Slab Room to a Designer's desk.
He is wearing his Uncle Bertie's dinner suit

Terry Skinnedar
A 'hardcase'. Early twenties. Snappy dresser
and *ersatz* Elvis. Bernadette's beau

Alan Downie
University student temporarily in the Slab Room.
He is dressed in his father's dinner suit
which is somewhat over-large for him

Lucille Bentley
A Sketcher and good-looking doll. Nineteen

Bernadette Rooney
Best chum to Lucille. Working as a 'temp'
in Dispatch. A stunner

Miss Walkinshaw
A maiden lady of indeterminate years.
At the dance on her own

Sadie
Stobo's tea lady. Also there solo.
Has it in for Miss Walkinshaw this evening
for some reason. Bad feet

Willie Curry
Design Room gaffer, ex-army. Mid-fifties

Scene

*The Annual Staff Dance of A. F. Stobo & Co.,
Carpet Manufacturers, at Paisley Town Hall
on a Friday evening in 1957.*

*Act One takes place in the Ladies' and Gents'
cloakrooms, Act Two on the terrace overlooking
the town. It is a starry night.*

Act One

Paisley Town Hall. A Friday evening (19 December 1957).
Ladies' cloakroom.

Bernadette (*off*) Yeh, all right, but make it a big one the next time, I can still feel my legs. And no ice, remember. (*She enters.*)

Gents' cloakroom. Enter Terry.

Terry No ice . . . check . . . no ice, that's cool.

Ladies.

Bernadette (*crosses to mirror*) Tch, look at that . . . 's all blew out. (*Tries to fix hair.*) Why doesn't he get shot of that stupid motorbike and get himself a car? That's hellish. Three hours under the drier and it looks as if I've been up all night with my head in the Hoover.

Gents.

Terry (*sings*) I'm all shook up!

Ladies.

Bernadette And what does he want to get engaged for? I know what he wants to get 'engaged' for! Elvis, for God's sake?

Gents.

Terry (*admiring himself in mirror*) Yep, it's the schnozzle, I reckon . . . that and the eyelids. Varoom . . . varoooooooom. (*Affects an American accent.*) Jes' make it a coupla fingers o' rye, honey . . . me an' the boys is

129

burnin' rubber down to Big Momma's Roadhouse for a rumble with the Barracoodas, ya dig? (*Sings.*) A-well, a-bless a-mah soul, a-what's a-wrong with me? Ah'm a-shakin' like . . . God, so I'm are . . . (*Stretches out hand.*) Look at that. Must be that clutch. Hey, c'mon, Li'l Joe, quit foolin' around wid dat switchblade, we gotta hit dem fish! Varoooooooooooom-a-bless a-mah soul!

Ladies.

Bernadette And him sitting there loving every minute. 'That's what I like about The Jolly Beggars . . . their bar staff's got what you cry "taste".' Taste?? She's hanging over the counter picking her ears with a cocktail stick. I'm glad I never asked for a cherry now. Elvis?? Since when did Elvis have blackheads all over the back of his neck?

Gents.

Terry I wonder if anybody's got a styptic pencil?

Ladies. Enter Lucille. She shouts back over her shoulder.

Lucille Well, you should've put another handful on the stays then, shouldn't you?

Gents. Alan enters, carrying a large golfing umbrella.

Alan Sorry, Lucille, but there was just enough to lubricate the brolly.

Ladies.

Lucille Oh, hi . . . Terry give you a backsaddle in?

Bernadette It's a Triumph Five Hundred, not a Triang three-wheeler.

Together Your hair's a right mess!

Gents. Alan shakes out umbrella.

Terry Heh, mind the threads! The gamp's damp, baby.

Ladies.

Lucille He couldn't get the hood up.

Bernadette The what up?

Lucille The hood.

Bernadette What'd he bring you in . . . a pram?

Lucille His dad's MG. (*Looks in mirror.*) Look at that! I went and had it done too. Blisters all over my scalp for nothing. Have you such a thing as a comb with soft teeth you could lend us?

Gents.

Alan Is that your bike in the car park?

Terry Oh, oh, dig the get-up . . . must be one of the bosses . . .

Alan The big Five Hundred job?

Terry Mebbe it is . . . and mebbe it isn't.

Alan I think we passed you in George Street. You and your girl were going into that little pub . . . The Jolly Beggars. Heavy on the juice, is she?

Terry Better watch what I'm telling this guy. No, just the odd vodka.

Alan No . . . mpg.

Terry Oh. I wonder if he's 'plain clothes'? Er . . .

Alan Bet he doesn't even know what mpg means.

Terry So-so . . . yeh, so-so.

Alan I've been trying to persuade my dad to let me get my leg over something like that for ages . . .

Terry What's he on about now . . . the bint or the bike?

Alan But he says they're very deceptive. Look as though they're fast but aren't . . . knock a great hole in your pocketbook . . . and they can be pretty painful on the crotch.

Terry Wonder when he was out with her? I'll wring her bloody neck. You haven't any oil on you, pal?

Alan 'Fraid not. Meant to stick some in the boot. D'you have to change it every thousand miles or so, is that it?

Terry It's for the hair.

Alan Yeh, I know. D'you have to change it every thousand miles or so?

Ladies.

Bernadette My mother said I should've put on a pixie hood when she seen the wee man coming out the barometer with his kilt over his head. Who did you say brung you?

Lucille The new guy that's started in the Slab Room.

Bernadette The Slab Room?

Lucille Yeh. Quarter to five before he plucked up the courage. I thought he was going to chicken out . . . after all the groundwork I put in. He started this morning. Only temporary . . . during his vac . . .

Bernadette Eh?

Lucille Holidays . . . from the university.

Bernadette Oh, a jessie?

Lucille He is not. Shut it, you . . . and quit hogging the mirror. You don't have to be a coal-heaver on a lugger to be attractive.

Bernadette It's the *Maid of the Loch* Terry's on . . . and he's a chef not a coal-heaver . . .

Lucille Well, you could've fooled me. All you get on them coracles is soggy chips and jet-black hamburgers.

Bernadette What d'you mean, jet-black? You must've been sitting next to the funnel . . . my Terry's dead particular. And when were the chips ever soggy? They're blotted on dishtowels before they leave the galley. Shift over, I can't see the back of my frock.

Lucille Just as well. What d'you call that stuff again?

Bernadette Cloth. Paws off.

Lucille D'you want a couple of safety pins for the hem?

Bernadette What's up . . . 's it hanging down?

Lucille Not so's you'd notice. Just watch you don't catch your heels on it . . .

Bernadette Oh, no . . . I thought the Yanks were dead knacky with hems? This just arrived in a food parcel from the States . . .

Lucille Maybe that's what's wrong . . . it looks like there's a couple of watermelons still up there.

Gents. Enter Hector.

Hector Hello, Alan. Hello, er . . .

Alan Hi, Hector. Wasn't expecting to see you this early.

Hector I got a lift in from Willie Curry in his new motor.

Terry Any Brylcreem, kiddo?

Hector (*to Alan*) You want to see it. 'S all chrome stuff round the bumpers. Did Lucille come with you?

Alan What?

Hector Lucille . . . have you brung her with you?

Alan Yeh, she's in next door.

Hector That's fine.

Terry Any hairgrease, son?

Hector (*to Alan*) We're having a sort of get-together on Sunday.

Alan Oh, yeh?

Hector Over at our place . . .

Terry Pomade . . . for the nut?

Alan Sorry, Heck, I promised to go on this trainspotters' outing . . .

Hector That's okay . . . wasn't going to be nothing much.

Terry Dressing, kid?

Hector You could've brung Lucille if you wanted. Or she could even come by herself if she felt like it. (*Gazes into mirror.*) God, whenever I think of her reaching up to get that jar of chrome yellow and the sun just caught the bloom on her arm . . . like the golden fuzz on a peach skin. And the smell of her body. I could've sank my teeth right into her. (*Takes home-made birthday card from pocket.*) 'Happy Birthday, Lucille.' Tch . . . what was it made her fling open the Slab Room door and chuck it on the floor for? I should've put 'From Hector' instead of 'From Guess Who . . . the Slab Room' . . . that must've

been what made her think it was Phil McCann had done
it. But what made her get so blazing mad and call him
a dirty-minded pig? That's what I'd like to know. All
I done was draw a wee scotty dog with a ribbon round
its throat and when you opened it up its tail went . . .
(*Opens up the card . . . this 'thing' pops up.*) Took us
nearly three hours and a book on oriental paper-folding.
Phil was beeling! Tied us up and put stuff down my
trousers.

Terry Cream, shorty?

Hector No . . . sticky gum! I could hardly squeeze out a
jobby!

Ladies.

Bernadette God, look at my face – you'd think this was
blanco I was banging on. Last time I looked as white as
this was in the RAI.

Lucille I never knew you were that Irish.

Bernadette The Royal Alexandra Infirmary, dummy . . .

Lucille When were you in the Infirmary? You never told
us.

Bernadette I did so. For TB . . . for a fortnight last Easter.
You were away. Yeh, you bloody well made sure you
were away. 'Oh, is that you, Bernadette? I'm that glad
you phoned. No, Lucille's not at home just now. Have you
been having a lot of visitors?' A wardful of pensioners
coughing their hearts out and not so much as a bunch of
grapes for company.

Lucille Last Easter? Oh, yeah, so I was. Never take
a Brownie pack berry-picking in Blairgowrie if you can
possibly avoid it. Drive you bananas. What did you say –
TB? Since when can they cure TB inside a fortnight?

Bernadette They only thought it was TB. They seen this shadow . . .

Lucille I remember one night one of the little dogs lit a hurricane lamp in the mess tent and the rest of the pack went hysterical. They seen this shadow . . . eh?

Bernadette On my lung.

Lucille Oh . . .

Bernadette Turned out it was a dirty development.

Lucille On your lung?

Bernadette In the dark room. Some guy with clatty mitts was handling all the X-rays.

Enter Miss Walkinshaw.

Miss Walkinshaw Good evening, girls. My, what a wild night. Hello, is this your chum, Lucille?

Lucille Hello, Miss Walkinshaw. Yeh, this is Bernadette – Bernadette Rooney. Miss Walkinshaw, from the Design Room . . .

Miss Walkinshaw How do you do?

Lucille Let me help you off with your wrap. God, this is really lovely . . . isn't it, Bernadette?

Bernadette Was you out shooting?

Lucille Bernadette's filling in for the lady that's off having her baby in Dispatch.

Miss Walkinshaw How nice. Are you quite enjoying that?

Bernadette 'S lousy.

Miss Walkinshaw Oh, dear. Mrs Lumsden seems to like it.

Bernadette 'S that her with the warts? Yeh, she would.

Lucille Do forgive her, Miss Walkinshaw, Bernadette's used to better. Her future fiancé's a flenser on a whaling ship. (*Whistles.*) That's a really beautiful gown you've got on.

Miss Walkinshaw Oh, d'you like it, Lucille? It's just an old rag of Mother's . . . been hanging in the closet for ages. I've had it altered to fit in with today's fashions, of course . . .

Bernadette Yeh, you can see that.

Lucille Did you manage to get a taxi all right?

Miss Walkinshaw Gracious me, I came on the bus.

Bernadette I wouldn't've came on a bus with that on.

Miss Walkinshaw Oh?

Bernadette In case it got crushed. What're you kicking us for, Lucille?

Gents. Enter Phil, followed by Spanky, who is carrying a paper carrier bag with the bottom hanging out of it.

Spanky I told you to hold on to it while I got a light for my fag off that old guy's beery nose and what d'you go and do?

Phil How was I to know it was sitting in a puddle?

Spanky Six big McEwans and a full quarter bottle of Rich Ruby down the stank. Honest to God, Phil!

Phil Straight from the loony bin – no dinner, no nothing – and I've got to listen to this? Shut up, will you? 'S not the end of the world, is it? Well, is it? (*Pause.*) What d'they have to take their false teeth out for anyhow? It's undignified having to greet when you're gumsy. What d'they think she's going to do . . . take them out and bite herself to death with them?

Terry Dig the jacket, pal. Pretty cool, eh?

Phil Fifty-eight stock . . . just new in. Got the old man to give it a press for us.

He turns and we see a scorch mark on the back. It is in the shape of an iron.

Hector Hey, Phil, there's a . . .

Spanky (*quickly*) And how're we doing, Heck, son? My, aren't we the swanky ones? Say another word and I'll put my fist down your throat.

Phil (*fingering Alan's lapel*) Am I wrong, kid, or is this still warm from the corpse?

Spanky Another crack, Phil, and the boy's going to mention the scorch mark.

Terry Don't let him away with that, son . . . make one back about the scorch mark.

Hector I'm glad I kept my mouth shut about the scorch mark.

Phil Whose is the Chad Valley mobo-horse outside?

Alan He's talking about your bike.

Terry Eh? 'S mines . . . how? And it's a five-hundred . . . cc.

Phil Okay, Pancho . . . keep the sombrero on, I was only asking.

Terry What're you asking for? And the name's Terry.

Phil 'S like the one Lee Marvin had in *The Wild One*, that was all . . . Terry.

Terry Oh . . .

Phil Did you see the movie?

Terry Course I did.

Phil D'you remember Lee Marvin in it?

Terry Er . . . I'm not very sure . . .

Phil You must. He was the one that couldn't keep up with the rest. Give us your comb, Spanks. Who is this guy?

Ladies.

Bernadette Who is this guy?

Lucille A dirty pig, that's who.

Bernadette What'd he get his books for?

Lucille Giving up cheek most likely . . . he's a cheeky swine. You want to've seen the birthday card he gave us.

Bernadette Eh? What's cheeky about that? Last time I got a birthday card I was in a nappy.

Lucille Bet you it wasn't filthy but.

Bernadette Course not, I was a very careful baby.

Lucille The card. What was it like, Miss Walkinshaw? A clatty bit of pasteboard with a drawing of a gorilla on it . . . and you want've seen what happened when you opened it up. What was it like, Miss Walkinshaw? I showed it to you, didn't I? Miss Walkinshaw nearly fell off her half-drop. This 'thing' popped up . . . it was dead obscene, wasn't it, Miss Walkinshaw? Miss Walkinshaw'll tell you. If I thought he'd be here tonight he'd be in for a doing.

Bernadette From the new boyfriend?

Lucille Don't be dense. He's from a semi-villa . . . they don't go in for that sort of stuff. From your Terry.

Bernadette My Terry?

Lucille He's done jew-jipsy, hasn't he?

Bernadette Jew-jipsy? Who told you that?

Lucille You did. You said he went to night classes for it.

Bernadette The only night classes my Terry goes to's for choux pastry.

Lucille What? You mean the only thing he could get the best of's a chocolate éclair?

Bernadette My Terry's a hunk! You point this joker out and Terry'll put his face in, right?

Lucille He probably willn't be here anyhow. I told you, he got his books today.

Bernadette Well, if he is here my Terry'll batter him for you. Bloody cheek. He can batter anybody, my Terry. What d'you think he's got all them muscles for?

Gents.

Terry Heh, shorty, going to get that bit at the back for us? My arm's getting tired.

Holds up comb for Hector to put the finishing touch to his DA. Hector takes the comb and draws it straight down the back of Terry's head and leaves it stuck there. Terry is stunned.

Ladies. Enter Sadie.

Sadie God, see that man of mines. (*icily*) Evening, Miss Walkinshaw. See that good for nothing bugger. Twenty minutes to seven still wasn't a bloody sign of him . . . so I gets the wean's coat on. 'Away down to The Jolly B's, sweetheart, and tell your granda to put a spurt on, your Granny's waiting to go to the dance.' Off he goes . . .

five minutes later I hear him coming up the close crying the eyes out. Do you know what that swine had done? Do you know what that . . . There it was on the back of the wee fella's leg: 'I will be home about nine. Having a few jars with Big Peter. His wife died this morning and never left his tea out.' What would you make of that? It was in copying-ink pencil. Took half an hour and a packet of Rinso before I could get the wee soul out to Devotions. Look at my fingers . . . they're like bloody prunes.

Lucille I thought you weren't coming tonight, Sadie?

Sadie What . . . and miss all the fun!

Gents.

Spanky Twenty-five bob for the weekend rental . . . Jackson's. And you get seven bob back when you hand it in.

Terry (*doing a crossword in the* Elvis Monthly) Heh, what's a three-letter word ending in 'x' that Elvis has got a load of?

Spanky The pox? God, is that my imagination or do I really feel a chill at my . . . (*Cautiously puts a hand round to trouser seat.*) Oh, no . . . she was right. 'You'll never get them breeks on with them things on your feet. And what have I told you about underpants?' What has she not told us about underpants? She's a world bloody authority on underpants. 'Well, you'll be sorry, my lad. Don't you dare give this address if you get knocked down, d'you hear?' Yeh, seven bob back . . .

Phil You were scalped, kid. I got mines from Caledonian Tailors last time. Fifteen shillings for the hire and they gave you a quid when you took it back.

Terry Mines was thirty bob.

Spanky We're not talking about to buy.

Phil (*to Alan*) Much was yours, kiddo?

Alan This wasn't hired . . . belongs to . . . Oh, Christ, I wish the floor would open up . . . belongs to my dad, actually.

Spanky He's not still in it, is he? There's enough room.

Phil Is that your sports buggy in the car park, Archie?

Alan Yeh, why?

Phil There's puddles all over the seats. You and Lucille stop off for a couple of beers, did you?

Alan Ha, ha . . . if you must know, I couldn't get it up.

Phil Oh, you had more than a couple of beers then?

Alan The hood, you . . .

Phil You what? C'mon . . . you what?

Terry Hey, cool it, you guys, cool it.

Spanky Freeze, hotrod, nobody's talking to you.

Phil Okay, you what? Come on!

Alan You know!!

Spanky Christ, I'm glad it isn't me. Put his face in, Phil!

Terry Let's cool it, huh?

Spanky What were you told, you? Don't make a move . . . don't make a move.

Terry I'm just asking your pal and this guy to cool it . . . to be cool. I better make a move or he'll think I'm feart which I'm are. Cool it, all right?

Spanky One more 'cool it' from you, knucklehead, and your noddle's going down that pan, d'you hear? Just stare him out . . . stare him out. Right??

Terry Right! Don't blink, Terry, don't blink. Okay, cool it! I wish he'd let go my shirt, I'm choking!

Spanky I should never've grabbed his shirt, I've got his dander up. Look at the way his eyes are sticking out!

Enter Curry.

Hector Thank God.

Phil God.

Spanky God.

Terry God.

Alan God. (*like an echo*)

Curry Godstruth . . . did you remember to lock the door on your side, Hector? The car door . . . did you remember to . . . Alan, hang that up, would you? (*Passes over coat.*) Eh? Hector. (*to Alan*) Trust that isn't your dad's racing car down there? The upholstery's sodden . . . shouldn't think he'd be too pleased about that. Farrell, would you remove this carrier bag, please? I needn't ask if it's yours. Go on, get it out of there. Hector . . . I'm surprised you're here, McCann. Even more surprised to see you've got yourself fixed up. P & O Line, is it? Hector?

Hector Yes, Mr Curry?

Curry Away down and make sure that door's locked. Oh, and if you bump into Bobby Sinclair tell him I won't be needing that stupid lectern . . . I'll be working without notes this year . . . (*Spreads out notes.*) And Hector . . .

Hector Yes, Mr Curry?

Curry If Mr Barton's arrived with the Acting Chief Constable, would you ask him to keep me an end seat at the top table so's I can get in and out easily? Thanks. Oh, and Hector . . .

Hector Yes, Mr Curry?

Curry Don't get lost, eh?

Exit Hector. Curry consults notes.

Curry Now . . . tum-ti tum-ti tum-ti tum . . .

Spanky *and* **Phil** Tum-ti, tum-ti, tum-ti, tum . . .

Ladies.

Sadie That's a lovely frock, Miss Walkinshaw.

Miss Walkinshaw Oh, d'you like it, Sadie? It's just an old rag of Mother's.

Sadie Aye, but it's still quite nice.

Bernadette He used to work for Frog Crichton, the butcher, before he went on the *Maid of the Loch* . . . him that was 'Mr Paisley'. . .

Lucille 'The Body Beautiful'?

Bernadette Yeh, and he gave Terry these big dumb-bells to practise on.

Lucille And can he get a tune out them yet?

Bernadette You want to see the arms he's got on him . . . like two legs of beef. And he does press-ups on the sun deck, hail, rain or shine. Fit as a fiddle, my Terry.

Gents.

Spanky *and* **Phil** Tum-ti tum-ti tum tum. (*imitating pizzicato violins*)

Curry I sincerely hope we are not going to have a repetition of last year's hooliganism from you pair of . . . I wonder if Mimi remembered to put in a handkerchief this time? I'll never forget the embarrassment of reaching in and pulling out that pair of . . .

Spanky Pair of what, Mr Curry?

Curry Pair of bloody underpants, and Mr Barton made that crack about the travelling salesman. (*to Terry*) And you can move over a bit, lad.

Spanky Underpants? I wonder if he's in league with my maw?

Terry Hey, I can't see in the mirror now.

Curry I should've thought that was a bonus.

Phil What hooliganism's this, Mr Curry?

Curry (*looking up from notes*) Eh? You know damned fine what hooliganism, McCann. It's taken Miss Walkinshaw a twelvemonth to get over it. Here, that's a nice touch . . . (*Pencils it in his notes.*)

Phil That wasn't us. Was it, Spanks?

Curry Too much blooming drink, that was your trouble. Hanging Hector upside down over the balcony and spitting hot peas at the Lord Provost might be your idea of a good night's entertainment but . . . oh, it's coming back to you, is it? Well, if there's anything like a repeat performance of that carry-on this evening . . . just watch it, right? (*Notes.*) Mr and Mrs Barton, Acting Chief Constable, boys and girls . . . Mr and Mrs Barton, Acting Chief . . . Acting Chief . . . we could all've been acting chiefs given the chance . . .

Spanky Are you going to be telling that one about the two moths, Mr Curry?

Curry Moths? Oh, yes . . . yes, I thought I might. Went down well last year, didn't it?

Phil And the year before that . . .

Spanky And the year before that . . .

Phil (*to Alan*) You want to hear this, son . . . 's a right ribtickler.

Curry Have you heard it, Alan? The one about the two moths, no? Well, there were these two moths . . .

Alan Yes, I have, Mr Curry, my dad . . . bugger! My dad told me it.

Curry Oh. (*to Terry*) Have you heard it? The one about the moths . . . the Daddy Moth and the Baby Moth . . .

Terry Moths?

Curry Well, there were these two moths . . . a Daddy Moth and Baby Moth . . .

Spanky Sit back, hotstuff, you're going to enjoy this.

Curry A Daddy Moth and a Baby Moth . . .

Phil Hope you haven't got a hernia, pal.

Curry D'you mind, you pair? Right . . . a Daddy Moth and a Baby Moth, and they're . . .

    Enter Hector.

Hector What was I to tell Mr Barton again?

Spanky *and* **Phil** Shhhhhhhhhhhhh!

Phil He's telling the one about the two moths.

Spanky The Daddy Moth . . .

Hector . . . and the Baby Moth? Oh, I like this one.

Curry Will you sit down and shut up?

Hector Sorry, I never realised . . .

Spanky *and* **Phil** Shhhhhhhhhhhhhl

Hector Sorry.

Spanky Accept our humbles, Mr Curry . . . do carry on.

Curry Right . . . there were these two moths . . .

Terry You needn't bother for my benefit . . . I'd just as soon not . . .

Curry Don't let them put you off! Now!

Phil Yeh, grit your teeth, you'll like it.

Spanky *and* **Hector** Shhhhhhhhhhhhh!

Phil I'm sorry!

Curry McCann!

Phil Sorry! I know . . . shhhhhhhh!

Spanky, Hector *and* **Phil** (*to Alan*) Shhhhhhhhhhhhh!

Curry There were these two moths! Right?? A Daddy Moth . . .

Spanky, Hector, Phil *and* **Alan** . . . and a Baby Moth . . .

Terry Huh?

Ladies.

Sadie You not with an escort this year, Miss Walkinshaw? They're not worth it, are they? By the time you're halfway through a St Bernard's their tongues is hanging out looking for a barrel of drink. See that bugger I've got? No, I'm forgetting . . . you know him as well as I do . . . how's the leg?

Miss Walkinshaw Oh, it's . . . fine, thank you, Sadie . . .

Sadie I think it was the window pole, myself . . . when the fella winkled yous out.

Miss Walkinshaw Yes . . .

Sadie That . . . more than the leapfrog, if you see what I mean.

Miss Walkinshaw Quite . . .

Sadie He was nice and relaxed . . . that's the secret, you see. Course, you weren't quite as blotto as he was, were you?

Miss Walkinshaw Good heavens, I hadn't had so much as a drop, Sadie.

Sadie That's right . . . neither you did . . . it said it in the papers . . . wonder how much that set you back, eh?

Bernadette How is he at the winching? Is he a good kisser?

Lucille I don't know yet, do I? And don't be so immature . . . a good kisser! He's at the university.

Bernadette I once went with a guy from Stow College and he was hopeless. He was going to be a woodwork teacher, this guy.

Lucille Well, personally I go for the brighter wincher myself.

Bernadette Doesn't need a blueprint to locate the catch on your brassiere?

Lucille Shut your face . . . Intelligent, I'm talking about.

Bernadette This woodwork teacher was intelligent. The only thing that put me off was he had contact lenses and

thumbs like baby beets. You don't have to go to university
to prove you're smart, you know. Take my Terry . . .

Gents.

Curry No, no, you don't seem to understand . . . piles
on carpets and piles on . . . oh, you explain it, Farrell,
I give up.

Terry It wasn't that I didn't get it, which I didn't, I just
don't get it. Is it supposed to be funny or what?

Spanky He did get it, Mr Curry.

Enter Hector.

Hector That's the band unloading their stuff, Mr Curry.
Can I go down and help them? Bobby Sinclair said
I could. Can I, eh? Him and Mr Barton are giving the
piano player a lift up the stairs . . .

Spanky Oh, God, it's not the Largie Boys again?? Oh,
Mr Curry . . .

Curry It's not me that orders the band, Farrell . . . kindly
be quiet. That's Bobby Sinclair's province. If there's
anybody to blame for the Largie Boys, it's him. Now,
shut up . . . I'm trying to go over these . . . Mr and
Mrs Barton, Acting Chief Constable . . .

Hector They've got something really exciting this year.

Phil Pockets on their jackets?

Hector An electric guitar! Can I go and help, Mr Curry?
Can I?

Curry Och, away you go! Jigging about there . . .

Spanky I'll come with you, Heck. What's it like . . . is it
a Fender? You coming, Phil?

Phil He's not going to come up out of the floor playing it. I'll see it after.

Alan Can I come? I'm quite keen to . . .

Exit Spanky and Hector.

Hey, wait for me . . . (*Hurries after them.*)

Pause.

Terry (*doing crossword in* Elvis Monthly) Six across: 'Abbreviated urinatory function coupled with regal proname features anatomically in King's stage act . . .'

Curry Have you been up to see your mother, Ph . . . Ph . . . McCann?

Phil What? Oh, yeh . . . yeh, she's all right. She's. . .

Terry Abbreviated urinatory funct . . . ?

Curry Yes, it's wonderful what they can do nowadays. We once had a big lad in our billet. It was the shells, you see . . . sent him back down the line first opportunity. Padre tried comforting him for a bit but it was useless . . .

Phil Good thing that priest arrived when he did . . . Otherwise I'd've killed her with them shears. Though, Christ only knows, he wasn't much good for anything else. Face went the colour of putty and his hands shook all the holy pictures out of his missal. And he might've took the clips off. I'm kneeling down next to the bed, my maw squealing blue murder, and he's standing there with these stupid bicycle clips on his trousers . . . right through two Hail Holy Queens and a dozen Memorares. Then, just as we get to the Fourth Sorrowful Mystery, off come the clips. Course, no sooner does he bend down to take them off than she's off . . . straight into the lavvy, locks herself in . . . starts running the bathwater full force.

Him and me's shouting at one another but we can't hear
a bloody thing. Then she starts singing 'Show Me the Way
to Go Home' and chucking shampoo bottles through the
window. That's when he wraps it up . . . the bike clips
are back on and he's at the front door. 'I'll call in again
tomorrow, Philip, see that your mother doesn't break her
fast now.' No, but she can break every other thing in the
bloody house for all he cares. It's him I should've killed
with the shears, the useless bastard!

Curry Quite comfortable, is she?

Phil Yeh . . . oh, yeh.

Curry She'll be well looked after. It's amazing what they
can do with these . . . these . . . yes, I think you'll see a
difference next time you pay her a visit.

Phil Sure. Her hair'll be grew over the rivets?

Terry Your maw not well, Jim?

Phil My maw's fine, Jim . . . and the name isn't Jim, Jim,
okay? She's locked up, that's all.

Terry Oh . . . jail, you mean?

Phil Shut up, eh?

Ladies.

Miss Walkinshaw (*offering girls a sweet*) Would you
care for a loose Merroll, girls?

Sadie How's your old mother these days, Miss
Walkinshaw? Last time we spoke she was at death's
door . . . How's she keepin' now?

Miss Walkinshaw Oh, not so bad, thank you. She
managed to get up just before I left and force down
a piece of poached hake.

151

Sadie What was up . . . was it annoying her? Aye, they need their nourishment at that age. What'll she be now . . . eighty-six . . . eighty-seven?

Miss Walkinshaw Eighty-five and still hale and hearty . . . though she does look much older . . .

Sadie Aye, you take after her, don't you?

Miss Walkinshaw She had me when she was almost fifty, you know.

Sadie Miraculous conception, was it? Aye, that's the age my mother was when she was took.

Miss Walkinshaw Took?

Sadie Fifty-one . . . coming up the stairs with the message bags . . . wee insurance man had to side-step her corpse to collect her premiums . . .

Miss Walkinshaw How dreadful. What on earth did you do?

Sadie We got a lend of the one-and-six from the woman down the stair. All Tommy got in his Christmas stocking that year was a nut and that fell through the hole in the toe . . . it was one of my mammy's . . . the stocking, not the nut . . . she hated nuts . . . that's how she couldn't thole cleaning for yous lot up the terrace . . . Monday mornings, half past five, right through to dinner time on a Saturday . . . course, that's what killed her . . .

Miss Walkinshaw Yes, she was never done, was she, Sadie?

Sadie Done? She was an old woman by the time our Thomas was in the go-chair.

Miss Walkinshaw No, I meant she was never . . .

Sadie And her feet! You never seen feet like these . . .
Like Halloween tumshies with toes on them. Down on her
hunkers in freezing-cold water summer and winter . . .
they never thought to put a light under the geyser in
these big houses, you know.

Miss Walkinshaw Oh, I'm sure I remember Mother
always seeing to it that . . .

Sadie The doctors put them into a book for medical
students . . . that's how bad they were. Course, that's
where I get these. (*Displays feet.*) Them's what you
describe in pathological terms as 'absolutely buggered'.

Lucille Who was it sent you the frock? Stay at peace,
will you? (*Pins up hem.*)

Bernadette Big Donna . . . her that was over last New
Year. . . see if you jag me!

Lucille Was that her I seen you with in the Silver Lounge?
Will you hold still, Bernadette?

Bernadette That's her. Imitation-crocodile shoes and
making googly eyes at the waiters . . . it was dead
affronting. Ohyah!

Lucille Where was it she came from again? Stop
shoogling about. Where?

Bernadette Battle Creek, Michigan. 'S that it? Where all
the corn flakes get made. You want've seen the outfits
she had with her . . . four cabin trunks and a celluloid
suitcase absolutely crammed . . .

Lucille Just got this last bit . . . Did she leave you
anything behind?

Bernadette Yeh . . . the crocodile pumps and a sloppy
joe with 'Kelloggs' on the back . . .

Lucille Is that all?

Bernadette No . . . it had 'Einstein Worked It Out With All-Bran' across the bust, but it looked daft so I gave it to Terry.

Lucille There. (*Finishes fixing hem.*) We're supposed to be going over next summer . . . to the States . . . me and my mum. Her sister's got a big ranch house in Kearney . . . just up the road from New York. She sent us over snapshots of it. 'S really beautiful. They're all standing on the front grass having a barbecue and you can see my Uncle Joseph in his lorry. They're dead well off, so they are. Dead generous too. Know what they sent my mum for New Year?

Bernadette No, what?

Lucille Two dried turkeys and a big tin of cling peaches.

Bernadette Terrific.

Lucille Yeh, they're dirt cheap over there, these things.

Gents.

Terry (*admiring himself in mirror*) Maybe I'll get across there some day to see him . . . the *Ed Sullivan Show*, maybe . . . 'Ladies and Gen'lemen, Elvis Presley!' Hello!! (*Sings.*) A-well a-bless a-mah soul a-what's a-wrong with me? Ah'm a-shakin' like a . . .

Phil Going to chuck that! That's twice I've dug that comb into my noddle.

Terry You ever been to the States?

Phil Where?

Terry I've been a few times . . . on the boats. New York, San Francisco, Tupelo . . .

Phil Tupelo?

Terry Tupelo – up the Mississippi where El was born. I was there two years ago with my Uncle Tex. He's a Yank.

Phil Your Uncle who?

Terry Tex.

Phil What does he wear . . . two-gallon chaps and cowboy raincoats? Uncle Tex?

Terry Yeh, Uncle Tex . . . His real name's Buddy but his family call him Tex 'cos he spent twelve years busting cattle in Wyoming . . .

Phil Oh, that figures . . .

Terry He was over here just recently. Gave me and the brother a hundred bucks each and a pigskin wallet with a longhorn carved on the front . . . 's dead handy for keeping stuff in.

Phil Oh, yeh, like your ration books?

Terry And he's sending us over some western gear.

Phil Western gear? What? A burlap sheriff's set and a plastic tommyhawk from Woolies?

Terry The genuine article . . . real McCoy . . . cowboy boots from a store in Denver.

Phil A right chookie you're going to look strolling down St Mirren Street in a pair of cowboy boots!

Terry There's nothing up with cowboy boots!

Phil They've got high heels, stupid.

Terry That's for keeping your feet in the stirrups.

Phil Oh, he's sending you a cuddy as well?

Curry Will the two of you give over? I can't hear myself think!

Phil I should've thought that was a bonus.

Ladies.

Bernadette Was I telling you I got a hurl down the road from work?

Sadie Was I telling you I got a hurl right up to the front door?

Lucille *and* **Miss Walkinshaw** Oh, who from?

Bernadette I was standing at the lights when this big shiny car drew up and a head came out.

Sadie D'you suppose that'll belong to him or will it go with the job, d'you think?

Bernadette Mr Barton. D'you know what the bugger was asking me?

Sadie And his wife sitting there in the motor with him.

Lucille *and* **Miss Walkinshaw** No, what?

Bernadette whispers in Lucille's ear.

Sadie If I'd fancy going up to do a bit of light dusting for them twice a week in my spare time . . .

Sadie *and* **Bernadette** Bloody cheek of the man.

Miss Walkinshaw Oh, I'm sure that he and Mrs Barton never intended . . .

Sadie Never intended what, Miss Walkinshaw?

Miss Walkinshaw Well, he would've heard about your mother and thought . . .

Sadie 'Oh, aye, this looks like another right mug,' is that what you mean? 'Let's see if this wee bachle'll

come and skivvy for a handful of washers like her daft
mammy,' eh? Listen, it was her feet she passed on not
her bloody IQ.

Miss Walkinshaw You're far too touchy, Sadie, I'm sure
Mr and Mrs Barton would never . . .

Sadie Never what? Send a lovely wreath like yous lot in
the terrace sent for my mother?

Miss Walkinshaw What on earth are you talking about?

Sadie Half-a-dozen scabby wallflowers in the shape of a
scrubbing brush?

Miss Walkinshaw For heaven's sake!

Sadie Talking of scabby wallflowers . . . how's your
dance card filling up?

Miss Walkinshaw Sadie!

Sadie I've got Mr Curry down for six rhumbas. Here,
was I telling you Mr Barton's wife was in the Rolls
Royce with him? Turquoise ball dress, purple hairdo and
a wee bolero jacket with rhinestones on it that would
choke a dug.

Miss Walkinshaw How charming.

Lucille And did she not say anything?

Bernadette All you could hear was –

Sadie – her grinding her wallies every time he took a
corner.

Gents.

Curry (*with notes*) How the time rolls by, eh? It hardly
seems a twelvemonth since I was standing at this mike
gazing out over an ocean of dickie-suits and a sea of
happy . . . a sea of happy . . . you've only yourself to
blame, McCann!

Phil Eh? What am I saying?

Curry Standing there with your face tripping you.

Phil I never said a word.

Curry It's about time you woke up. The world and A. F. Stobo don't owe you a living, you know.

Phil Nobody said they did.

Curry There's young Downie there . . . he's not going to find it easy in the Slab Room but he's willing to buckle to . . . There's a lot worse off than you, you know . . . a lot worse.

Phil Name a hundred.

Curry Pull yourself together, for God's sake. Good grief, if you'd seen limbless ex-servicemen turning their hands to making baskets . . . What was that? Listen, you, if you had been born twenty years earlier . . .

Phil I could've been one of your paraplegic weavers? Yeh, missed my chance, eh?

Curry You're in for a rude awakening, my boy. Just think for a minute how you're going to fare outside without me giving you the feedlines. A crack like that'll earn a crack in return . . . right on the mouth!

Enter Hector.

Hector That's them nearly set up, Mr Curry. Bobby Sinclair's putting another plug on the amplifier. He says it takes a three-prong. You want to see the guitar, Phil . . . it's yon size . . . and it's got switches all over it. (*to Terry*) You ever seen an electric guitar?

Terry Course, I have, shorty. Out of my road . . .

Hector Sorry. Quit shoving . . .

Enter Spanky.

Spanky That's them nearly set up. Bobby Sinclair's just phoning home for some fuses. Hey, you want to see the boy's guitar, Phil. 'S like that one Charlie Gracie plays . . . big black job with knobs all over the joint. (*to Terry*) You ever seen an electric guitar?

Terry What is this, *Double Your Money*?

Spanky (*to Phil*) Bobby says if he can get another plug on the amp he can work the fairy lights off it as well.

Ladies.

Miss Walkinshaw I can't think what's got into you tonight, Sadie. You seemed quite hunky-dory this afternoon.

Sadie Well, I'm not so hunky-bloody-dory the night, am I? Still, it's not every day you get insulted in a limousine, is it?

Miss Walkinshaw I'm sure they were trying to be kind. We've known the Bartons all our lives and I'm quite, quite certain they weren't in any way whatsoever trying to insult you, Sadie.

Sadie No? What was it, then . . . a bloody compliment? I'm sitting there in my good frock and he's rattling away about how nice it would be for me to go up and muck out for him and his missus . . .

Miss Walkinshaw There's no one forcing you to do it. It would be kindness that prompted him to ask . . .

Sadie Has he asked you?

Miss Walkinshaw Don't be silly, Sadie . . .

Sadie Aye, well, I wonder what it is in me that brings out this kindness in people like the Bartons, eh? Kill you with bloody kindness if they thought they'd get away with it.

Miss Walkinshaw For goodness' sake, he'd only be looking to supplement your salary . . .

Sadie My what? It's a tea trolley I steer about the Design Room, not the bloody Bristol Brabazon.

Bernadette D'you not think he's like him?

Lucille Who like who?

Bernadette Terry . . . like Elvis?

Lucille Elvis?

Bernadette Elvis Presley. What's funny about that? He got taken for him in the pub tonight . . .

Lucille Oh, do they both use the same pub? That's understandable, then. Hey, there's two stills missing from that *Picturegoer Annual*, by the way. *Jailhouse Rock*.

Bernadette Don't look at me . . . never tore them out. (*Clips nails.*)

Lucille They weren't torn . . . they were snipped . . . with nail scissors.

Bernadette Somebody else's done it.

Lucille I don't lend my *Picturegoers* out.

Bernadette You lent them to me, didn't you?

Lucille Yeh, but I used to like you.

Gents.

Curry (*still with notes*) . . . and so, friends, would you give a warm Stobo's welcome to our principal guest for this evening – a gentleman I'm sure you all know from his work with juvenile delinquents . . .

Spanky When's this frolic getting under way, Mr Curry? You not fed up, Phil?

Curry Would you welcome, please . . .

Spanky Eh, Mr Curry . . .

Curry Would you welcome, please . . .

Spanky When? God, we could still've been in The Jollys, Phil . . .

Curry What is it, Farrell?

Spanky Just asking when they lift the hatches . . . my feet are itching.

Curry Small wonder in those things. Good God, there'll be tyre marks all over the parquet.

Spanky (*to Alan*) You any dough on you, Big Tux?

Curry Farrell!

Spanky Only asking the boy for a small bung so's we can beetle off and give you peace, Mr Curry. (*to Alan*) Well?

Alan How much d'you need?

Curry Put that away, Alan, you'll never see it again. Quiet, Farrell.

Spanky You got anything you could lend us, pal?

Terry You don't mean me, do you?

Curry I don't think you'll find that chap as daft as he looks.

Terry Eh?

Spanky Don't look at me, it was him that said it.

Curry Quiet, for God's sake.

Phil (*to Alan, who is putting his purse away*) What're you saving up for . . . a twinset?

Curry You get that into a Post Office book . . . get yourself a good holiday. Those buggers'll only be wanting it for booze.

Phil Yeh, there's nothing like a holiday for setting you up, son. A fortnight in Girvan in a prefab . . . week one, heaven . . . fish teas, red faces, Nivea Cream . . . week two, stony broke . . . red necks, train home. Yeh, I can let you have an address . . . you can take the towels back for us . . .

Ladies.

Lucille I wish they'd hurry up. Can your Terry jive?

Bernadette He's a champ. Can yours?

Lucille He goes up the Papingo, doesn't he?

Bernadette That doesn't mean to say nothing. Where d'you say he went?

Lucille The Papingo – it's a jazz club in Glasgow.

Bernadette Jazz?

Lucille Yeh, jazz. Me an him's going up there next weekend.

Bernadette That's only for intellectuals, all that stuff. What's he taking you for?

Lucille Some of us can tell the difference between Elvis Presley and Aldous Huxley, you know.

Bernadette Al does what?

Lucille Huxley. (*Pause.*) He plays up the Papingo, ignorant.

Gents.

Terry Play anything – rockabilly, bluegrass, bit of jazz . . .

Alan Oh . . . d'you improvise?

Terry If a string breaks, you mean? Sure, you just get a pair of pliers and . . .

Spanky Hey, Phil, just think . . .

Phil Just think what?

Spanky Just think . . . this is the last Staffie for the Stobo's Slab Boys . . . when we'll all be together . . .

Phil So?

Spanky So . . . d'you not feel nothing?

Phil Yeh . . . I feel exhilarated.

Spanky D'you feel anything, Heck?

Hector Maybe I'll get that empty desk right next to hers . . . then I could talk to her all day. Where's my desk to be, Mr Curry?

Curry Mmmmm? What're you mumping about now, Hector? What desk?

Hector My Designer's desk . . . what you're moving me out of the Slab Room for. I was wondering where it was going to be, that was all. Where is it going to be?

Curry In the blooming Design Room, where else?

Hector Yeh, but whereabouts, Mr Curry? There's a spare one next to Lu . . . next to Miss Walkinshaw with the shoogly legs, but you could get the joiner to come up and put a nail in them, eh?

Curry Tch, for goodness' sake stop interrupting me. There's time enough next week to think of that . . . now, please . . . shut up.

Hector I was just wondering.

Spanky When the bloody hell am I getting a desk? 'This is the Slab Room, folks . . . and this elderly gent over here is our Mr Farrell. Mind you don't give his crutches a dunt as you pass. Yes, we're all very fond of Mr Farrell . . . a genuine antique . . . Carry on, Aged One. No, no, I shouldn't imagine he'll ever get put onto a desk . . . there's so few of them with oxygen tents, you see.' You ever thought of the future, Phil?

Phil Shut up, eh?

Ladies.

Sadie Brung it all back, didn't it?

Miss Walkinshaw Pardon?

Sadie (*gazing at the acknowledgements column in the newspaper*) 'In Memoriam Cissie Jowett, Beloved Wife and Mother, died this day, December 19th, 1922.'

The cherubim rejoiced on High
The day that flower was born,
But when the blossom withered, tears . . .
A rose without a thorn.

'Inserted by her loving daughter, Sadie. Sacred Heart, have mercy.' You can keep the plaster on a currybunkle for so long but underneath it's suppurating away . . .

Drumroll.

Here . . . fling us over them sandals, flower. (*Puts on 'Carmen Miranda'-style sandals.*) God, I hope I can rhumba at this altitude.

Gents.

Curry God's truth, and I haven't committed a bloody line of these to memory. Mr and Mrs Acting Barton, Chief Inspector . . . bugger . . . (*Exits.*)

Ladies.

Lucille 'S my hair all right, Bernadette? Oh God . . .

Bernadette How's my dress at the back? God, I hope nobody steps on it.

Gents.

Alan This is it, then. Please God, I remember all those turns my dad showed me. Damn! Coming, Heck?

Exeunt Alan and Hector.

Ladies.

Sadie You'll be putting something in a hanky for Mother, won't you, Miss Walkinshaw? Aye . . . what about a few drops of ether? They say they go out like a light at that age.

Exeunt.

Gents.

Spanky Can you see anything, Phil? (*Bends over.*) There's quite a stiff breeze . . .

Ladies.

Bernadette How's my hem?

Lucille (*overlapping*) How's my hair?

Exeunt. Another drumroll.

Gents.

Phil and **Spanky** (*together*) I wonder if the drummer's still injecting himself with daily Delrosa?

Spanky bends to fix his shoe.

Phil Right, Spanks . . . head up, shoulders back, best foot forward . . . oh, and do keep a weather eye open.

Spanky in hunchback pose.

Who knows . . .? Esmeralda might be here.

Spanky Yeh . . . I've got a hunch she could be.

Exeunt. Terry is left onstage. He strikes an Elvis pose.
End of Act One.

Act Two

The terrace overlooking the river and town.

Curry (*off*) Thank you, the Largie Boys . . . that was
a Viennese waltz, I'm led to believe. And now, at the
special request of our own Mrs Barton . . . Hector, would
you hand that across to the chap with the cummerbund
and braces? Thanks. No, hang on till he's finished
blowing his nose. 'Roses of Picardy', boys and girls.
What? Och, go to buggery, Bobby!

*Enter Terry and Bernadette. Terry is eating a
meringue.*

Terry Who is this guy again?

Bernadette What guy?

Terry The guy I'm supposed to batter for Lucille . . .
mmmmm, these are good.

Bernadette You're not battering nobody, Terry Skinnedar,
d'you hear?

Terry Quit nudging us!

Bernadette Stop acting the dumb-bell.

Terry Quit nudging us, I said! Look at that . . . the arse's
fell off my fucking meringue! Yeh, and what was all that
about dumb-bells?

Enter Phil and Spanky. Spanky is eating a meringue.

Phil What movie?

Spanky The one where the guy's got amnesia . . . wish to Christ I could remember the name of it.

Terry What were you telling her?

Bernadette Nothing . . . just about them dumb-bells you got off Crichton the butcher.

Terry What dumb-bells?

Phil (*eyeing Bernadette*) How come we've never seen her before?

Spanky She works in Dispatch.

Phil I'm sent. What'd you say her name was again?

Bernadette Thon metal things that you can't even lift off the mantelpiece.

Terry Them's not dumb-bells. That's my father's trophies from the Thread Mills Bowling Club – two silver-plated bobbins . . .

Bernadette Eh?

Terry And I can so lift them. I done it for my maw when she was looking to see if he had a plank. We found fourteen and six.

Bernadette Aw, shut up. See if you act the nitwit when we bump into Lucille . . . you're for it.

Terry I was only asking what the guy was like. So's I can keep out of his road.

Bernadette He was in the cloakrooms with yous earlier on, she said. Go and get us a drink.

Terry Oh, yeah, there was a guy going on about 'Lucille, Lucille' . . . a skelf with goggles . . . that's all right then. Leave it to me, Lucille baby . . . by the time I'm finished with this guy his own mother's not even going to recognise me.

Bernadette And no ice, remember.

Terry Check. (*Exits.*)

Spanky Hold on . . . it starts with a 'B'. Same as that doll's in that other movie . . . the one where the Virgin Mary comes down for one of her personal appearances . . . *The Song of* . . . then it gave you the doll's name . . . same as hers . . . Mmmmmm, these are good.

Phil *The Song of* what? C'mon . . . *The Song of the South*, was that it? That had Brer Rabbit in it . . .

Phil Bunny?

Spanky Yeh, you can see a million Catholics queuing up for *The Song of Bunny*. No . . . *The Song of.* . . *The Song of* . . . *The Song of Belinda*, that's the one! Me and my father seen it up the Bug Hut. It was all about this deaf and dumb lassie in Nova Scotia and Our Lady comes down and tells her to warn all the fishing folk but this doll can't hear so Our Lady works a miracle and the doll's head lights up. It was a religious picture.

Phil Who was in it? (*Combs hair.*)

Spanky Her with the the big . . .

Phil (*examining comb*) Nits!

Spanky Eh? (*Has a look.*) White powder paint from the Slab, ya mug.

Phil God, I got the wind up there . . . she's hardly going to go a bundle on somebody with nits, is she?

Spanky Oh, I don't know . . . they're funny, dolls.

Enter Alan and Lucille.

Alan (*looking down at feet*) What d'you mean? They are on the right feet, Lucille . . .

Lucille Well, they sure weren't a minute ago . . . they were on mines. God, it's boiling in there.

Alan Would you care for a drink, perhaps?

Lucille Yeh, get us a highball . . . plenty of ice cubes.

Alan Right . . . fine . . . will the chap know what that is, d'you think? His shelves looked a bit sparse . . . what was it again?

Lucille I'll get it myself! (*Exits.*)

Bernadette spots Alan for the first time.

Bernadette Hello, get a load of that. If it wasn't for the King Kong jacket and the Globetrotter shorts this might well pass for a fine boy. Wonder who he's came with?

Spanky Heads. No, tails. No, heads.

Phil Make up your mind.

Spanky Sorry, tails.

Phil You're just after saying heads.

Spanky Yeh, but I meant tails.

Phil Tails, you're sure?

Spanky All rights, heads.

Phil For definite?

Spanky Yeh, definitely tails. Heads, I mean.

Phil Listen . . . tails, you get to talk to her first . . . heads, I do . . . right?

Spanky Right . . . flickeroonie.

Phil tosses coin into the air. There is a bang and flash from inside hall. The lights go out.

Phil Where'd it go? Where'd it go?

The band grinds to a halt.

Curry (*off*) No panic, boys and girls . . . just a little electrical fault . . . I told you it was folly running those fairy lights off that bloody amp, Bobby . . .

The fairy lights flicker back to life, the ballroom remains dark.

Bernadette The luck of the Rooneys . . . just about to stroll over and get him to hitch up his strides for a sashey round the hangar when the end of the world arrives . . .

Phil Give us up your foot, Spanks . . . where are you?

Curry (*off*) Attention . . . will the gents with lighters make their way to this end of the hall, please? Gents with pocket lighters . . .

We can dimly perceive Bernadette feeling her way towards Alan.

Bernadette Does this happen every year?

Alan Oh, er . . . I've no idea . . . this is my first time . . .

Bernadette Snap. Brilliant, isn't it?

Spanky What was it, Phil?

Phil Half a dollar.

They are on hands and knees.

Spanky Aaaah!

Phil Great!

Spanky Sorry . . . it was a pigeon.

Curry (*off*) What d'you mean, they can't locate the fuse box? No, don't you go, Bobby . . . will someone stop that chap! Hector, away after that bugger . . .

Bernadette You here on your tod?

Alan Er . . . not exactly. I did come with a girl but she doesn't seem to . . .

Bernadette 'S nice with the lights out, isn't it?

Phil What about that bicycle lamp you got for your Christmas, Spanks?

Spanky That was in nineteen forty-nine, Phil . . . the battery's done.

The lights go back on. Lucille appears in the doorway with drink. She sees Alan and Bernadette standing very close.

Lucille *and* **Bernadette** (*together*) Damn!

Spanky and Phil look at Alan and Bernadette, then at Lucille, who has moved across to front of stage.

Curry (*off*) Right, thanks, Bobby. Okay, boys and girls, back in business once more. Will you take your partners, please, for a 'ladies' choice' . . . a 'ladies' choice' . . . thank you.

Band strikes up.

Bernadette (*grabbing Alan's arm*) C'mon, I'll lead . . .

Exeunt.

Lucille Aaaargh!

Spanky That kind of drops the shutters on us, eh? Think I'll go and give Lucille a sympathetic shoulder. . . this one, I reckon . . .

Phil follows Bernadette and Alan into hall. Spanky crosses to Lucille.

Spanky Now's your chance, Spanky boy . . . don't throw it away. Be casual . . . casual but sparkling. My clothes are all sticking to us . . . how's about you, Lucille?

Lucille What?

Spanky Not getting nowhere with that line, son . . . better try a more sophisticated approach. The Grosvenor Pie was tasty though . . . it's the boiled egg in the middle that makes all the difference if you ask me.

Lucille Who's asking you? Going to give it a by?

Spanky The sympathetic patter might do the trick. I know how you feel, Lucille . . . same thing happened to me with a doll I took up the Bug Hut. Found her up the back stalls with the checkie . . .

Lucille Tch!

Spanky You've got her now, kiddo! Yeh, and his torch was off!

Lucille throws her drink over him and stomps off.

I think I'll have a squint for that half-dollar . . . buy myself some blotting paper.

Enter Miss Walkinshaw.

Miss Walkinshaw Cooeeeee . . . I was just wondering if there were any gents out here?

Spanky hides. Exit Miss Walkinshaw. Enter Sadie.

Sadie I was just wondering if there were any gents out here? No? Thank God. Ooooohhhh . . . (*nurse's feet*) Look at that . . . (*Takes off shoe.*) . . . soles are like tishy paper . . . ninety denier? I'll wear my prescription stockings the next time . . . to hell with glamour.

Enter Curry.

Curry Ah, Sadie . . . come on, it's a 'ladies' choice'. . .

Sadie Oh, is it? Fancy that . . .

Enter Miss Walkinshaw.

Miss Walkinshaw Ah, Bill . . . come on, it's a 'ladies' choice' . . .

Curry Oh, is it? Fancy that.

Miss Walkinshaw grabs his arm and leads him towards door. Exeunt.

Spanky Handkerchief, Sadie?

Sadie Oh, help my God! See you . . . Is that yous slittering drinks yous? It's bibs yous boys need. Here . . . (*Gives him hanky.*)

Spanky Ta. Feet away again?

Sadie How the hell did Carmen Miranda ever manage to walk in these bloody things?

Spanky I've got the same problem with underpants . . .

Enter Bernadette and Alan.

Alan Sorry to break off there but I've got to go through to the bar and look for someone . . . Anything I can get you . . . er . . .?

Bernadette Bernadette. No, it's all right, Terry's bringing us something.

Alan Right. Thanks for the dance.

Bernadette My pleasure. Hey – I never caught your name . . .

Exit Alan. Enter Phil.

Phil Phil . . . good name, eh?

Sadie (*to Spanky*) You carry these for us, son. (*Hands him shoes.*) God, you're that like our Tommy, so you are. He got tablets for it.

Exeunt.

Phil Belinda . . . now there's a name for you.

Bernadette Eh?

Phil *Johnny Belinda.* Jane Wyman was in it.

Bernadette What's this we're getting? Oh, yeah? I wish Terry would hurry up.

Phil Yeah, she plays this deaf mute doll that Lew Ayres teaches how to talk with her fingers and she gets dead good at it. He's the local quack, you understand. Anyhow, her old man's a crabbit pig and the only way he can shut the doll up is to get her to wear these mittens . . .

Bernadette Are you collecting for something?

Phil Eh?

> *Enter Terry, a Bloody Mary in one hand and plate of Chicken Maryland in the other.*

Terry Vodka 'n' tomato juice . . . plenty of ice. (*Spots Phil.*) What're you wanting, pal?

Phil Ah, that's very kind of you, hotshot . . . I'll have the Chicken Maryland.

Terry Beat it, wise guy! I've had about as much as I can take from you! (*Holds out drink, the glass rattles loudly.*) I wish she hadn't asked for ice!

Phil Okay, okay, cool it, don't lose your cool, just cool it, okay? Quite hard getting that out with your heart in your mouth but I managed it, thank God. Okay, okay, don't cool your lose . . . fuck! Don't just cool it, lose it, okay? Okay. (*Exits.*)

Terry I thought you weren't going to talk to guys if I brung you!

Bernadette (*grabs drink and takes quaff*) Aaaaargh! My fillings! See you!

Exeunt. Enter Hector.

Hector Hello . . . 'S anybody seen Lucille? Lucille? She promised us a dance . . . (*Exits. Off*) Lucille?

Enter Lucille.

Lucille I knew this was going to happen . . . I just knew it . . . I can't keep nothing to myself. Aaaargh!

Enter Miss Walkinshaw.

Miss Walkinshaw All right, Bill . . . I'll just be out here. Gosh, it's like a hothouse in there . . . this is the first breather I've had all night . . . My, isn't it refreshing now that the rain's let up? Mmmmm. . . (*Takes deep breath.*) One can almost smell the ozone coming up from Largs.

Enter Hector.

Hector Oh, you are out here, Lucille, I've been hunting all over the place. How's about that dance now?

Lucille What dance?

Enter Alan.

Alan Oh, you are out here, Lucille? I've been . . .

Lucille (*to Hector*) Oh, that dance? (*Grabs him. Pulls him towards exit. Stops.*) Hold on. (*Plants a juicy kiss on his lips.*) Okay?

Hector Okay? Okay? Godallbloodymighty, is this a dream or what?

Exit Lucille.

I'm coming, Lucille!

Miss Walkinshaw Gosh, it's like a hothouse in there . . . this is the first breather I've had all night . . . (*Pause.*) Are you on your own too?

Alan What? Er . . . no, not exactly, Miss, er . . .

176

Miss Walkinshaw My, isn't it refreshing now that the awful rain's let up? I shouldn't let it worry you unduly . . .

Alan What?

Miss Walkinshaw We were all a wee bit flighty at that age . . .

Alan Sorry. I'm not. . .

Miss Walkinshaw I remember my first Staff Dance . . . I think I danced every number with a different partner . . . and I had six of them wanting to run me home. Not that things have changed that much . . . though I don't think I should find the back step of a bike all that comfy nowadays . . .

The Town Hall clock strikes.

Gosh, is that the time? I'd better give Mum a wee tinkle. I do trust she hasn't thought to light up one of these cork tips that Mrs Cruise left . . . she can't keep a grip on them with her top set out . . . Would you care to take my arm, Alan? Thank you. Gosh, don't you look smart in that suit . . . (*Exeunt.*)

Enter Bernadette.

Bernadette Good God, is that him she's dancing with? How the hell did he ever get near a university?

Hector appears in doorway.

It's like somebody put togs on a greenfly.

Lucille (*handing Hector her bag*) Here, hold on to that, I'll be back in a minute.

Enter Hector, clutching bag.

Bernadette Ho, ho, now's your chance, hen. Hello, handsome . . . come and perch over here. Lucille said I was to keep you warm till she got back.

Hector, still starry-eyed, wanders over. Pause.

God, he hasn't got much patter for an egghead. (*Pause.*) I was seriously debating with myself whether to come here tonight or stay in and listen to my Al 'Diz' Huxley records.

Pause.

Hector Eh?

Bernadette Yeh, you can see the intelligence close up. I've been trying to get hold of his LPs for ages but it's not every shop that has jazz discs . . . I've even tried the Co-operative. Keep going, Bernadette, you're getting through. Yes, I much prefer him to guys like Satchmo and Bert Weedon . . . there's so much more to get your gnashers into . . .

Hector Pardon?

Bernadette Of course, he's not to everyone's taste . . . not what you'd cry Lucille's cup of tea . . .

Hector Who isn't?

Bernadette Big Al . . . him that goes up Pipongo jazz club.

Hector Yeh, that's true. I thought she really liked him at first but now I know for definite.

Bernadette Bullseye, hen! Yeh, it's dead stimulating a daud of that stuff, isn't it?

Hector (*placing a finger to lips*) Yeah . . .

Bernadette whisks him into a dance. Enter Lucille.

Lucille Where did that stupid mug Alan get to. It was a reaction I was after, not a vanishing act. Oh, there's that Jezebel. Hoi.

Hector Oh, you're back, Lucille!

Bernadette I should've danced Brainbox here into the stadium, dammit! (*to Lucille*) You weren't long . . . thought you were away doing up your face?

Lucille That's how I wouldn't be long then. Unlike some folk I've only got the one.

Bernadette Somebody across the river you're shouting at?

Lucille Don't come the Little Bo Peep, Rooney, you know who I'm talking to . . .

Bernadette Talking? There's windows getting flung up in Possilpark!

Lucille You were exactly the same at the Abercorn Primary . . . couldn't keep your sticky mitts off nothing of mines, could you?

Bernadette We're not getting the saga about the pencil case with your initials burnt into it again, are we?

Lucille And there was Davey Smythe with the limp and the big boy with the moustache in the qualifying class!

Bernadette This is only supposed to happen when you're getting drowned, all this. What are you on about, Bentley? As if I didn't know. What are you on about?

Lucille As if you didn't know. Well, not this time, Rooney!

Hector Er . . . Lucille? (*Gets knocked out of the way.*)

Lucille That's the last safari you make into my ballpark, buster! Okay, so we can all understand the roving eye considering that chimp you brung along that thinks it looks like Elvis but . . .

Enter Terry.

179

Terry Hi, you cats, what's going on out here?

Bernadette Nothing . . . she's just eaten up with jealousy, that's all.

Exit Lucille.

Terry What's she got to be jealous about?

Bernadette (*drily*) 'Cos she thinks you're a dead ringer for Presley and I've got you.

Terry (*pleased*) Oh, does she?

Bernadette Yeh, come on. (*Exits.*)

Hector (*polishing his spectacles*) Lucille?

Terry Oh, there's that clothes peg that I've to give the doing to. Hey, jumping bean.

Hector Eh?

Terry You the guy that done the birthday card for Lucille?

The lights flicker and go out.

Hector What if it was? Lucille, your wee bag, your wee bag, Lucille . . .

Terry God, listen to that . . . she said he was a cheeky bastard. C'mere.

There is a thump. Hector falls to the ground.

Okay, Lucille baby . . . anything else you want just whistle 'Don't Be Cruel' . . . God, my hand . . . (*Exits.*)

Curry (*off*) For Christ's sake, Bobby, this is worse than the bloody blitz . . . Eh? What the hell would I be doing with three-amp fuse wire?

Enter Miss Walkinshaw.

Miss Walkinshaw Who on earth would be telephoning the terrace at this time of night? Unless Mother's trying to phone out. . . Oh, God, I just hope she's not trying to phone here . . . No, it's come off the hook . . . that's what's happened. She's caught it on one of those tassle things on her smoking jacket . . . Oh God, what has she got up for? I shoved the commode right up next to her bed . . .

Enter Phil and Spanky with two pints of beer. Spanky is holding on to Phil's jacket as they stumble in.

Phil In the land of the halt the one-legged dwarf is king . . . (*Bumps into Miss Walkinshaw.*) Oops, sorry Mr, er . . .?

Miss Walkinshaw Who's that?

Phil No, no, I asked you first. Hold on . . . Bobby Sinclair?

Spanky Don't be stupid, Bobby's got a light-up dicky-bow.

Phil Well, if it isn't Bobby Sinclair with the neon cravat and it isn't the gorgeous Miss Walkinshaw whose voluptuous body drives us pimply youths absolutely . . .

Miss Walkinshaw Is that you, Philip?

Phil Oh, is that you, Miss Walkinshaw? Do forgive my chum's coarse reference to your frame but he's never been the same since I showed him that corselet ad in the *Tit Bits* . . .

Miss Walkinshaw Are you tight, Philip?

Phil Tight, Miss Walkinshaw? Not me . . . right, Spanks? There's a half-dollar lying about the balcony here you can have a lend of. Came away without any dough, have we? Take your shoe off and have a feel about with your toes, Spanky . . .

Miss Walkinshaw I don't know what they're thinking of, serving strong drink to young chaps like you . . . one of you'll be on the floor before the night's out . . .

The lights come back on. They see Hector lying on the ground. He comes to groggily. He sits up holding his nose.

Hector Ohyah . . .

Miss Walkinshaw Tch, tch, tch . . . what did I tell you? That is disgusting, Hector. I'm surprised at you.

Exits.

Curry (*off*) Thanks again, Bobby . . .

Hector Somebody hut us.

Phil God, look at the beak.

Hector I was shouting to Lucille to give her back her bag when this voice says 'C'mere,' then the lights went out and this voice just hut us . . . for nothing. Ohyah!

Spanky You point this voice out to us, kiddo. Right, Phil? (*to Hector*) Going to not hold your face over my pint?

Enter Alan.

Alan Lucille, are you . . .? (*Sees Hector.*) Excuse me! (*Exits.*)

Enter Lucille.

Lucille 'S anybody been out here looking for us?

Spanky Well, there was a dinner suit walked in a second ago but it was hard to tell if there was anybody inside it.

Hector (*trying desperately to get up*) I'm here, Lucille . . .

Exit Lucille. Spanky and Phil hang on to Hector.

Spanky On your marks . . .

Phil Get set!

Hector Let us go!

Phil And they're off!

Hector races out.

And into the first bend goes the Lovesick Pixie followed by a Trail of Blood but Elusive Lucille is just behind Big Pants and as they come to the Canal Turn it's over to Michael O'Hare!

Spanky Thank you, Raymond . . . and they're just coming into view over Beecher's and Elusive Lucille is just ahead of Big Pants and the Lovesick Pixie . . . and who's this coming up on the Stand Side? Yes, it's Bobby Sinclair on Voltage Drop and as they head out into the country I'll hand you back to Raymond Glendenning!

Phil Thank you, Michael! And it's Elusive Lucille, Big Pants, the Lovesick Pixie, then Voltage Drop, followed by Willie Curry on Colonel Bogey, and Sadsack Sadie, the filly dogged by hoof-rot all season, making a brave run for home . . . Michael!

Spanky Oh, and there's a faller there! Wacky Walkinshaw, the grey, has taken a tumble . . . and as Big Pants takes up the running with just two strides in it it's back to Raymond Glendenning at the Winning Post! Raymond!

Phil Christ, sorry, I missed that, Michael . . .

Enter Curry and Sadie.

Curry They weren't all rhumbas, for God's sake. That last one was a Dashing White Sergeant . . . lassie in the ATS taught me . . .

Sadie Aw . . . it wasn't the Gestapo, then?

Curry What's up with you pair? Away through and take turns with Miss Walkinshaw . . .

Sadie Our Tommy was a wonderful ballroom dancer . . .

Phil We lost some dough, all right?

Sadie He never had the bequest of the feet, you see . . .

Spanky Half a dollar . . .

Curry Och, here . . . (*Hunts out some change.*)

Sadie I mind my mammy was that tickled when he and the wee lassie up the street brung home third prize in the John Boscoe Black Bottom.

Curry How much did you say?

Spanky Half a crown . . .

Phil Each. (*Takes two half-crowns from Curry's outstretched palm.*)

Sadie And a cruet set in the shape of the Vatican.

Phil Thanks . . . this way, Spanks.

    Exeunt.

Sadie She put it up on the sideboard next to the photo of Matthew, Mark, Luke and John . . .

Curry Bloody corner boys. Are you up to the next one, Sadie?

    Enter Miss Walkinshaw.

Miss Walkinshaw Bill?

Sadie Much as I am loath to say it . . . thanks, hen.

Curry Oh, Lord . . . what is it now, Elsie?

Miss Walkinshaw You left me standing there in the middle of the floor . . .

Curry Oh, did I?

Miss Walkinshaw Just standing there . . . I felt such a fool . . . Bobby Sinclair had to come and rescue me on the pretext of looking for a set of welding rods . . .

Curry I'm dreadfully sorry, Elsie . . . I used to do the very same with Mimi.

Sadie Aye, what's up she's not here like how she wasn't here last year either? Missus Curry . . .?

Curry Eh? Oh, er . . . distemper.

Sadie Distemper? Christ, I thought I was bad with my feet.

Curry Yes, the pup's got distemper and Mimi stayed home to nurse him . . . we're keeping our fingers crossed the budgie doesn't catch it next . . . Look, Elsie, why don't you go back inside and I'll join you shortly, hm? You'll only catch your death out here in that thin frock . . .

Miss Walkinshaw I'm perfectly all right, Bill, it's fully lined, thank you.

Sadie I wondered what the bumphles were. (*Gets up and moves towards exit.*)

Curry You're not away, Sadie?

Sadie Oooohh, that wet stone's sending a shooting pain right up my back. Pass us up them sandals, will you, Miss Walkinshaw? Thanks. Constipation? I go through absolute purgatory.

Miss Walkinshaw Heavens.

Curry Hell . . .

Sadie I'm away in for a Limbo . . . (*Exits. Pause.*)

Miss Walkinshaw It's so unbecoming, Bill . . .

Curry Sorry, what was that, Elsie?

Miss Walkinshaw Now, if it were some young bitch with a big bottom . . .

Curry Pardon?

Miss Walkinshaw That poor Mimi was having to play second fiddle to . . .

Curry He's a cocker spaniel, Elsie . . .

Miss Walkinshaw I can't for the life of me fathom what the attraction is . . . those feet!

Curry Paws, Elsie . . . paws, dear . . .

Miss Walkinshaw Yes, and I wish you would, Bill . . . just for a moment . . . before it's too late . . .

Curry It already is. I'm after shelling out for the licence – five shillings it was. Here, that reminds me . . . McCann, Farrell . . . (*Heads for exit. Stops.*) Say a wee prayer that Sonny doesn't get it.

Miss Walkinshaw Who?

Curry Sonny Tufts . . . the budgie. McCann! (*Exits.*)

Enter Terry and Bernadette.

Terry It's the schnozzle, I reckon . . . that and the eyelids, know what I mean? (*Sings.*) Love me tender, love me true . . . all my dreams fulfil . . .

Bernadette Get us a vodka . . . that's really hellish.

Terry Check. (*Sings.*) For, my darling, I love you . . . D'you want any ice?

Bernadette No! You always ask us that.

Terry (*sings*) And I always will. (*Exits.*)

Bernadette See, guys . . .

Miss Walkinshaw Yes . . .

Bernadette You're not married, are you, Miss Walkinshaw?

Miss Walkinshaw I haven't had the pleasure so far . . .

Bernadette No, I wasn't asking that . . . I was asking if you were married? My mum keeps warning me, 'See, if you come home with some guy and say you're getting married I'll break your bloody jaw.' Your mum ever say that to you? Course it'll be that long ago you won't be able to remember . . .

Miss Walkinshaw Thank you. Yes, as a matter of fact, she did say something along those lines . . . though why I should be telling you I can't think . . . you're Lucille's friend, aren't you?

Bernadette Used to be . . . yeh. Her and I's fell out . . .

Miss Walkinshaw Oh, that seems a shame.

Bernadette Not really. You know how it is with best friends . . . we can't stand one another.

Miss Walkinshaw Quite . . .

Bernadette I mean, what would I be wanting with some crummy stills from a five-bob movie annual when I can have all the ten-by-eight glossies I want just by dialling our Dennis . . .? That's my young scud . . .

Miss Walkinshaw Scud?

Bernadette Brother. He's in the film business . . .

Miss Walkinshaw Oh . . . how exciting . . .

Bernadette Yeh . . . him and another boy from Paisley got a lift down to London last Fair holidays. You want to see the flat they've got. Right next door to Piccadilly tube station . . . and they don't pay rent or nothing too. Their manager says they're really going places. Yeh, trust our Dennis to land on his feet . . .

Miss Walkinshaw Yes . . . it's a funny place, London . . .

Bernadette Wish everywhere was as funny.

Enter Hector holding his nose.

Hector I can't find her anywhere . . . ohyah . . . hello, Miss Walkinshaw . . .

Miss Walkinshaw Tch, tch, tch, tch . . . (*Exits.*)

Enter Phil and Spanky. They join Hector.

Spanky When've you to give the suit back to Pinnochio, Heck?

Bernadette I don't blame him for holding his nose next to that pair. (*Smiles across.*) Look over here, ya wee pig.

Phil (*catching Bernadette smiling*) Oho . . . dig the sun's come out. Must've left the button on 'Delay' when I switched on the movie patter. Better move in and consolidate . . .

Strolls across, followed by Spanky.

Give her the 'I know you from somewhere, don't I?' routine this time (*to Bernadette*) Was it the Ice Rink, maybe?

Bernadette Was what the Ice Rink?

Spanky Gave you that bum?

Phil (*gives Spanky a look*) No . . . there was a doll used to be the Pirates' mascot . . . went to all their games. Me and him's pally with the guy that's their goalminder now. Lives across the backdoor from us in Feegie. Comes from Manitoba, he was saying.

Spanky That's right . . . he was at Benediction the other night . . . Red Indian dabbities all over his jerkin and these terrific shitecatcher trousers on . . . doesn't genuflect or nothing, this guy. (*Gets another 'sinker' from Phil.*) Sorry . . .

Phil That's right . . . he was at Benediction the other night . . . Red Indian dabbities all over his jerkin and these terrific shitecatcher trousers on . . . doesn't genuflect or nothing, this guy . . .

Spanky (*wistfully*) Wish I could do patter like that.

Exit Hector. Bernadette follows him out.

Bernadette (*to Phil*) Is that a Mountie's hoofprint you've got on the back of your jacket? (*Exits.*)

Enter Alan.

Alan Has anyone been looking for me?

Spanky Yeh, us . . . d'you want to refill these? (*Holds up tumblers.*)

Alan What with?

Spanky Developing a nasty sense of humour, this boy. D'you not drink or something, smart talk? Not got a head for it, is that it? What was it like last year, Phil? You want to've seen this, son. Did we ever show you the photos of us vomiting into Miss Walkinshaw's evening bag?

Phil Yeh, that was some Staffie, that.

Spanky Top table sent us down a tray of drinks when we both lost our kelly bows down the lavvy. (*Holds up tumblers.*) Phil's is a pint of heavy and mines is two pints . . . just whenever you're ready.

Enter Hector.

Hector Has she been out here?

Alan turns away. Enter Lucille.

Lucille Well?

Hector Oh, hello, Lucille . . . I've still got your handbag and I bought you a drink . . . look.

Lucille Are you going to stand there and let me buy my own?

Hector I bought you one, I said.

Lucille What's up, are you deaf or what?

Hector No, it was just a smack in the nose . . . d'you not fancy a Martini and Vimto?

Lucille It's a Manhattan I'm after . . .

Hector Oh . . . right . . . I'll not be long . . . (*Exits.*)

Lucille Well? What about my Manhattan?

Alan He's gone to fetch it . . .

Lucille I'm talking to you, dummy. Well?

Alan But I thought . . .

Lucille And get a move on, I'm parched. Plenty of ice, okay?

Alan Yeah, sure . . . I thought . . . yeah, right. (*Exits.*)

Spanky (*loudly*) And we'll have a couple of . . .

Lucille Don't you dare, Alan!

Phil Thanks, Lucille.

Lucille Can it. And stop staring at us, the pair of yous.

Enter Bernadette looking back into hall.

And you can stuff your eyeballs back in their sockets, Rooney. He is not for sale, understand?

Bernadette I was looking to see if Terry was coming. Who wants to look at what you've dragged along? God, she could've brung him in her purse.

Lucille I never dragged no one along . . . he brung me in his da's sports car.

Bernadette Did you work the pedals for him?

Lucille It's a cut above hanging from the back of a clapped-out moped to scruff.

Bernadette My Terry is not scruff!

Spanky Yeh, he is . . . me and him recognise scruff when we see it. Right, Phil? Okay, Lucille?

Phil You speak for yourself, Farrell. (*to Bernadette*) D'you want to sit over here, sweetheart?

Bernadette Eh? I wouldn't be seen dead sitting over there beside that. (*Indicates Lucille.*)

Lucille And you did so clip them *Jailhouse Rock* photos out.

Phil (*to Bernadette*) Great movie that, wasn't it?

Lucille Shut up talking to her, you! And you stop trying to sook in with him, Rooney!

Bernadette Look what's talking! The biggest one at the Abercorn . . .

Lucille Just what exactly are you implying?

Bernadette All I'm saying is, once a sook always a sook. It's a well-known phrase . . .

Spanky (*quickly*) . . . or saying, that's right. They had it on *Beat the Clock* last Sunday, only the woman put 'Sook, sook, only a once always' . . . She got turfed.

Phil Yeh, I seen that.

Bernadette *and* **Lucille** (*together*) The both of yous blow, this is confidential.

Bernadette As I was saying, once a sook, always . . .

Enter Terry.

Terry Heh, they're having a go-as-you-please through there . . . how about – (*Sings.*) You ain't nothin 'but a hound dog, just a –

Bernadette Shut up, Terry.

Terry What'd I do now?

Bernadette Shut up and sit!

Terry Right, right, sit! Woof, woof . . . good boy! Right!

Enter Alan with drinks.

Alan Sorry I took so long . . . he'd never heard of a Manhattan . . . is a gin and pineapple all right?

Lucille That'll have to do . . . c'mon.

Alan Sorry . . . where are we going?

Lucille Bring them with you. (*She moves to exit.*)

Alan Sorry?

Lucille Bring them with you, I said . . . the dance hall . . .

Alan Right. Er . . . would you all like to come through to the . . . er . . . ?

Lucille The drinks, softie!

Lucille *and* **Alan** (*together*) Aaaaaargh!

Exeunt. Enter Hector with trayload of assorted drinks.

Hector I got you a selection, Lucille . . . the guy said he'd never heard of a . . . Lucille? (*Exits. Off*) Lucille??

Spanky Well, what now, Phil? Mines is off into the fray with the Seven League Breeks and yours is sitting there quite content with Blueto.

Phil Let's choke one another.

Spanky Good idea.

They grab each other by the throat and fall to ground.

Terry Hey, that looks a right laugh, doesn't it?

Bernadette Yeah, why don't you join them, Terry? Stupid pigs.

Lights flicker and go out.

Phil (*sings*) Dark night has come down on this rough-spoken world . . .

He is joined by Spanky.

And the banners of darkness are boldly unfurled . . .

Bernadette Hang off, Terry!

Enter Curry and Miss Walkinshaw.

Curry Och, I give up, Elsie . . . where the devil are you going?

Miss Walkinshaw I'm making sure I'm not beached through there . . . this way.

Curry God, it's like walking into the middle of a liquorice allsort . . . Elsie? I'll murder that bugger Sinclair . . . Elsie?

Miss Walkinshaw Over here, Bill.

Curry Oh, that's very helpful . . . where's 'over here', in the name of God? (*Stumbles about.*) Oucha!

Miss Walkinshaw Look, there's the most wonderful view . . . you can see right up-river. Isn't it beautiful with the moonlight just catching it?

Curry (*stumbling about still*) Oh, Christ!

Miss Walkinshaw Like a silver thread dropped willy-nilly . . .

Terry She off her napper?

Bernadette Shut up, Terry.

Curry Who's that?

Miss Walkinshaw It's me, Bill . . . I was saying how fine the river looks . . . over there . . .

Curry Where the hell's 'over there'?

Phil *and* **Spanky** (*sing together*) Over there . . . over there . . . oh, the Yanks are coming . . .

Curry Who is that? There's somebody out here . . .

Miss Walkinshaw Come and see, Bill. Look, there's the harbour just catching the moon . . .

Curry Oh yes . . . D'you realise that's where the first American troops to set foot on European soil landed, Elsie? (*Joins Miss Walkinshaw at balustrade.*)

Phil, Spanky, *and* **Terry** (*together, singing quietly*) Oh, the Yanks are coming, the Yanks are coming . . .

Bernadette . . . the Yanks are coming over there . . .

Curry I'm sure there's somebody out here . . . Shhhh . . . can you hear anything? Listen . . .

Silence.

Miss Walkinshaw I can't hear anything . . .

Curry Aye, not unless it suits you.

Miss Walkinshaw What was that?

Curry Nothing, nothing . . . what was I saying? Oh, yes . . . about the Yanks . . .

The singing starts up quietly again.

Yes . . . Paisley Harbour, nineteen forty-two . . . that's when the balloon went up.

Spanky Does he not mean Pearl Harbour?

Curry Eh? There it goes again . . . listen.

The singing goes quietly on.

Miss Walkinshaw Don't be silly, Bill . . . carry on . . . Paisley Harbour, nineteen forty-two . . .

The singing goes quietly on.

Curry Yes, well, the reason I know is that an old girl-friend of mine swears she bumped into Clark Gable in that wee sweetie shop in Well Street and he let the cat out of the bag . . . though how that bugger would know beats me . . . he wasn't even in the first wave . . . I wish I could remember what her name was.

There is a giggle.

There! You must've heard that . . . Who is out here? Come on . . .

Miss Walkinshaw You wouldn't have thought such people would be partial to boilings, would you?

Curry Sorry, what was that, Elsie?

Miss Walkinshaw Film stars. Of course, a lot of them don't have their own teeth, you know.

Curry Who is that?

Miss Walkinshaw Oh, God, that reminds me . . . I best give Mother a ring. You know what she's like with those bloody cork tips?

Curry Eh?

Exit Miss Walkinshaw. The remaining fairy lights go out and the terrace is plunged into darkness. Pause. Then all the lights come up. There is a ragged cheer from inside the hall. Curry looks round the now deserted terrace.

That's funny, I could've sworn . . .

Exits. Spanky and Phil appear from hiding.

Spanky God, that's heady stuff that Younger's. 'Many pints would you say we had, Phil?

Phil I'm not very sure . . . two, I think.

Spanky D'you feel it running down your legs?

Phil I sincerely hope not.

Spanky 'S like an electric current . . . d'you feel it? 'S like a current getting passed through your members . . .

Phil Yea, and I say unto you that it is easier for a current to pass through your members than it is for that prune Bobby Sinclair to light up the Kingdom of Heaven. Book of Proverbs, two-and-nine at all good fruit shops.

Spanky (*whistles*) Look at the moon . . . 's huge. (*Slight pause.*) That'll not be helping your maw none.

Hector (*off*) Lucille? Oyah!

There is a crash of broken glass.

Lucille . . . ?

Spanky And just look at all them stars . . . 'S dead romantic, isn't it? There must be thousands of the bastards. Heh . . . look! One of them's moving!

Phil Where?

Spanky There . . . just next to the Great Bear's bum . . . see? Aw, it's went out . . .

Phil Maybe it was the Sputnik with the mutt in it . . . ?

Spanky No . . . I think you can only see that through a smoky-flavoured dog biscuit . . . It was a shooting star.

Phil Don't be ridiculous . . . what would a shooting star be doing over Paisley?

Spanky Yeh . . . right enough. Heh . . . how's about all them graves in the Abbey? Who's all buried there, d'you reckon?

Phil Dead people mostly.

Spanky I remember when my da went . . . me and the bree were sitting watching a clip from *Merry Andrew* on the TV when my maw came through and said, 'That's him away, then.' The bree started bawling his eyes out . . .

Phil Yeh, I hear it's not too hot a movie, *Merry Andrew*.

Spanky They put a collection round his work for a floral tribute but they never got enough so my maw got a headsquare with Pat Smythe on it and a statue of the Whistling Boy instead . . . bit like old 'Rusty Spats' down there. Who was that again?

Phil That, my dear Spanks, was Sir Tiny Cottonbuds, the mill-owner and social reformer . . . one of the town's most illustrious sons.

Spanky Aw, yeh?

Phil Yeh . . . it was him that built all them convalescent homes at the seaside for the unfortunate herries that went down with tuberollesis from working in his thread works . . .

Spanky Very enlightened man by the sounds of it.

Phil That's his church up the High Street there . . . (*Points.*) Once described by Berenson's buddy, Kenneth Clark, as 'a symphony in sandstone to the Greater Glory of God and the Dignity of Labour'. Holds about four thousand, that joint. There's a big crucifix above the High Altar that's fashioned entirely from the thigh bones of local weans that died with the rickets.

Spanky Amazing . . .

Phil I wonder if it helps being a cripple?

Spanky Helps what?

Phil Look at Lautrec . . . hardly bum-high to a palette knife, but he done it, didn't he?

Spanky Art School again, is it? I could break your legs if you like.

Phil And there was Matisse and all. Sitting there in his wheelchair . . . Goolwazz clenched between the teeth and the brushes glued to the end of his walking sticks . . .

Spanky That'd be for sweeping up the dowts, yeah?

Phil D'you know what it's like being able to draw? It's the most exciting thing in the world . . . bar none. You don't need to send anybody up there to see what the world looks like. You only have to open a book of Ingres' drawings . . . there we are . . . you . . . me . . . him . . . her . . . them . . . us . . .

Spanky You going to try again next year maybe?

Phil Take the first time you heard 'Heartbreak Hotel' . . . the first time you pulled the laces tight on a pair of blue suede shoes . . . the first time you sat in the movies with a doll and realised there was better things in life than gorging yourself on Butterkist . . . and it's that – (*Snaps fingers.*) – compared to sitting there with a sheet of paper and a Black Prince pencil.

Spanky D'you think we'll ever get away from here, Phil?

Phil Sure . . . straight after the Last Waltz.

Spanky Paisley, I mean. I don't want to end up across there. I wonder what it is like being dead?

Phil Listen, kid . . . you're nineteen with a wardrobe full of clothes . . . you've got everything to live for.

Exeunt. Enter Miss Walkinshaw.

Miss Walkinshaw And what's that supposed to mean. . . 'You're never here when I need you, Elsie'? For goodness sake, Mother! A night out at Gwyneth's once a month and the Raffia Circle on alternate Thursdays . . .? Never there? And what the hell does she go and put the cork tip on the seat of the commode for in any case? She must've realised she'd get her arse scorched. 'Oh, Elsie dear, the humiliation.' Well, it serves you right, you old pig. I just wish it had been a half-corona!

Enter Terry and Bernadette.

Terry (*sings*) Blue moon, you saw me standing alone. . . (*Speaks.*) Hey, dig that . . . (*Looks up at moon.*) 'S like a big million-seller.

Bernadette It's right creepy over there, isn't it?

Terry All them crazy catafalques? Yeah. (*Pause.*) What d'you suppose they'll do when the King cops his lot?

Bernadette He has. Nineteen fifty-two . . . we got the day off school.

Terry Big El, I'm talking about! 'Many kings d'you think there is? What d'you suppose they'll do when he dies?

Bernadette Let his mother know?

Terry D'you not think they'll organise a world tour or something?

Bernadette For a stiff?

Terry Why not? It's about the only chance we'll ever get to see the bastard!

Bernadette D'you not think cremation's a good idea? Our next-door neighbour got cremated.

Terry 'S that her that had the chip-pan blaze?

Bernadette Don't try and be funny, Terry, it doesn't become you. That was my Auntie Sylvia and she's just after having thirteen skin grafts. (*Hauls him towards the exit.*)

Terry Oh . . . and how were the chips? (*Exeunt.*)

Enter Sadie.

Sadie I hope that man of mines remembers to bring the bogie with him when he comes to pick us up . . . oh, you're out here, Miss Walkinshaw . . . I thought you'd be through there in the bar with the Chief Constable . . . that's where Curry is . . .

Miss Walkinshaw And what made you think that, Sadie?

Sadie Well, if it wasn't one you were trying to hang on to all night it was the other . . . does he not come from up the terrace . . . PC Forty-Nine?

Miss Walkinshaw I'm sure I've no idea . . .

Sadie Aye, well he does . . . take my word for it . . . My
old mother used to sluice out that clatty house of theirs
after she'd done yours and your mammy's. They used
to give her the left-over fish wrapped in the *News of the
World* every Sunday for a bonus. I used to go out with
the bugger. Oh, I didn't always used to look like this,
you know. I was a fine-looking lassie in my time. Wanted
me to get engaged at one point. I know what he wanted
to get 'engaged' for! And him six months married with
a bungalow in Ralston? Our Tommy soon wiped the
smirk off his chops . . . couldn't get his helmet on for
a fortnight. Hell mend him. I never did like the way he
spoke about his wife. Nor has he changed a jot. He's
through there with a pint of rum and pep telling the
entire world what a washout she is. And he was spotted
up on the balcony earlier on with the trousers off sitting
on a jelly. What's up . . . have I upset you?

Miss Walkinshaw No, it's not that, Sadie. . .

Sadie What is it then? You're as white as thon sheets on
your beds never was . . . what is it?

Miss Walkinshaw It's Mother . . .

Sadie You forgot to phone her?

Miss Walkinshaw No, worse . . . I didn't forget. She's
mutilated herself.

Sadie She's what?

Miss Walkinshaw With a cork tip . . . on the backside.

Sadie Tch, tch, tch . . . and they try to tell you the toffs
know how to behave, eh? Aye, I mind of reading of one
of these cases in them *News of the Worlds* the rotten fish
was in . . . only this happened in Torquay and it was a

big Chinese man that done it to a sailorboy . . . I've never come across somebody doing it to theirselves . . . still . . .

Miss Walkinshaw D'you think I ought to get a taxi home? Look at that . . . my hands are shaking . . .

Sadie What you're needing's a wee drink, flower . . . you sit where you are . . . I'll get these to drag my aching body through to the bar and buy yous a stiff one . . . no, no . . .

Waves Miss Walkinshaw's protests aside.

My pleasure, hen . . . it'll draw you together . . . Have you got some change? I spent my last buying the bandleader a drink so's he wouldn't play any more rhumbas. Thanks, sweetheart . . . now, you just sit there and shake in peace . . . I'll not be long . . . ooohhh . . . (*Exits.*)

Enter Alan and Lucille.

Lucille I told you it would, stupid, trying to jive to that! 'S as if you've got the ship's cat up your trousers.

Alan Sorry . . .

Lucille Where did you hire that suit – the Brobdignag Naval Outfitters?

Alan I'm really sorry, Lucille . . .

Lucille Sorry, sorry. sorry! My nerves are like piano wires with 'I Apologise' getting played on them!

Alan Sorry.

Lucille Jack it in!

Alan Right . . . Lucille . . . sorry. Ooops, sorry. Aaargh, sorry! Sorry. Sorry, sorry, sorry!

Lucille 'S that you got it out of your system, d'you think?

Enter Hector.

Hector Ha . . . found you at last, Lucille . . .

Lucille What're you wanting?

Hector I brought you a drink out . . . I'm afraid I couldn't get exactly what you asked for but I got the next-best thing . . . a Bronx Cheer with a twist. Oh. I never knew Alan was . . . ?

Lucille Never knew Alan was what? A good wincher? Well, we'll soon see, willn't we? He can't dance, that's for certain. Now, beat it! And give us back the bag, worm.

Alan Lucille, I don't think . . .

Lucille No? Well, don't start now . . . you've dragged us out here, so winch, will you? (*Gets him in a clinch.*)

Hector So you might not make it on Sunday?

Lucille What were you told? Scat! And the nose isn't funny, okay? (*to Alan*) Right, you. (*Hauls him off into dark corner.*)

Hector What's happening? One minute I'm the bee's knees, the next I'm lower than a gnat's anklesocks. Scat! What's that supposed to mean? Oh, hello, Miss Walkinshaw, I never seen you there . . .

Miss Walkinshaw Oh. (*Comes out of her reverie.*)

Hector It's your frock . . . I thought you were a statue . . . Scat! What d'you make of that? Scat, she says. (*Takes a slug of the Bronx Cheer.*) Yeugh . . .

Miss Walkinshaw You really oughtn't to drink, Hector. See, you're like me. . . you don't even like the filthy stuff.

Lucille Okay, okay . . . I'll go on this trainspotting caper on Sunday, but I'm not sitting on wet seats again, get that straight.

Alan I know it's not everyone's idea of a day out, but as long as you think you might come along . . .

Lucille I'm after telling you for definite . . . no 'thinks' or 'mights' about it. As long as that hood goes up, okay? And listen, going to quit with the Mr Nice Guy act? That went out with waspies and moonie haircuts, all right? And don't hang your head either.

Alan Sorry.

Lucille You go through that palaver again and you're playing solitaire, bub . . . Now, what time are you picking us up at?

Alan On Sunday? Let's see . . .

Lucille Saturday . . . you're taking us to the La Scala.

Alan Oh, I think I've maybe seen that . . .

Lucille You'll see it again then, won't you? The La Scala, right? Six . . . half-six . . . foot of the road and don't pump your horn . . . it's dead annoying.

Alan Right, half-six, then.

Lucille You weren't listening, Alan . . . I said, six . . . half-six, okay?

Alan Okay.

Lucille Good . . . I'll be ready about seven.

Exeunt. Hector and Miss Walkinshaw sit in mutual misery.

Curry (*off*) Thank you, the Largie Boys . . . Right, boys and girls, the moment you've all been waiting for . . . no,

204

not my speech, ha, ha . . . that comes later . . . no, the tombola. Where's Miss Walkinshaw? Hector?

Hector Scat! What's that supposed to mean?

Curry (*off*) Hector . . . away and see if you can find Miss Walkinshaw . . . Hector?

Miss Walkinshaw 'You're never here when I need you.' What's that supposed to mean?

Curry (*off*) Miss Walkinshaw, please!

Hector I think you're wanted . . .

Miss Walkinshaw Mmm?

Curry (*off*) Hector? Elsie?

Hector *and* **Miss Walkinshaw** (*together*) What's that supposed to mean?

Exit Miss Walkinshaw. Enter Terry and Bernadette.

Terry But, how not? The tickets are only a tanner and the first prize is a two-pound fruit cake . . . I'm starving.

Bernadette Stop affronting us, Terry. (*Spots Hector. Walks towards him.*) Oh, hello there . . . are you not . . .?

Hector turns.

My God, what happened to your face?

Hector Somebody hut us.

Bernadette What! Who would want to . . .? Terry!!

Terry Don't look at us like that . . . he had his specs off.

Bernadette What did you go and hit him for?

Terry What did I go and hit him for? 'Cos he's the guy that done the birthday card for your pal . . . (*to Hector*) Aren't you?

Hector Yeh, but . . .

Terry See?

Bernadette He's at the university, you mug . . . aren't you?

Hector No.

Bernadette See? Eh?

Hector I'm Hector . . .

Terry (*grabs Hector*) You are this guy, aren't you?

Bernadette Put him down, Terry! He's the guy that goes up the Pipongo . . . he's just new started in the Slab Room . . . aren't you?

Hector I've just new left the Slab Room . . . Hector McKenzie . . . hang off!

Terry You wee . . .

Bernadette (*overlapping*) What did you go and lead us on like that for!

Terry You're asking for a doing doing that . . . trying to kid me on you were the one that was asking for a doing . . . you're for a doing!

Enter Phil and Spanky.

Bernadette That's the guy, you lunk! (*Exits.*)

Terry Oh, God . . . (*Releases Hector.*)

Hector Aaaaahhh, my oxters . . . (*Exits.*)

Phil Sundays . . . that's when me and my old man saunter up to see her . . . take her to the tea-rooms . . . slip her some pocket money. Three of us sit there, heads down, staring at the French cakes, him and me wishing that the bell would go and her hoping to Christ there's

a Gillette blade inside the ten-bob note we gave her . . .
Give us a match.

Terry I had a feeling all along it was going to be one of
these wiseguys . . . I wish there was something to eat . . .
my stomach's turning over.

Bernadette appears in doorway with Lucille.

Bernadette Well, we'll soon see, willn't we? Terry!

Terry What?

Bernadette Or that Elvis Fan Club record's going on top
of the cooker.

Terry Oh, you wouldn't! There's only six of them in the
whole country.

Bernadette I've only to pick up the phone to my daddy.
He would be delighted . . .

Terry Okay, okay, okay.

*Tries to collect himself. Spanky comes up behind and
taps him on shoulder.*

Aargh!

Spanky Got a light, Jim? What's wrong . . . your trousers
seized up?

Terry How would you like a . . .? (*Draws fist back.*)

Bernadette Not him stupid! The other one.

Terry Oh? Er . . . 's your pal about? Say he's went home,
will you? Eh?

Spanky This palooka looks as if he means business,
what'll I tell him? Maybe he has . . . maybe he hasn't.

Terry Oh, he's went home, has he?

Spanky If I say yeh, he'll maybe put one on me. No, no, wait and I'll give him a shout.

Terry No, don't strain yourself, pal.

Spanky He's over there . . . see you sometime, eh? (*Exits.*)

Terry (*to Bernadette*) I think he's went home, hen . . .

Phil strolls up and taps Terry on shoulder.

Terry Aaaargh!

Phil Got a light, Jim? What's wrong . . . your trousers sei . . .?

Terry Right, you cheeky bastard! How'd you like that fag rammed down your throat? Christ, did I say that?

Phil Christ, did he say that? Eh?

Terry What? I never said nothing.

Phil Thank God for that . . . must be the drink, Phil. You going to give us a light or . . .?

Terry Or what? I'm doing it again! Or what?

Phil What's up with him? Or what? he says . . . Jeeesus. Or what, what?

Terry What d'you mean, or what, what? Or what, what, what? Did I get that right?

Phil I'll never get this right. He said, or what, what, what? Now, if I say back, 'Or what, what, what what?' it's going to sound really infantile. Let's cool it, eh?

Terry What d'you mean, let's cool it? Everything is cool, right? Right? Too many 'rights' maybe? No, his face hasn't creased.

Phil One too many 'rights' there, pal . . . that just wasn't cool. Right, right, right . . . everything's absolutely . . . (*Sniffs.*) Everything's . . . (*Sniffs again.*) Every . . . what've you got on your hair, Jim?

Terry Grease! From the Chicken Maryland.

Phil Doesn't half make you smell henpecked.

Terry Listen, you!

Makes a lunge. The lights go out.

Miss Walkinshaw (*off*) It's all right, Bill, I can make out the bumps on the balls . . . all the threes, twenty-six.

Curry (*off*) No, no, hold on, Elsie, oh Christ . . . hold on. Where's Hector?

Miss Walkinshaw (*off*) Forty-six . . . unlucky for some.

Enter Curry.

Curry (*shining pen torch about*) Hector? Who's that? Oh . . . look, you girls nip through to the buffet and see if you can find Hector . . . he's away with Bobby's scout knife with the screwdriver on it . . . on you go . . . Who else is out here?

Phil Nobody.

Curry Is that you, McCann? You can take the cloakrooms,

Phil Ach, away to . . .

Curry Please, McCann . . .? Mrs Barton's just waiting on one number for a 'house' . . . Thanks. Who's that with you? Is that you, Farrell?

Terry Skinnedar . . . Terry.

Curry Right, Skinnedar, Terry, you have a shufti in the bar, he can't be far away.

Terry What was the description again?

Curry Small, horn-rim specs, stupid . . . hurry up . . .

Terry The blade, man . . . the blade . . .

Curry Big, horn-rim handle, very sharp . . . get a move on.

Exit Terry.

You've got my permission to give his ears a box.

Miss Walkinshaw (*off*) Two and six . . . was she worth it?

Curry For crying out loud, Elsie . . . (*Exits.*)

Phil is left standing alone in the semi-dark. Enter Hector.

Phil You haven't got a match, have you, kid?

Hector chucks over a box.

Eh? What's a mite like you doing with matches? (*Examines box.*) Ah, safeties . . .

Hector They were for lighting the soot bombs in the good room for Sunday . . . you can't get a chimney sweep at the weekends.

Phil And, lo, as I extricate this single fagaroonie from its handy crushproof pack and place it to my lips – (*Puts bent Woodbine in his mouth*) – I am at once reminded of the lonely Tommy and the legless Jock somewhere in a foreign field sharing their last gasper and contemplating the ways of the Lord. You're to give Bobby back his machete, Heck . . . Mrs Barton's sweating on a line.

Hector I'm desperate, Phil.

Phil And as the young Tommy draws the smoke deep into his lungs . . . the brave Jock brings forth a deck of cards from his kitbag and, spreading them out on the sand, says to the Tommy, 'Cut you for the tabby.'

Hector Phil, I'm desperate!

Phil God, so am I . . . must be them pints . . . you lead the way, Heck son . . . you can give Bobby back his . . .

Hector Stay back! I'm desperate, I said!

Phil I know, I know . . . so am I . . .

Hector Take one more step and I'm going through with it!

Phil Christ, what's that you've got? C'mon, Heck baby, quit the capering . . . is it a piggyback to the lavvies you're after?

Hector Cut the patter, McCann . . . this is it! You and Farrell think you're so smart, don't yous? Well, you're both going to be sorry . . .

Phil D'you want me to shout him through so's you can knife him?

Hector Shut up!

Phil C'mon . . . what's up, Hector?

Hector Shut your face . . . it's too late asking 'What's up?' Stay where you are! You wouldn't listen . . . none of yous . . . you wouldn't listen.

Phil I'm all ears now, kid, fire away . . . is it a cuddle you're wanting? (*Moves towards Hector.*)

Hector Stay back, you fucking bastard! Aaargh!

The lights come back up. Phil and Hector stare at the knife through Hector's wrist.

Phil *and* **Hector** (*together*) Jesus Christ!

Hector drops to ground.

Phil That's the white tux upstaged.

Curry (*off*) No, don't squeeze the balls, Elsie.

Miss Walkinshaw (*off*) Piss off, Bill . . .

Curry (*off*) Elsie!

Enter Spanky with leaking fountain pen in hand.

Spanky Look at this, Phil . . . I was just about to write a few adagio numbers when the nib . . . bang goes my deposit.

Phil Give us a hand, Spanks . . .

Spanky It's not the knife they were looking for? What's it doing through his . . . Oh God, is he dead?

Phil Walloped his napper off the flag stones . . . feel.

Hector Ooooohhhh . . .

Spanky Pull yourself together, Heck . . . it's mostly red ink.

Holds up ink-stained hands. Lights go out.

Has he lost a lot, Phil?

Phil Red ink? 'S hard to tell, Spanks.

Hector (*coming to*) Oh, Mammy, Mammy . . . what am I doing down here?

The lights come back on.

Phil Don't look, kid, there's a knife right through your wrist.

He holds Hector's wrist up while Spanky points to knife.

Hector Aaaargh,

Phil I told him not to look.

Enter Alan. The lights come back up.

Alan Holy Christ! What's happened?

Spanky My pen burst . . . look at the suit.

The lights go off.

Alan Out of my way, for God's sake . . . Hector? Hector?

Spanky Hang off.

Alan We better get something round his arm to stop the blood . . . quick, give me your tie!

Spanky *and* **Phil** (*together*) Right.

Phil and Spanky pull off clip-on bow ties and hold them out.

Alan Christ!

The lights start to flicker.

Spanky D'you not think we should ease the knife out?

Alan Hold on . . .

Spanky They're needing it for the fuse box.

Enter Terry.

Terry Hello? I couldn't find that wee . . . (*Terry sees Hector.*) Aaaaargh! (*Faints.*)

Phil Oh, well done, sir.

Spanky Nifty crumple, the boy.

Alan You're going to be all right, Hector, there's help on its way. Someone fetch Mr Curry!

The lights go out.

Sadie (*off*) I'm telling yous, it was a 'house' . . . (*Enters.*) May God strike me down dead this instant . . . Aaaargh!

The lights go up. Sadie is on ground in a heap.

Terry (*coming to*) Hey, what happened . . .? (*Struggles to feet. Sees Hector. Slumps down again.*) Oooohhh . . .

Alan God in heaven . . . will someone fetch someone! C'mon, you! (*He prods Terry.*) Go and tell Mr Curry. Hurry up!

Spanky Stop shouting at the poor bloke, can you not see he's peely-wally? (*Helps Terry to his feet.*)

Alan Get a move on, will you!

Spanky We're going, we're going. Want anything while we're away, Phil?

Alan For fuck's sake!

Exeunt Terry and Spanky. The lights go out.

Sadie Who's that doing all that swearing? 'S that you, Philip McCann? Help my Christ, these bloody Carmen Mirandas. Is there none of yous boys can give us a hand up?

Hector Ooooohhh, Jesus . . .

Sadie No, you stay where you are, Hector son, I'll manage, sweetheart . . . (*Sees Hector.*) Ooohhhh, my God!

Enter Curry.

Curry What the hell's going on out here? That pair said . . . Sacred heavens! Has he got a tourniquet on his arm?

Phil No, just a tattoo with 'I Love Lucy'.

Curry rushes over to Hector.

Curry What's he done, Alan?

Sadie Sacred Heart of Jesus, what's happened to my wean? (*Goes over to Hector.*)

Hector Oh, Mammy . . . Mammy . . .

Sadie What have they done to you, flower? Oh, my God, that's hellish. That bloody thing's probably red with rust . . . he'll give himself lockjaw.

Phil No, no . . . *au contraire*, Our Lady of the Bunions, this bobby-soxer with the bobby-pin through his wrist will soon be pouring his heart out to the witch doctor with the blue chin and the six biros. 'Tell me, Mr McKenzie, was it the hurlyburly of modern life that drove you to it or was you just at a loose end? Nurse, take our man across to the Deep Therapy Unit and plug him in . . . it takes a three-prong. We don't want a blackout with Mrs McCann on the premises, do we? Many thanks.'

Sadie Away, you . . .

The lights come up.

Curry Alan, nip down and dial nine-nine-nine . . .

Sadie You're going to be all right, sweetheart. The nice boy's away to phone.

Curry And don't take any lip from that janitor.

Alan punches Phil on the way out.

Phil You bastard!

Exit Alan.

Curry Give us a hand with him, Sadie. We don't want the lad getting carried past the top table on a stretcher . . . you know what that bunch are like. Ready? Lift . . .

Sadie Hold on . . . ooohhhh. There's always something at these bloody do's, isn't there?

They stagger towards exit.

Curry Could you possibly make it look as if you're dancing with him, Sadie? Just till we get him past Mr Barton and the polisman . . .

Sadie C'mon, honeybunch . . . we'll have a stab at a rhumba.

Exeunt. Enter Miss Walkinshaw unsteadily.

Phil (*catching her*) C'mon, Miss Walkinshaw, we've just been through all that.

Miss Walkinshaw God, I feel sick.

Phil C'mon, brace your knees . . . that's it.

Miss Walkinshaw Have you ever had a mother, Philip? Take my advice, darling, they're not bloody worth it. If I'd known forty-whatever years ago what it was going to be like I'd've asked the midwife just to stuff me back up, put in a couple of stitches and tell the old cow it was wind.

Phil Steady now. D'you want to hang over the parapet for a bit? That usually brings you round . . . the smell of the river. There, look at that . . . the Abbey in all its moonlit splendour . . .

Miss Walkinshaw Like a Woolworth's biscuit tin.

Phil Steady.

Miss Walkinshaw D'you know what she said when I brought him home? D'you know what the swine said?

Phil Who was this?

Miss Walkinshaw 'If you're thinking of marrying that, Elsie, you've got another think coming. You're wasting your time, dear.'

Phil Oh, yeah?

Miss Walkinshaw And he just sat there footering with his bloody glengarry . . . couldn't even look me in the eye. That's where the wedding was to've been . . .

Phil Where?

Miss Walkinshaw Across there in that bloody biscuit tin. 'I don't like him, dear . . . I just don't like him.' Hell, I didn't bloody well like him, did I? That was hardly pertinent, was it? (*Slumps forward.*)

Phil Steady.

Miss Walkinshaw Anyway, I'd much rather have run off with Clark Gable. Did I ever tell you how I bumped into him outside that sweetie shop in Well Street?

Phil Never.

Miss Walkinshaw Well . . .

Phil joins in.

I was going into town to collect Mum's weekly sweetie ration. I'd just got home on leave from the ATS – stop me if you've heard this – when who should step out of Humphrey's Confections . . . ?

Phil I've no idea.

Miss Walkinshaw You couldn't even take a wild guess?

Phil A jelly-baby in a siren suit?

Miss Walkinshaw Clark Gable!

Phil Get away . . .

Miss Walkinshaw Gosh, I couldn't believe my eyes. Rhett Butler in khaki and me, scarlet with embarrassment, just standing there gawping. He'd to stretch out and haul me onto the pavement otherwise I'd've been knocked down. Well, he seemed a bit surprised at first but after he'd got

over the initial shock he told me I had to keep cavey as
he was supposed to be back home at his sweetheart's
funeral . . . she'd just been rather unfortunately killed in
an aeroplane crash, poor dear . . . That's when I gave
him the poke of sweeties. He seemed terribly grateful.
Of course, Mother was positively livid when I got back
to the terrace . . . practically accused me of devouring
the wretched things on the way home. In front of Old
Cruise, too. It was humiliating. They had me in tears,
the pair of them. People can be so bad, can't they? And
Mother lying there with that twisted smile on her face as
if to say, 'Oh, Elsie dear, you're such a soft mark.' It was
so Clark Gable . . . I'm not stupid. I'll never forgive her
for that. Still we mustn't dwell on these things, must we?
(*Gathers herself.*) Her dentures are going down the
thunderbox tonight. (*Totters towards the exit.*) Teach
the old bugger a lesson. Goodnight, Philip . . . (*Exits.*)

Enter Terry and Spanky. Phil is lying down.

Terry I seen the same thing happen to a guy at the
skating. Tried bodychecking this doll with a tumbler
in his hand . . . glass went straight through his neck,
tumbled backwards over the barrier and broke his . . .
hey, that's it!

Spanky Eh?

Terry Six across. Pelvis!

Spanky You all right, Phil?

Enter Lucille and Bernadette.

Bernadette Maybe it was that guy you wanted battered?

Lucille No, it couldn't have been him . . . could it?

Bernadette Thought you never liked him?

Lucille sees Phil lying on ground.

Lucille Aaaargh!

Phil Don't be stupid . . . it was Heck.

Lucille I hate you!

Terry He swapped me his hockey boots for a polo-neck jersey, this guy . . .

Spanky What?

Terry The guy that got the tumbler through his throat and broke his 'abbreviated urinatory funct –'

Phil, Spanky *and* **Bernadette** Shut up, Terry!

Lucille Where's Alan?

Phil He's downstairs, waiting for Fred Emney to pass so's he can give him back the suit.

Spanky He's waiting for the ambulance.

Lucille Oh. (*to Terry*) How's your jiving, big boy?

Terry Fantabuloso.

Lucille (*to Bernadette*) You don't mind, do you?

Bernadette Carry on, you make a lovely couple.

Terry (*sings*) Well, you can do anything but lay offa ma . . .

    Bernadette looks down at his white shoes.

So? Nobody's perfect.

    Exit Lucille. Terry sings.

Just put a chain around ma neck an' lead me anywhere . . . (*Exits.*)

Spanky D'you not feel nothing, Phil, eh? You listening? I said, d'you not feel nothing?

Phil Yeh, I feel exhilarated! Feel? 'S like an electric current . . .

Spanky You're a lousy bastard!

Phil How's about a song, Bernadette? Listen, the Largie Boys are goose-stepping into 'O, Mein Papa'. (*to Spanky*) Don't wait up for us, kid, you've got your work on Monday, remember. Have a gaze out over the future. There it is, spread out before you like a great tapestry. Big Weaver's made some job of it, eh? Okay, so he buggered up the woof here and there but the warp's still fairly evident, all right? (*to Bernadette*) Hey, did I ever tell you the one about the two moths?

Bernadette Moths?

Phil Yeh . . . the Daddy Moth and the Baby Moth . . .?

Bernadette Is there some point to this?

Phil Not really . . . just that the Baby Moth fluttered too close to the flame and got burnt . . .

Spanky Yeh, you can see the scorch mark!

Phil Listen, try not to be too upset about the boy, Spanks. Couple of months in the psychiatric ward'll sort out his cutlery problem. Besides, it gives you a better chance of getting onto a desk now.

Spanky Yeh . . . it's an ill wind, eh?

Phil That's the stuff . . . look on the bright side for a change. You know what they say, kiddo: 'Better the wound that heals than the heel that wounds . . . for upon the first a scab may form which is benevolent but the second is a scab which no man should pick for fear of what lies beneath.' Health and Safety at Work . . . Post-free from any branch of HM Stationery Office.

G'night, Spanks . . . (*to Bernadette*) This way for the magic carpet, doll. Any dough for the fares?

They move towards exit.

Ta. Ever notice how most straitjackets button up the wrong side?

Exeunt. Spanky is left alone on stage. Pause. Suddenly bends down and picks up half-crown. Examines it.

Spanky Wouldn't you just know it . . .? A fucking dud! Thanks, McCann! I hope yours is and all! So . . . who cares? I'm nineteen with a wardrobe full of clothes . . . I've got everything to live for!

Lights out for last time. Curtain.

STILL LIFE

Still Life was revived at the Traverse Theatre, Edinburgh, on 30 December 2003. The cast (in order of appearance) was as follows:

Phil Paul Thomas Hickey
Spanky Iain Robertson
Lucille Molly Innes
Jack Hogg John Kazek
Workman Michael Mackenzie

Director Roxana Silbert
Designer Neil Warmington
Lighting Designer Rick Fisher
Sound Designer Neil Alexander
Assistant Director Lorne Campbell
Voice Coach Ros Steen
Stage Manager Dougie Wilson

Deputy Stage Manager Gemma Smith
Assistant Stage Manager Kenna Grant

Still Life was first performed at the Traverse Theatre, Edinburgh, on 27 May 1982. The cast (in order of appearance) was as follows:

Phil McCann Billy McColl
George 'Spanky' Farrell Gerard Kelly
Lucille Elaine Collins
Jack Hogg Andrew Gray
Workman Alexander Morton

Directed by David Hayman
Designed by John Byrne
Lighting Design by Colin Scott
Costumes by Anya Glinski

Characters

Phil McCann
An artist. Thirty. Formerly a Slab Boy
with A. F. Stobo, Carpet Manufacturers

George 'Spanky' Farrell
Lead singer and rhythm guitar with The Sparkling
Casuals. Twenty-nine. Like McCann a former Slab Boy

Lucille *née* **Bentley**
Twenty-nine. Attractive. Fashionably dressed

Jack Hogg
Thirty-two. Runs his own gents' outfitters in Paisley

Workman
Elderly. Does things at his own pace

Scene

*A corner of a municipal cemetery in Paisley known as
'The Garden of Remembrance'. A number of gravestones
dating from 1946 are dotted around this section. There
are more in evidence beyond. The ground is marshy,
uneven, and rises to a modest hillock towards one
corner. Part of a drystane dyke encrusted in lichen and
ivy separates 'The Garden of Remembrance' from
the rest of the cemetery.*

*The action in Act One spans a morning in the winter
of 1967, Act Two a winter's afternoon five years later.
In Act Two Mrs McCann's recently turned-over grave
is revealed.*

Act One

Hawkhead Cemetery, Paisley. Winter 1967. Morning. Phil McCann and Spanky Farrell standing among the gravestones.

Phil Look at all this junk. If they broke it all up into chuckies you could have a gravel path from here to Death Valley and back.

Spanky Christ, I feel hellish . . .

Phil Did you drive up this morning?

Spanky Got the train. Somebody showed us the paper after the gig.

Phil Where are you, anyhow?

Spanky The Barracuda . . . Herne Bay. Four nights. It's murder. Christ . . . sorry. No, it's not all that hot . . . bugger! Did you see much of the boy recently?

Phil Just the tail end of his coffin disappearing into the furnace . . .

Spanky I don't feel too well . . .

Phil Put your head between your shoulder blades and say a good Act of Contrition.

Spanky I had to sit up all night in the guard's van with a battalion of the Black Watch singing every number in the Top Twenty from nineteen fifty-seven . . . It was agony. You don't have a drink on you, do you? God, I can still see that coffin. Did his old dear make it, d'you know?

Phil No . . . Co-operative joiners, I think.

Spanky Did his old dear make it to the crematorium, I'm asking?

Phil Aw . . . No . . . didn't see her. Too upset, I would imagine. Not every day your only child gets battered to death.

Spanky Hellish, eh? Wonder what got into the guy?

Phil Christ knows . . .

Spanky What was it he used again?

Phil A brick.

Spanky Jesus . . . Did you get to have a look?

Phil No, they took it away wrapped in a towel, I'm told. It was just an ordinary household brick . . . nothing special about it . . .

Spanky A look at the boy.

Phil How would I get to look at the boy? He was coming from the police mortuary, wasn't he?

Spanky I wonder if he was wearing his specs? I'm just trying to remember what he looks like without them . . .

Phil Do they not incinerate all that sort of stuff separately? Walking frames . . . artificial limbs . . . specs . . . Yeh, I'm pretty certain they do. 'There you go, Mrs McKenzie . . . you'll find the remains of his personal effects in this envelope and his ashes in this one. Mind, they're still hot. You got them? So, that's his ashes in this one . . . no, hold on . . . his ashes are in that one and . . .'

Spanky Did they know each other, d'you know?

Phil Who?

Spanky The boy and –

Phil The brickie? No . . . I don't think they were pals or anything . . .

Spanky A knife you can understand – a hatchet even – but what was this guy doing with a brick at the swimming baths?

Phil They weren't in the swimming . . .

Spanky No?

Phil They were in a changing cubicle.

Spanky Together? What were they up to in there? Christ, there's hardly room in one of those joints to swing a . . .

Phil Well, apparently there is . . . just.

Spanky Jesus . . .

Phil Papers described it as a *crime passionel* . . .

Spanky Yeh, I seen that . . .

Phil Not, of course, to be confused with a 'cream tea' . . . though, funnily enough, the pair of them were spotted beforehand having a cosy *tête-à-tête* over a rock cake and warm Tizer in the City Bakeries across the road from the Baths . . .

Spanky Thought you said they never knew one another?

Phil They didn't.

Spanky But you're just after . . .

Phil Aaahh . . . No, no . . . they only 'knew' one another in the Biblical sense.

Spanky You mean . . .?

Phil Right. Pair of them went round the doors flogging gospel tracts for some Yankee evangelist outfit.

Spanky Eh?

Phil Neo-Baptist Non-Conformist Mormons with a toe in the Jehovah's Witnesses' pond, from what I can gather. It was all he could get after he got out of hospital the second time round . . .

Spanky He was back inside? Jeez . . . I never knew that.

Phil They didn't seem all that concerned at him being a head case. In fact, it suited their books. Two cents commission on every pamphlet sold plus half a dollar if the client further invested in one of their tie-dye patchwork evocations of Holman Hunt's *The Light of the World* in pre-shrunk faded denim.

Spanky He should've stuck to his Designer's desk . . . I don't know how many times I said that to him. He even got to be a dab hand at them cabbage roses you and me always used to make a pig's arse of . . . just before I chucked it. Done a beautiful one-off Axminster floral for the boss's anniversary present that Jimmy Robertson only had to touch up a bit round the borders. Jesus, I never knew he went back into the bin . . .

Phil Yeh . . . I had a chat with him through the bars when I was up with a box of New Berry Fruits for my old dear . . . oh . . . must be about three years ago. I was off down to London with the rejects from my Diploma Show. No idea who I was. Didn't look a well boy at all. Head was shaved into the wood and he had on this boiler suit effort that looked as though it had once belonged to Muffin the Mule. He gave us a lend of the belt to hold my canvases together . . . Bastard snapped at Scotch Corner and I lost two of my best life paintings off the roof rack . . .

Spanky I never knew he went back in the bin . . .

Phil I reckon it was Lucille getting hitched that tipped him over the edge finally . . .

Spanky What?

Phil Lucille . . . getting married. You know what he was like about her . . . Bananas is not the word.

Spanky Yeh . . .

Pause.

Phil How is she, by the way?

Spanky Aw . . . fine.

Phil And the kids?

Spanky Kid. We've only got the one.

Phil Aw, yeh . . . sorry. (*Slight pause.*) Pity Lucille couldn't've been here today.

Spanky Jack it in, eh?

Phil Yeh, that was what done for him mental health-wise, if you ask me . . . Lucille getting spliced.

Spanky Nobody's asking you.

Phil You know how he used to sit and drool through the Slab Room windows at her . . .

Spanky Chuck it!

Phil As she sat there at her Sketcher's desk slowly crossing the gams and toying with her Number Three sable . . .

Spanky Chuck it, I said! Lucille had absolutely nothing to do with the boy going haywire. He was heading that road anyhow . . . especially after all thon stuff we done to him . . . no, no – correction – all the stuff you done to him.

Phil Me?

Spanky Well, it certainly wasn't yours truly that dipped his noggin into the drum of Mahogany Lake, glued up his eyeball with gum arabic and sent him out into the Design Room to ask Miss Walkinshaw if she fancied going down the canteen for some black-eyed bagels with Sammy Davis Junior . . .

Phil Who was it then?

Spanky And what about that time you stapled his shirt and pullover to the waistband of his pantaloons and fed him a cake of chocolate laxative from a Five Boys wrapper?

Phil God, I'd forgotten about that . . .

Spanky Or the Staff Dance where you got him to stick a bayonet through his wrist?

Phil That was me, was it?

Spanky Jesus God, Lucille did everything she could to help the guy . . . we all did. She even went up to visit him once or twice. No . . . twice . . . I remember. Her and old Walkinshaw. For all the bloody thanks she got. It wasn't her fault he went ape. Christ Almighty, she was even going to invite him to the bloody wedding.

Phil That was the two of us missed it, then?

Spanky What?

Phil Me and Hector.

Spanky You were in London! (*Pause.*)

Phil When d'you go back down to . . .?

Spanky Herne Bay. This morning. Depends if there's a sleeper.

Phil Then where to?

Spanky All over the bloody shop – Sunderland, Skegness, Leamington Spa, Huddersfield . . . then it's the American bases again. God . . .

Phil Lucille still travel about with you?

Spanky No.

Phil The kid! Yeah . . . You never think of moving from Paisley?

Spanky Never think of anything else.

Phil Lucille . . . yeah?

Spanky Her old lady's here. Looks after the kid sometimes.

Phil What age is he now?

Spanky She. It's a girl.

Phil Aw . . . better luck next time.

Spanky She'll be three in November . . . what d'you mean, better luck next time?

Phil Not me . . . it was you that always said you wanted a boy.

Spanky What?

Phil If you ever got married you wanted a boy. I don't think you realised in those far-off days that it's quite possible to beget without necessarily tying the knot.

Spanky Pardon me if I don't give myself a double rupture. When did I ever say that? I don't remember saying I wanted a boy . . .

Phil Course you did. The night you and me got pissed at Jack Hogg's farewell party. Christ, you must remember Plooky Jack's farewell party . . . I was in first year at the Art School and you were taking over Jacky Boy's desk. It was in a back room at The Jolly Beggars . . .

Spanky The desk?

Phil The party . . . quit acting it. Hector was there. You must remember Heck being there. It was him that brought up The Jordanaires. . . along with a plate of fish and two pokey hats virtually intact. You were going to call this future son of yours after one of them . . .

Spanky Yeh, 'Pokey Hat' Farrell sounds terrific, I must say.

Phil One of The Jordanaires, ya clown.

Spanky I don't remember that . . .

Phil They were on that Elvis album Hector brung along – the one he got for his Christmas that year . . .

Spanky What Elvis album?

Phil The one you were using as a drinks tray.

Spanky Aw, is that what that was?

Phil Then after we got papped out of The Jollys, you, me, and Heck went back up to Jacky Boy's place and he had all these autographed photos sellotaped to his furniture . . . d'you remember now? There was Brenda Lee on the tallboy, Buddy Knox and Frankie Avalon atop the sideboard, Jo Stafford inside the wardrobe, and . . .

Spanky There's bits of it coming back to me . . . yeh . . . Aw, God . . . (*He is feeling a bit queasy.*)

Phil Wait a minute . . . was one of them not supposed to be the wee guy's second cousin or something? Hector . . . One of The Jordanaires . . . ?

Spanky So he kept saying. You didn't believe him, did you?

Phil I don't know so much. It was Heck got them to sign Jack Hogg's lavatory seat . . . up at the Odeon. They came across one time sans Elvis for a religious concert . . .

Spanky It might've been true . . . he wasn't a bad singer, right enough . . . Heck. When we let him join in, that is. Sorry . . . when I let him join in. You were forever thumping the back of his neck with the gumspoon . . .

Phil What was it we used to sing again? Christ, it's that long ago now . . .

Spanky (*sings*) Your eyes are the eyes of a woman in love . . .

Phil That's the one!

Together And, oh . . . how they give you away . . . Your eyes are the eyes of a woman in . . .

Phil Sssssssshhh. Listen.

Spanky What?

Phil Shhh. (*Pause.*) Quiet, isn't it?

Spanky Ya bastard. You had the hairs on the back of my collar going there. God, it's funny though . . .

Phil Not half as funny as when the three of us sang it.

Spanky No – about the wee guy being away for good . . .

Phil Jack it in, eh?

Spanky We'll never see him again . . .

Phil We could still make the charts with just the two of us. Aw, come on . . . you're not going to start bubbling, kiddo . . .

Spanky Hah . . . nobody's called me that in ten years.

Phil What, 'kiddo'? I should hope not . . . you're hitting thirty, for God's sake.

Spanky I'm twenty-nine.

Phil Twenty-nine is hitting thirty, Spanky son.

Spanky Christ, there's something else . . . nobody's called us that either. When you packed in Stobo's everybody went back to calling us George . . . even Hector dropped the 'Spanky' bit . . .

Phil Quite right. There's something not quite kosher about grown men with nicknames.

Spanky But I wasn't a grown man . . . I was nineteen, a boy. It was such an abrupt change . . . One day I'm Spanky, the next I'm George. It was a shock to the system, Phil.

Phil You'll get over it, George.

Spanky Cut it out . . .

Phil What does Lucille call you?

Spanky Depends what I call her first, doesn't it?

  Slight pause.

God, twenty-nine . . . Doesn't half fly in, eh?

Phil What's twenty-nine?

Spanky Old.

Phil Not for getting murdered . . .

Spanky Yeh, but in my line . . . I promised Lucille I'd have a Number One before I hit twenty-two . . . then it was twenty-five . . . then twenty-seven . . . and now it's thirty's the deadline . . .

Phil Think you'll manage it?

Spanky I've got till the end of the month.

Phil All the best . . .

Spanky Mebbe this time though . . . We've just done a cover of 'Mr Kite'.

Phil Mr Who?

Spanky 'For the Benefit of Mr Kite' . . . off the Beatles album.

Phil Thought you were only going to record your own stuff? You and that bum guitar player from Elderslie . . .

Spanky He is not bum. And he comes from Pollokshaws.

Phil Aw . . . sorry.

Spanky There's one him and I wrote on the B side . . . we've put it in the stage act. They've played it a couple of times on *Top Gear*. You ever listen to that show.

Phil 'S that the one that replaced *Workers' Playtime*? No . . . I'm never up that early . . .

Spanky Anyhow, Eddie thought it would be a good idea if we done one of the Beatles' first . . .

Phil Ah . . . then you could step in and take his place, is that the plan? How about Ringo? You and him's about the same build. Who's Eddie?

Spanky New manager we've got.

Phil God, we are getting serious. Guitar player's maw jack it in, did she?

Spanky This guy is really ace. Went to the Academy. Knows your Jim, he was telling me.

Phil What's his second name?

Spanky Steeples.

Phil Steeples? Not Big Eddie Steeples from Darkwood Crescent that's mammy used to sell toffee-apples through their lavvy window? Jesus . . . fingers crossed you don't make the big time, kid . . . you'd never clap eyes on a solitary tosser. You haven't signed anything yet, I trust? Aw, no . . . don't tell me.

Spanky It's only a contract . . .

Phil Listen, son, the only 'contracts' Big Eddie understands is for shooting people.

Spanky He seemed perfectly okay to me when I was in his office . . .

Phil He's a header, Big Eddie. Used to bite the kneecaps out of whippets for a giggle. What office?

Spanky Up the City. West Nile Street . . .

Phil Aw, he's packed in the corrugated shed at the back of the slaughterhouse, has he?

Spanky You want to see this joint . . . even the close's got flock wallpaper . . .

Phil He's only after doing seven years for GBH, ya mug.

Spanky Oh . . . He never mentioned that to me. He was trying to sign up Donovan at one time, you know.

Phil What – to hang in the back window of his motor?

Spanky He's got quite a number of clients on his books.

Phil And quite a few more on his conscience . . .

Spanky 'Live Acts . . . Recording Artists.'

Phil There's probably one or two of his 'Live Acts' in here somewhere. (*Reads from gravestone.*) 'Jerry Lee

240

McAllister . . . Number Two in East Kilbride . . . Now Upstairs with the Big Bopper . . .'

Spanky He's okay, Big Eddie.

Phil Sure he's okay . . . Eddie's always okay . . . it's you I'm worried about, pal.

Spanky You don't need to worry about me . . . I can take care of myself. God, you talk as if you knew the business inside out . . .

Phil I know Eddie Steeples inside out . . .

Spanky He's going to be starting up a 'co-operative' . . .

Phil You try collecting you 'divvy' . He's a crook, Spanky boy. You want to've resisted the temptation and signed up with a London management . . . or were they not all that interested in the The Sparkling Casuals?

Spanky Aw, they're not crooks. And you know we've chucked calling ourselves that stupid name . . . stop annoying us.

Phil Of course . . . you've signed up with Eddie . . . what is it now . . . The Sparkling Morons?

Spanky Shut your face, will you?

Phil Christ, he was in 2F at the Academy, Spanks. The guy is an idiot.

Spanky Yeah? Then what is he doing in Manchester right now?

Phil Sunbathing?

Spanky Only fixing it for us to appear as the Mystery Guests on a special edition of *Juke Box Jury* . . .

Phil Thought they took that rubbish off?

Spanky They want us on with the Stones . . .

Phil Aw . . . . you carry stones about with you? That'll be for smashing the guitars, right?

Spanky Just you keep an eye on the Twenty, pal. Even getting slagged on that show can shift a helluva lot of records.

Phil (*'lifting' a flat gravestone*) I'll just open this up and slide in, will I? God almighty, you and me used to sit in your living room soaking your maw's good settee at that shite. (*Sings signature tune for* Juke Box Jury.) Daraa, ra, raaa . . . dara, dara, daraaa . . . 'Hi . . . and on tonight's Jury the man who put the Dick back into *Doxon of Dick Green* . . . Jack Warner. Steady, Sarge. And sitting on Jack's helmet, the ever-lovely song thrush Miss Joan Regan – welcome, Joan, that's an interesting gown you're falling out of . . . my . . . And peering down Joanie's décolletage, that rising young star of *In Town Tonight* and *Variety Bandbox* . . . yes, it's Digby Wolfe . . . And finally, the man who knows just about everything there is to know about the music that makes today's kids 'groove' . . . yes . . . it's Jimmy Wheeler! Take it away, Jim!' Ahyah! (*Topples over with 'heart attack'.*)

Spanky Is that you?

Phil Ah . . . ah . . . you'll know all about it when you hit the Top Thirty, m'lad . . . Jesus . . .

Spanky We might not get on it anyhow . . .

Phil You want on it, George, you go on it. Never heed what anybody says. Never mind who laughs . . . if it's what you want . . . you and the boys . . . if it's what you and the boys want . . . Just one thing . . .

Spanky What?

Phil Give the face a runover with the flannel before going on camera . . . okay?

Spanky Eh?

Phil It's a very poor advertisement for the Paisley rock scene to have one of its alumni going on the box with a manky kisser . . .

Spanky What're you talking about? I was home and had a bath before I got here . . .

Phil Well, it's either your schnozzle casting a shadow on your top lip or . . . ah, sorry . . . you're trying to grow a moustache . . . sorry!

Spanky Yeh, very good. I am growing a moustache.

Phil No, you're *trying* to grow a moustache. Moustaches've got hairs in them. I don't think lugging a Hofner President about the country's agreeing with you, son . . .

Spanky Shut up, eh?

Phil Aaahh . . . I've got it. The Beatles've got them. Next thing you know you'll be sauntering into The Bobbin Bar with the wife's loose covers on . . .

Spanky Quit mocking, will you? There's a lot of good things going down right now . . .

Phil I'm sorry . . . I didn't quite catch that?

Spanky You heard . . .

Phil Well, St Mirren went down into Division Two fairly recently but . . . aw, you're talking about karma and all that keech? Sorry. I'm with you now, Spanks . . .

Spanky That's right . . . go on. Listen, there's going to be a lot of changes . . . a lot of changes. A New Generation . . .

Phil I don't believe this. What have you been smoking, Youth Dew Emulsion? You're a child of the fifties, Farrell . . . you're too old for this 'New Generation' malarky. You grew up with sweetie coupons and Stafford Cripps, not hash cookies and fluorescent underpants.

Spanky I'm only seventeen months older than Paul McCartney!

Phil That is not going to see you through life, Spanky.

Spanky You were always the bloody same, you. Mock, mock, mock. 'Many years've we known each other now? Twelve . . . something like that?

Phil No, I'm sorry, Eamonn . . . I can't quite place that one . . . Have a heart, I've only bumped into you twice in the last ten.

Spanky And that was accidental, believe you me, pal. You were exactly the same in Stobo's . . . anything you done was terrific, anything anybody else tried was up for laughs . . . especially me. What is it with you? Eh?

Phil (*falls to his knees*) Bless me, Father, for I have sinned . . .

Spanky Well, not any more, buddy boy. You're the one the laugh's on, Phil. Look at you. Yeh, okay, so I'm humping a crap guitar and a bunch of deadbeats round the country in a fucked-up baker's van . . . what've you done since you quit Art College, eh?

Phil (*sings*) Pat-a-cake, pat-a-cake, baker's van . . .

Spanky Couple of months in London, nineteen sixty-four, one lousy painting in the 'Young Contemptibles' . . . then it's back home to your mammy and spongeing pints off art students so you can shoot them a load of shit about how you used to drink in the same boozer as that balloon from Edinburgh that wouldn't know a filbert from a sash tool . . .

Phil Knock it off, Spanks . . .

Spanky Call yourself an artist? Christ, you've not even had a bloody show.

Phil I have had a bloody show . . . two bloody shows as a matter of fact!

Spanky When? First I've heard of it.

Phil Well, you don't exactly grope your way around the demi-monde of High Art, do you? Nineteen sixty-five . . . Van Eyk Gallery, Cardiff . . . and last year in Dunoon.

Spanky Dunoon!?

Phil Yes . . . Dunoon! What're you sniggering at?

Spanky That is sad, d'you know that? Is this the guy that cartwheeled out the door of A. F. Stobo's Slab Room in nineteen fifty-seven to go fifteen rounds with Pablo Picasso? 'And there goes the bell for the First Round and . . . oh, fuck me! It's an uppercut from the Spanish boy but McCann is still on his feet . . . a left and right to the head . . . the young challenger is on his knees in the Blue Corner – no, he's up – another right and left – oh, Christ, he's down! He's on the canvas . . . but hold on, folks, the Paisley featherweight is desperately trying to draw himself together – yes, he's got the Black Prince pencil out of the trunks but the dusky Dago's too quick for him . . . a left jab to the solar plexus and it's all over! TKO, Round One!'

Phil You're asking for a punch in the mouth, pal!

Spanky That's your answer to everything, isn't it? 'You're asking for a punch in the mouth, pal.' For God's sake, get a grip. You can't go around punching the entire world in the mouth . . .

Phil No, but I could start with you. 'Love and Peace' we're getting, is it?

Spanky All I'm saying is, that stuff's negative . . . right?

Phil Is this off a Beatles album?

Spanky Violence is negative . . . positively negative . . .

Phil What've you been taking?

Spanky You don't have to take anything to see how futile it all is . . .

Phil We should've got you to have a word with the guy with the brick . . .

Spanky Yeh, yeh . . . drop out into the old familiar territory, Phil . . .

Phil I don't think I'm hearing right. What was that remark you made in the crematorium again? Something about 'a wee white coffin . . . the kind they use for toddlers'? Eh? Okay, so Hector was on the short side, but . . .

Spanky I was upset!

Phil So was I. If it had been one of them wee coffins they could've got Topio Gigio for one of the pall-bearers.

Spanky You bastard.

Phil And as for 'dropping out', you're the one that's done that, sweetheart. Chanking out C, G and F on a Hong Kong Stratocaster with a gang of zombies is not exactly what Sophocles would see as 'Squaring it with the Cosmos'.

Spanky And having exhibitions in Dunoon is, I suppose?

Phil At least my work's got something to do with reality –
with the real world!

Spanky Aw . . . we've jacked in painting wee guys with
big ears and babies floating about on cotton-wool clouds?

Phil What??

Spanky Moved on to the harsher landscape of the Big
Rock Candy Mountain and Never-Never Land, have we?
I see . . .

Phil What're you talking about!

Spanky You don't remember the wedding present you
gave us? I'm hurt, Phil . . .

Phil That was below the belt, you shite. And anyhow,
that was three years ago!

Spanky Four . . . you can cut the innuendo!

Phil That's the last time you get a wedding present from
me!

Spanky I wasn't complaining . . . we like the bloody
thing!

Phil It's shit and you know it.

Spanky We put it in Lindy's room. Lucille's very fond
of it . . .

Phil Yeh, she would be.

Spanky Meaning what exactly?

Phil Well, she never did have 'impeccable' taste, did she?

Spanky It was you that painted the fucking thing! And
watch your mouth – Lucille happens to be my wife . . .
right?

Phil I knew this would happen. You do somebody a favour and it comes back to haunt you! Aaaaaargh! (*Falls to the ground, head in hands.*)

Spanky Och, get up, will you? Come on . . . Every painter's done shit . . .

Phil See!! Ahyah! Ahyah! Ahyah!

Spanky Come on . . . can you see Botticelli getting up to this kind of carry on?

Phil Leave me alone!

Spanky Right, I'm off. You can lie there the rest of your life if you like . . .

Phil Where're you going?

Spanky I'm off, I said.

Phil You can't go just like that . . . we're in the middle of a trauma.

Spanky Correction . . . you're in the middle of a trauma. Me? I'm off. What the bloody hell am I doing hanging about a cemetery at half past ten in the morning, for Christ's sake?

Phil We're discussing art . . .

Spanky The one day off you get in seven weeks and this is it?

Phil Yeh . . . most inconsiderate of the boy to go and get himself bumped off like that, I do so agree, Spanky.

Spanky George to you. You don't know what it's like sitting up night after night with your head between somebody's knees in a bloody baker's van . . . the guy next to you being sick into his guitar bag . . . the drummer beating merry fuck out of the side-panelling

248

'cos he's gobbled Christ only knows how many sheets of blotting paper . . . the roadie freaking out on Certofix . . . the slag with her legs round the driver's neck as we hurtle through the Potteries to another 'sellout' gig only to discover the road map's covered in honk and we should be two hundred miles away in Egham. And the smell! Jesus . . . the smell!

Phil It sounds a riot . . .

Spanky It's no joke, I'm telling you. See you sometime, eh?

Phil That's it, is it!

Spanky Eh?

Phil We don't see each other for four years and it's, 'See you sometime, eh?'

Spanky What d'you want . . . a kiss?

Phil We've hardly touched on the boy's demise, for God's sake.

Spanky And that's my fault?

Phil I'm going in to see his mother . . . d'you want me to tell her anything?

Spanky Yeh, yeh . . . tell her I'm sorry . . . okay?

Phil It was her son she lost, not the fucking budgie!

Spanky What d'you want me to say? What d'you want me to say? Tell me and I'll say it! You're the one that's supposed to be eloquent! I'm sorry! That's the best I can do! I'm sorry . . . right! If I'd had more warning I could've wrote something out for you!

Phil I wasn't saying that! I know you're sorry . . . I'm sorry. Christ, it isn't enough, is it?

Spanky Nothing is ever enough for you, Phil, nothing!
Tell her I'm awful sorry . . . how's that? (*Exits.*)

Phil I wanted to talk about it! (*Pause.*) Look at all this
junk! (*looking up*) Your old dear had the right idea,
kid . . . (*Reads gravestones.*) Elizabeth Boyle . . . 1954 . . .
Sorely Missed. Agnes Ritchie Roberts . . . Now with
Isobel, Raymond, Ronnie, Arthur, Henry and Little
Campbell . . . March 12, 1951. Thomas Quick . . .
October 8, 1957 . . . Goodbye. Is that it . . . 'Goodbye'?
Could they not've put 'Goodbye, Dad' or something?
(*Reads.*) Aged Two Years and Seven Months. Maybe not.
Still, it is a mite bald. Two years seven months . . .?
Hardly time to learn how to pluck the wings off a frog.
(*Looks up.*) Think yourself fortunate, Heck . . . there's a
kid here probably never even saw a fairy cycle much less
came to work on one. (*to gravestone*) Keep your eyes
peeled for a wee guy with blisters and a big hole in his
napper . . . don't lend him any of your Dinkys, you'll
never see them again. What? No, no . . . just somebody
we used to work beside . . . me and the fella that just
left. Three of us spent the twilight of our teens grinding
up powder paint for a Design Room full of galoots
battering out rug patterns not a boot in the Broadlooms
from here . . . nineteen fifty-seven. Hey, that was the year
you turned in your Tufty Club badge, Tommy son. Fancy
that, eh? Yes, those were the days . . . when a tuppenny
single was fourpence and you could go from here to
Seamill for the price of a second-hand Ferrari . . . Yes,
I remember it well . . . George Elrick was still doing
Housewife's Choice and Plooky Jack Hogg was just
cutting his first pimple. Of course, you wouldn't know
Plooky Jack, kiddo . . . He was the guy in the hand-
crotcheted face that sat next to Lucille . . . a source of
constant entertainment to us Slab Boys in those far-off
days. Every morning there was a fresh crop . . . pink

ones with green heads . . . green ones with puce heads . . .
and if you were really lucky . . . the Great Yellow . . .
right on the tip of the snorter. We used to draw lots to
see who would get to wander past his desk and casually
flick it with the end of a palette knife . . . God, you
wonder what becomes of these people, eh? Last I heard
old Hoggbottom had his own remnant business . . .
drives about Paisley in a pre-war Dodge with black
windows . . . or so Hector was told. (*Looks up.*) What
did you have to go and get done in for, ya wee bastard!

Lucille (*off*) Is that you, George?

Phil No, it's me. What did you go and get killed for!?

Enter Lucille.

Lucille George . . .? Oh . . .

Phil Eh?

Lucille Good God . . .

Phil Lucille?

Lucille I don't believe it . . . What're you doing here?

Phil I came to take some rubbings . . .

Lucille I thought you were in London?

Phil Off and on. I thought you weren't coming?

Lucille I'm looking for George . . . he should've been
home ages ago.

Phil George?

Lucille Have you seen him?

Phil Ah . . . of course. (*as if just remembering who George
is*) How foolish of me. Did he forget his playpiece?

Lucille Are you ever going to grow up? I thought they might've knocked that out of you down there. God, you look terrible . . .

Phil It's been a harrowing morning . . .

Lucille Have you seen him or haven't you seen him?

Phil We did toss a few casual phrases to and fro across the sarcophagi, yeah . . . then he went off in the huff. God, you're still a good-looking doll, Lucille.

Lucille See if he's gone to that pub . . . what?

Phil Something pressing was it? I can give him a message if you like?

Lucille No. Yes . . . bugger! If you do see him tell him to get home straight away . . . Eddie Steeples phoned from Manchester.

Phil Steeples . . . Steeples?

Lucille The rest of the group are making their way from Herne Bay in the van, tell him. Oh, yeah, and say I'm going to murder him when I get a hold of him . . .

Phil Any other time that might just've been faintly amusing . . .

Lucille What? What d'you m – Oh, Christ . . .

Phil (*looking up*) Sorry about that, Heck . . .

Lucille Cut that out . . . you're disgusting. If I could have come I would have.

Phil You're here now . . .

Lucille This is an emergency!

Phil Ah . . .

Lucille I couldn't just drop everything and come; could I? And who are you to talk? If I had come I would've polished my bloody shoes for a kick-off. Look at you . . . you're a mess.

Phil Thanks.

Lucille What'd he go and get himself done in for anyhow?

Phil I'm just waiting on a reply . . .

Lucille Well, he's better off if you ask me . . .

Phil Yeh, that's how I'd like to go . . . brick through the noddle.

Lucille What!

Phil That's how he got killed . . . didn't you know?

Lucille I thought it was a knife . . . Somebody said he got knifed in a homosexual toilet.

Phil Yeh . . . granted that would have been marginally more apposite, but a brick it was, I'm afraid. What's a 'homosexual toilet', by the way?

Lucille You know what I mean . . .

Phil Anyway, it was the Baths . . . where it happened. In one of the changing booths.

Lucille God . . .

Phil Guy was a header apparently . . .

Lucille Yeh, I know . . . Miss Walkinshaw and I went up to visit him a couple of times.

Phil The other guy. . .

Lucille Oh . . .

Phil Don't you read the papers?

Lucille I couldn't . . .

Phil He was apprehended on board the Finnieston Ferry trying to get his leg over the Purser.

Lucille Stop it, will you! I only came here to look for George . . . It's not my fault the guy's dead. Well, is it? And stop looking at me like that!

Phil How am I looking at you? I'm only looking at you. How should I be looking at you?

Lucille Honest to God, it's embarrassing . . . I wouldn't have come but for my mum. What's a man of thirty doing playing rock 'n' roll for anyhow?

Phil Twenty-nine, doll . . .

Lucille Twenty-nine then – it's still bloody embarrassing.

Phil You never know – he might make it yet.

Lucille And you know who's to blame, don't you?

Phil For what? That he hasn't had his kisser on the front of the *Melody Maker* so far? He wants to get along to the nearest Tao clinic and have that unsightly superfluous hair removed from his upper lip. That's what's holding him back, if you ask me. They do it with hypnosis . . . and a red-hot poker.

Lucille You know damn fine what I mean . . . filling his head with all this stupid nonsense about 'making it'. It's been going on for years. I'm sick to death of it. I wouldn't care if he was happy, but I don't know if you've ever sat up half the night listening to somebody vomiting down the lavatory just because they've got a gig in some Masonic Hall in Lochearnhead, Lochgoilhead, or bloody Budleigh Salterton . . .

Phil Still at it, is he? He should've taken that up instead of the banjo . . . Hey, where're you going, Lucille?

Lucille You're exactly the same as you were ten years ago . . . only worse!

Phil No, don't go . . . I'm sorry . . .

Lucille Let go my arm.

Phil I said I was sorry . . .

Lucille My arm, I said.

Phil Listen, there's something I want to tell you.

Lucille What is it with you? Let go! You're hurting me.

Phil Look at me.

Lucille Look at me what?

Phil Look at me and tell me you haven't thought of me in ten years.

Lucille What? I do not believe this . . .

Phil Tell me!

Lucille Tell you what?

Phil I've thought about you . . . a lot.

Lucille Yeh, fine . . . we'll send your prize on to you . . . now let go my arm . . . please.

Phil I've never stopped thinking about you . . .

Lucille Is it being in a graveyard that's doing this to you?

Phil Cut the jokes . . . I'm serious. Well?

Lucille You keep saying 'Well?' You keep asking me questions . . . you keep staring at me . . . What am I supposed to say? Tell me and I'll say it!

Phil I love you, for Christ's sake.

Lucille Ow!

Phil Sorry . . . (*Lets go her arm.*)

Lucille That was really sore . . .

Phil Didn't you hear what I said?

Lucille I've just had this coat cleaned.

Phil I've just told you I love you . . . after ten years. You could say something.

Lucille (*shaking arm*) I don't think I've any feeling left . . .

Phil I did try to phone you one time but I was drunk . . .

Lucille You're not drunk now, are you?

Phil Then you went and got married to Spanky . . . sorry . . . George. What did you go and do that for?

Lucille I'd just had my hair done that day. What d'you think I did it for? And you've cut off the circulation in this!

Phil I remember waking up in this flat in Harlesden . . . the wireless was on and this guy was talking to one of the Beatles . . . then he played 'I Wanna Hold Your Hand' . . . twenty-second of February, nineteen sixty-four . . . that's when it hit me. Like a ton of bricks . . .

Lucille gives a glance heavenwards.

I was in love!

Lucille Who with . . . John, Paul, George or . . .?

Phil You! I was in love with you!

Lucille Weren't you always?

Phil No . . .

Lucille Thanks a million . . .

Phil I thought, Jesus . . . is this how it feels? I felt as if somebody had punched a big hole in my skull and the sun was shining in . . . I felt terrific and terrible at the same time . . .

Lucille You could sell that one to Hallmark Cards . . .

Phil Listen to me. For the first time I can remember I was actually caught unawares . . . I wasn't even thinking about you.

Lucille I'm supposed to be flattered by all this?

Phil I felt something I never expected to feel . . .

Lucille Look, I'll have to go . . .

Phil Hold on!

Lucille Would you mind grabbing the other one this time?

Phil C'mere . . .

Lucille C'mere what?

Phil Just c'mere. . .

Lucille I've got to get back . . .

Phil I love you . . .

Lucille Mind out for my arm.

They embrace.

What took you so long?

Phil To let go your arm?

Lucille To tell me . . .?

Phil I'm telling you now.

Lucille I could kill you . . .

Phil Kill me . . .

They embrace even more passionately.

Lucille What do we do now?

Phil I've got a coat . . . (*Starts taking it off.*)

Lucille About George?

Phil You're not thinking of telling him, are you? (*Lays coat on ground.*) I mean, not straight away?

Lucille I've got to. Eddie's not going to be phoning again – he was in a call box . . .

Phil Eh?

Lucille It's really important to him . . . him and the boys. This could be their big chance.

Phil Yeh . . . there's nothing like getting everything into perspective, is there? Bloody hell, you're just after going on about how stupid it all was . . .

Lucille Yeh, I know . . . but at least this'll put the lid on it once and for all. Either he breaks into the Big Time and the past three and a half years have been worth it or he jacks it in, flogs that stupid guitar, and goes back to Stobo's.

Phil Aw, yeah? 'Welcome home, Spanky-stroke-George, we've had one of the juniors keeping your desk warm for you. Sorry to hear you made an absolute wombat's udder of it . . . seen you on *Juke Box Jury* . . . say no more, eh? Would you like Miss Walkinshaw to fetch you a wee mouthful of humble pie in her toothmug?'

Lucille Anything's better than being a bloody waster.

Phil Like me, you mean?

Lucille I never said that.

Phil You don't need to say it . . .

Lucille Look, I'll have to go . . . I've left Lindy with my Mum . . .

Phil That's it then, is it?

Lucille I've got to . . .

Enter Jack Hogg.

Jack Hello? Excuse me . . .?

Phil When will I see you?

Jack Excuse me. . .

Lucille I'm not sure . . .

Jack Could you tell me which way to the crematorium?

Phil Christ, who's this?

Jack There's a sign pointing up that way but . . . good heavens, Lucille . . .

Lucille Hello, Jack . . . excuse me, I'm just going . . .

Jack I'm not too late, am I? I'm sure the paper said . . .

Phil What is this, the Magic Grotto? Plooky Jack . . . minus the plooks . . .

Jack Sorry . . . should I know you? Oh, God . . . I might have known.

Phil Hey, don't go, Lucille . . .

Lucille Nice seeing you again, Jack.

Jack How's Georgie?

Phil Lucille . . .

Exit Lucille.

Jack Knock me down with a soggy test strip, I never expected to bump into you again . . . bugger me, eh? How've you been?

Phil Lucille . . .

Jack Sorry, did I interrupt something?

Phil You, Jack?

Jack How long has it been . . . seven years – eight even?

Phil Ten.

Jack You're kidding. Really? As much as that, eh? You're looking well . . .

Phil You think so?

Jack That is not a bad bit of material. Terylene, isn't it?

Phil What?

Jack Tend to bring me out in a rash, man-made fibres. Best of barathea this – (*referring to his own coat*) – half-lined, one hundred per cent silk . . . Suit's cashmere, wouldn't wear anything else . . . What time do we get rolling? Eleven isn't it? The lad's send-off.

Phil The lad's been sent off, Jack.

Jack I wonder if Willie Curry'll turn up? He did for old Elsie Walkinshaw's mother. Well, I suppose we better tag along after Lucille. . . she seemed to know where she was going. Dreadful business this, eh? I didn't know a damn thing about it till I set foot in the shop this morning. One of the girls showed me the newspaper. Just back from Harrogate . . . Woollen Fair annual junket. Got absolutely stinko on the overnight train.

Phil You're not listening, Jack . . . the lad's been sent off. And this is not Terylene.

Jack You're joking. Let me feel. Bugger me, I could've sworn.

Phil Ten o'clock . . .

Jack Yes, that was quite a good year for Terylene.

Phil D'you mind?

Jack What size chest are you if you don't mind my asking? Forty . . . somewhere around that area? Got some beautiful blazers coming into the shop this morning. Italian. Hand-stitched lapels. Pop in and try one on when you've got a few minutes to spare. (*Gives Phil a card.*) One of the girls'll look after you if I'm not there . . . here, I'll stick the old nom-de-plume on that.

Phil Keep it, Jack.

Jack No, no . . . give you a nice discount. Ten, did you say? Shit. There you go . . . ask for Morag. How'd it go? The lad's whatsit?

Phil How did you expect it to go? It was miserable.

Jack I was only asking. No cause to get narked. Pity. I would've liked to've seen some of the old familiar faces. Quite a few from the Design Room there, were there?

Phil There was nobody there, Jack. Just me and Spanky Farrell . . . that was all.

Jack Bugger me. What was it took him off, anyway? Godstruth, he was hardly any age at all . . . what . . . twenty-eight . . . twenty-nine? I know he had respiratory problems at one point.

Phil Especially when he got his head stove in.

Jack He got what?

Phil Suffering God, this is getting more and more like bloody Cluedo. The victim . . . Hector . . . the boy whose puny remains have just been done to a turn at Gas Mark Seven . . . was murdered by a blow to the head with a blunt instrument, to wit . . . one household brick . . .

Jack Bugger me . . .

Phil You want locus and perpetrator as well?

Jack All it said was 'Hector McKenzie. Suddenly on Tuesday.'

Phil Well, it's hardly going to say 'Done in with a brick. No Flowers,' is it?

Jack I suppose that's why the delay . . . of course . . . Post mortem, right?

Phil Hardly needed much of a post mortem, his napper crushed like a nut.

Jack You saw him?

Phil I saw the brick. Or at least, I saw a photograph of the brick . . . *Paisley Express*. Breeze block . . . about this size. Hector must've given the guy a hand to carry it into the Baths.

Jack They know who did it, then?

Phil Caught the guy.

Jack Bugger me . . . who would want to do a thing like that? I wish I'd known. God, suddenly I don't feel so good . . . (*Makes to sit.*)

Phil Uh, uh . . . you're just about to sit on our wee chum.

Jack What?

Phil Tommy Quick. Here . . . have a squat on Betty Boyle . . . Sorely Missed. (*Helps Jack.*)

Jack Thanks . . . (*Sits.*)

Phil Mind the cashmeres on the pigeon shite.

Jack I feel as though I want to throw up . . .

Phil I felt the same when I first heard. Feel free, Jacky Boy.

Jack Murdered? It doesn't seem possible somehow. . . Him and I got quite pally towards the end . . . before I quit, that is. Got him a fair-sized discount on a nice pair of tweed slacks, I remember. You don't happen to know offhand what he was wearing when . . .? No . . . I don't expect you would. Bugger me, I wish I hadn't had that egg now . . .

Phil Fried, was it?

Jack Yolk was runny.

Phil I would take off the barathea topcoat if I was you.

Jack It conjures up such a horrible picture.

Phil Just let her rip, Jack.

Jack Oooooohhhhh . . . (*Is sick behind gravestone.*)

Phil Did you get the entire egg up?

Jack Bugger me . . . aw . . .

Phil D'you want a hanky? (*Holds out a handkerchief.*)

Jack Ta. (*Wipes hands and face.*)

Phil No . . . you hold on to it. So, how's the remnant business doing?

Jack Gent's outfitting . . . I gave you a card.

Phil So you did. . . (*Takes it from breast pocket.*) 'Jack's'. What gave you the idea for the name?

Jack He sat right next to me . . . after he got his promotion that time . . . Between me and Miss Walkinshaw. She'll be choked. She wasn't at the service, was she?

Phil There was me, Spanky Farrell, the undertaker, and a bloke modelling hairshirts.

Jack Was his mother there?

Phil Yeh . . . she strolled in at half-time and gave us 'Sonny Boy' on the nose-flute. What d'you think?

Jack Bugger me. I don't know anybody that's ever been murdered before.

Phil That's one for the diary, then.

Jack You forgot about Lucille.

Phil Don't be soft. She only came looking for hubby.

Jack Oh . . .

Phil The Sparkling Casuals or whatever they're calling themselves nowadays've to be on *Juke Box Jury*.

Jack Eh? I thought they'd scrapped that? You're joking.

Phil Would that I were, Jack.

Jack What're they doing for outfits?

Phil What were you thinking of . . . some nice eye-catching off-the-shoulder slightly shop-soiled 'Barrier Reef' overcoats?

Jack They'll want to look their best, surely?

Phil That's true. You want to get a hold of their management, Jack . . . They've just signed up with Eddie Steeples.

Jack Steeples? Where've I heard that name before?

Phil He's got premises in West Nile Street.

Jack You know him, do you? (*Takes out a pocket diary.*)

Phil Vaguely. Ex-Paisley Grammar . . . nice quiet big chap. Does a fair amount of prison-visiting, I hear . . . He'll be in the book . . .

Jack Right . . .

Phil No . . . hang on . . . he's down in Manchester at the moment. TV studios. They should be able to put you in touch with him . . .

Jack Bugger me, I'm going to Manchester tomorrow . . . (*Holds out diary.*)

Phil Couldn't've worked out better. What about some of them Tally blazers you're getting in?

Jack The very dab . . . I could chuck some in the car . . .

Phil Good advert for you . . .

Jack Just what I'm thinking. And we've got some very nice flares in just now. . .

Phil You could get some big labels printed. . . 'Jacks's Remnants . . . Three Doors Down from Crichton the Butcher'.

Jack I mean, I wouldn't charge their management full price . . . how many are in the group, d'you know?

Phil Twelve, I think.

Jack Come on . . . how many?

Phil Not counting the hunchback? Let me see . . .

Jack Now you are kidding. Come on . . . there isn't a . . . you know . . . is there?

Phil You not got a blazer that would fit him?

Jack They're off-the-peg . . .

Phil Just leave the peg in one of them . . .

Jack You don't know of a phone box about here, do you?

Phil 'S this to apologise to Hector for being late?

Jack Stop reminding me, will you? I feel bad enough as it is . . . To ring this chap . . .

Phil Steeples.

Jack I think I passed one at the foot of the road . . . (*Starts getting up.*)

Phil I think you may also have passed one on Betty Boyle . . . Sorely Missed . . .

Jack Eh?

Phil No . . . sorry . . . it was a pigeon. Give us a look at the arse of your cashmeres . . .

Jack Oh, no . . . are they manky?

Phil Hold on . . . (*Rubs his hand in some muck and wipes the seat of Jack's trousers.*) There . . .

Jack Ta . . .

Phil My pleasure, Jack . . .

Jack By the by, how's the old painting going? I hear you had some sort of show in Dunoon just recently . . .

Phil You would . . .

Jack We must have a chat about maybe getting you to do something for the shop . . . sort of 'fresco' thing perhaps. Along those lines, anyway . . . Well, stick in. You never know, eh?

Phil Thanks, Jack.

Jack Right, I best get up the road . . . got a lunch date with some reps . . .

Phil Don't forget that phone call.

Jack You kidding? Hey, tell me something . . .

Phil What?

Jack Is it true that you wangled your way into Art College that second time?

Phil What!

Jack No, no, don't get me wrong . . . *pardonnez moi* . . . That's what your chum told everyone . . . straight from the horse's mouth, he said. Not that I believed a word of it, but there were plenty of others that did . . . you know what they're like in Stobo's. Well, so long . . . nice seeing you again.

Phil The bastard!

Jack I just wish I'd known about the lad . . . Bugger me, eh? (*Moves off.*)

Phil Yeh . . . bugger you, Jacky Boy. . .

Jack Ciao.

Phil Bugger the lot of you. Heh, you never told us how you got shot of the plooks.

Jack Sorry?

Phil Nothing. I just hope you catch something off that telephone call.

Exit Jack.

The bastard . . . Wangled my way in?? The bastard . . . The jealous bastard. I only sat up every bloody night for three solid months getting a bloody portfolio together after that first fiasco . . . Three solid months . . . Every night for three months and what d'you get? If I ever see that bastard again . . .

Enter Spanky.

Spanky Who're you talking to?

Phil Aw . . . you're back?

Spanky I've lost my bloody train ticket. Halfway to The Jolly Beggars, dives into the pocket for a fag . . . nothing. You haven't seen it kicking about, have you?

Phil Never heed the ticket . . . I've got something to discuss with you, Farrell . . .

Spanky It was inside a see-through, half-timbered, plastic wallet with 'Tudor Travel' on the front . . .

Phil Just what were you telling that bunch of arsebags about me getting into Art School that time? Eh?

Spanky What bunch of arsebags? Going to lift your feet a minute?

Phil That bunch of clowns from the Design Room . . .

Spanky Aw, yeah . . .? (*Carries on hunting for ticket.*)

Phil Yeah . . . Jack Hogg was saying . . .

Spanky 'S not under your coat, is it?

Phil's coat is still lying on the ground.

Phil Hang off that and listen to me, will you!

Spanky What is it?

Phil I've a good mind to punch you in the mouth, pal!

Spanky What the bloody hell's up with you now?

Phil I'll tell you what's up . . . three solid months, that's what's bloody up! And quit shouting, will you! You're in the Garden of Remembrance!

Spanky Well, I wish to Christ I could remember what I done with that ticket!

Phil Bugger your bloody ticket . . . and give us that coat! (*Snatches coat.*)

Spanky I wish to God I could fathom what's biting you. Here, you've dropped your scarf . . . (*Picks up brightly coloured scarf which Lucille has left behind.*)

Phil You thank your lucky stars you're in a cemetery, boy, otherwise I'd . . .

Spanky Hold on . . . hold on . . . (*Staring at scarf in hand.*) Where did you get this?

Phil Get what?

Spanky This . . . this! You've been seeing her, haven't you! Haven't you? (*Grabs Phil.*)

Phil Seeing who? What're you doing!

Spanky What've you been up to, ya bastard!

Phil Hey!!

Spanky I bought her this in Wakefield . . . how long has this been going on, eh? She's been here, hasn't she!? Hasn't she?

Phil You're choking me! Who's been here? Ahyah!

Spanky I might've guessed . . . what the fuck was she doing here . . . you fucking pig, Phil!!

Phil She came looking for you, ya moron! Hang off! What the fuck're you doing! Hang off, will you! Ahyah! Something about your manager phoning! Let us go!

Spanky You're a liar! You would've said straight away . . . I'm going to kill you!

Phil It's true . . . it's true . . . honest to God . . . I was going to tell you after I punched you in the mouth . . . aaaaaaaargh!

Spanky The only mouth that's going to get punched is yours, ya lousy double-dealing bastard!

Enter Lucille.

Lucille George!

Phil Thank Christ . . .

Lucille What the hell d'you think you're doing?

Spanky You stay back, ya bitch! Think I'm stupid, do you! I know what you've been up to!!

Lucille Have you told him!

Phil About *Juke Box Jury*? Yeh . . . but I don't think he believes me . . . ahyah!

Lucille Let him go, George Farrell!

Spanky Eh? What about *Juke Box Jury*?

Lucille Eddie phoned . . .

Phil See?

Lucille I came looking for you and he said you were away to the pub so . . .

Spanky Aw, Jesus . . .

Lucille What were you calling me a bitch for?

Spanky Aw, Christ . . .

Phil Going to quit strangling me now?

Spanky Aw, Jesus . . .

Lucille Eh? And what in God's name are you pair fighting about? You're rolling about there like a couple of two-year-olds.

Phil We weren't fighting . . . he was choking me to death.

Spanky Look, Phil . . . Aw, God . . . look, I'm really sorry. What can I say? Jesus . . .

Lucille Never mind about him just now . . . you've to get down to Manchester straight away for a test . . .

Spanky Test?

Lucille You don't imagine they're going to shove the lot of you straight in front of a camera, do you? Be sensible. One of you could be a hunchback for all they know . . . and what're you doing with that scarf? Give us that . . . you're bad enough with that moustache . . . Don't you go wearing anything stupid if you do get on, d'you hear me? You weren't thinking of knotting this round your head, were you?

Spanky At this moment I feel like knotting it round my throat . . . What can I say, Phil?

Phil Just say 'cheerio' and beat it . . .

Spanky Listen, I'm really sorry, Lucille . . .

Lucille What're you apologising to me for? It was him you were asphyxiating. Here . . . (*Hands him car keys.*) You'll need to put more petrol in. And phone me, right?

Spanky Right.

Lucille The rest of the boys are making their way from the Barracuda Club. You've all to meet up at the BBC studios not later than half-four . . . and don't go building up your hopes, you know you take a lousy snap . . .

Phil And if Eddie Steeples tries to force you into blazers tell him where to shove them . . .

Spanky Blazers?

Lucille Get moving . . . it's almost half-eleven. I'll say 'bye to Lindy for you.

Spanky Right. Right . . .

Phil Good luck, kiddo.

Spanky Jeez, I'm sorry about that mix-up, Phil . . . still pals? (*to Lucille*) Say 'bye to Lindy for us . . .

Lucille Will you go, George!

Spanky I'm going . . . I'm going.

Lucille The car's at the front gates . . .

Spanky You don't want dropped off . . . no?

Lucille Lindy's at my mum's . . . I'll get the bus. Hurry up, will you!

Spanky Great.

Phil We'll be watching for you . . .

Lucille Don't forget to phone me!

Phil See you sometime, eh!

Spanky (*cheerily*) Bastard. (*Exits. Off*) Yahooooooooo . . .

Phil Jesus . . . (*Sits.*)

Lucille What the bloody hell happened!

Phil He found your scarf.

Lucille That much I had gathered . . .

Phil Look . . . I'm shaking like a leaf . . .

Lucille What d'you think I'm doing . . .?

Phil God, my throat. Must be playing that guitar every night . . . What in Christ's name did you come back for? Not that I'm not grateful, you understand . . .

Lucille I had to make sure. It was only when I was in the car that it got through to me . . .

Phil What did?

Lucille You said you loved me.

Phil Did I?

Lucille Phil McCann!

Phil I'm being jocund, doll. A set of fingers round the windpipe does that to a chap.

Lucille He's away now . . .

Spanky I wouldn't be too sure. He's probably just away to get the starting handle to beat the living dung out of me . . .

Lucille Tell me again . . .

Phil He's probably just away to get the starting handle to beat the . . .

Lucille Tell me properly!

Phil Ow!

Lucille Say it!

Phil Okay, okay . . . I love you.

Lucille Say it right!

Phil I love you, Lucille . . .

Lucille I love you too . . .

They embrace. Enter Jack Hogg with a selection of blazers.

Jack Hell . . . o.

Phil Christ!

Lucille Hell!

Jack It's only me.

Phil What're you playing at, creeping up on people!

Jack I wasn't creeping . . . it's these shoes. . . vulcanised crepe welded to a doeskin upper. Hi, Lucille . . . that's a very nice outfit, if I may say so . . .

Lucille What do you want, Jack?

Jack I just remembered I had a few samples in the back of the bus. I thought you . . . er . . . I thought maybe . . . (*to Phil*) Would you like to try one on?

Phil Me?

Lucille (*to Phil*) Did you not mention something to George about blazers?

Jack I spoke to the wardrobe mistress in Manchester . . . terribly nice woman . . . said if I'd like to drop them in sometime tomorrow . . .

Lucille What is this?

Phil Eddie Steeples wants The Casuals to wear blazers on the show . . .

Lucille How d'you know that?

Phil Free blazers?

Jack Here, try this one . . .

Phil What're you doing?

Jack is helping Phil off with his jacket.

Get to . . .

Lucille You're not going down to Manchester, are you, Jack?

Jack Tomorrow lunchtime . . .

Lucille (*to Phil*) Get the blazer on.

Phil Eh?

Jack 'Venice Blue'. (*helping him on with blazer*)

Phil It feels damp.

Lucille What other colours've you got, Jack?

Phil This is bloody ludicrous . . .

Lucille Shut up.

Jack Oh . . . 'Palermo' . . . that's a sort of greeny grey . . . 'Sienna' . . . nice shade of donkey brown, that . . . 'Napoli' . . . and of course black . . . 'Nero'. There, how's that?

Lucille *Que bella.*

Phil Have they never heard of oxters, the Tallies?

Jack D'you think he'd fancy a set of bells?

Lucille I'll ask. (*to Phil*) D'you fancy a set of bells?

Phil A set of what?

Lucille (*to Jack*) No . . . a nice gold pendant, I think.

Jack No, for Georgie.

Lucille Oh . . . Would those not go better with kaftans, no? Sort of temple bells are we talking about?

Jack No . . . polyester mix . . .

Phil *and* **Lucille** Eh?

Jack Four shades . . . self-support waist . . . graduated flare . . .

Lucille Yeh . . . yeh . . . why not? That would be really nice, Jack. (*to Phil*) Cut it out.

Jack Right . . . terrific . . . (*to Phil*) No, no . . . keep it on. If you and Lucille decide you like it you can settle up any time . . . no rush. Otherwise drop it into the shop . . . Tuesday's our half-day.

Lucille He likes it.

Phil It's horrendous.

Jack Any message for Georgie boy? Just in case we bump into each other down by . . .

Lucille Did you say you had a few more of these in stock, Jack?

Jack (*to Phil*) You really suit that colour . . . brings out the baby blue in your eyes . . . Ciao.

Lucille Bye, Jack . . . and thanks.

Jack It's twenty-one pounds nineteen and eleven, by the way. That includes your ten per cent discount. Cheers. (*Exits.*)

Phil The slimy . . .

Lucille Get that off, you look ridiculous.

Phil Give us a hand then . . . the sleeves are cutting off my circulation! Twenty-two quid!

Lucille It's cheap at the price . . . shut up, will you?

Phil If I could get my hands on that slug . . .

　　Re-enter Jack.

Jack Oh . . . what colour, Lucille? For the boys . . .

Phil It's a good thing for you I can't bend my arms, Hogg!

Lucille It's only monochrome, Jack . . .

Jack Yeh, but you want to give the studio audience a treat, don't you?

Lucille Yeh, that's true. Black blazers, white bells.

Jack Bugger me, I wish I'd thought of that. (*Exits.*)

Phil Come back here, ya slimy blackmailing bugger!

Lucille Are you going to take that off or do I have to scream!

Phil I'll take it off and we'll both scream. (*Takes blazer off.*) Ready? Aaaaaaargh!

Lucille For Christ's sake, we're in the Garden of Remembrance!

Phil (*looking up*) This is all your fault, Hector!

Together Aaaaaaaaaaaaaaaaaaaaaaargh!

End of Act One.

Act Two

Hawkhead Cemetery, winter 1972. Early afternoon.
Phil stands facing upstage. There is an additional grave,
sans headstone. He is wearing the same overcoat as
in Act One.

Phil The Garden of Remembrance . . . So, what's to
remember? I love her . . . I love her not . . . You
embarrassed me. Are you listening? I said, you
embarrassed me. No, no . . . not because you were
mad . . . for me that was a bonus. Not everybody in
the street had a mad mother. Some had collections of
Marvel Family comics . . . some had army badges . . .
Me? I had you . . . transparent . . . uneducated . . .
And you never spoke right, either. How come you
never said 'yous' . . . or 'ben the room'? You were
stupid enough, weren't you? And what did you hanker
after a 'writing bureau' for? Trying to act the toff,
were we? Eh? Christ, you couldn't even write right.
For me? Did you want it for me? Thanks a million.
(*Turns. He now sports a moustache.*) What d'you want
a stupid headstone for anyhow? You think I'm going
to forget you? Ha! 'Annie Rose McCann . . . October
18th, 1972 . . . Good Riddance.' Well, what d'you
want me to put? I don't want to feel sorry for dead
people. I don't want to remember them even. You've
got to've done something while you were here. Being a
loony just isn't enough, Ma. What d'you want a stupid
headstone for? You left your monument. I'm carrying
it round with me. What d'you think this is . . . a bloody
humph!

Enter Spanky Farrell. He is dressed in fringed jacket, cowboy boots, Levis, 'Che Guevara' beret. He is clean-shaven. His hair is longer.

Spanky Phil McCann . . . one, two, three!

Phil Bugger!

Spanky Is that all you can say?

Phil Where did you spring from, ya bugger!

Spanky That's more like it. How are we, kiddo?

Phil What in God's name are you doing here?

Spanky Just fell off the plane . . . phoned your place . . . little lady told us where to find you. Helluva job tracking you down . . . Where the fuck is this cowp? (*loudly*) It's okay, Chico son . . . we've found the bastard! (*to Phil*) New driver . . . picked him up in LA. Lovely wee guy . . . Spanish American boy . . . used to be one of the road crew for Canned Heat . . . total juicehead. (*loudly*) Take her round the block a few times . . . I'll be there in a minute! (*to Phil*) New motor . . . picked her up at the airport . . . lovely big number. Well?

Phil Well what?

Spanky It's really great to see you again . . . no, really. Hey, listen . . . no, listen . . . I was really choked to hear about . . . you know . . . No, really . . .

Phil When did you get back?

Spanky Told you . . . just fell off the plane . . . 'bout twenty minutes ago. Took us nearly half an hour to locate this dump. So how've you been . . . eh?

Phil I'm okay.

Spanky It's really great to see you again . . .

Phil You said that . . .

Spanky Is this her? (*Stands beside new grave.*)

Phil Yeh . . .

Spanky Jesus . . . When did she actually . . . ?

Phil Last month. Just came up to check on the installation.

Spanky She is down there, yeah?

Phil Her headstone.

Spanky Aw . . .

Phil Supposed to've been here this morning . . .

Spanky You don't have anything to drink, do you? Christ, it's freezing . . .

Phil Promised the old man I'd come along and get a snap of it . . . to send off to his sister Fay, in Canada. He's not able to get about much at the moment . . .

Spanky Ah . . . the old arthritis?

Phil No . . . new pub at the foot of his road. Left him breaking his heart into a big Newcastle . . . totally legless. So, how was America?

Spanky Unbelievable.

Phil Yeah?

Spanky Fifty-four cities in sixty-two days . . .

Phil That's a load of . . .

Spanky . . . ballparks? Right. First gig we done was Sausalito. Twenty-seven thousand headbangers blissed out on free wine and 'red roosters' screamin' blue fuckin' murder for seven solid hours. You want've seen this. It was beautiful, man . . . really beautiful. By the time we got on to blow, the moon was up and whole band was flying high. God . . . Just wait till we go back headlining. Jeesus. Hey . . . guess who we met up with in Newport, Rhode Island?

Phil Frog Crichton from up the Crescent?

Spanky Kris Kris-fuckin-stofferson!

Phil 'S that what he's calling himself now?

Spanky C'mon . . . you know how much I love that dude . . . And you know what? He is really beautiful. He is one beautiful guy . . . no, really . . . you would've loved him, Phil . . . no shit. Him and me got pished out of our skulls six nights on the trot. Came on the bus with us . . . it was really beautiful. Christ, I love America. . . I just love it. Brung along his axe . . . we sat up the back of the bus together . . .

Phil Chopping lumps out of the seats?

Spanky Uh?

Phil Nothing. Carry on . . .

Spanky No . . . sorry . . . I'm still coming down . . . It was really . . . really beautiful . . . yeah? Hey, listen . . . tell us about your old dear. You must be really cut up, yeah? I wish I could've been here . . . no, really. So?

Phil She lived . . . she died.

Spanky Yeah . . . right. (*Slight pause.*) How did she actually . . . ?

Phil *Dementia praecox* on top of the 'flu.

Spanky Yeah . . . right. Still . . .

Phil She's better off if you ask me . . . yeah . . . (*Slight pause.*) How's, er . . . ?

Spanky Benita? Fantastic . . . really beautiful. Yeah . . . really fantastic. I want you two to meet sometime, you know? She's a Theatre Arts major . . . really into all that stuff . . . yeah? We'll get Eddie to arrange something when they get back . . . right? I've sent her and the kids to Jersey for a couple of weeks . . . That's it . . . soon as they get back I'll get Eddie to organise something . . .

Phil Whatever you like. . .

Spanky I'm in the studios next month but as soon as that's in the can we'll put it together . . . yeah?

Phil Sure . . . sure . . .

Spanky We've bought this shack just outside Luss. Twelve acres and a sawmill at the bottom of the garden . . . are you into that? It's off its head, man . . . no kiddin'. First time we went out there Benita wandered about just touching stuff . . . she couldn't believe it. Hey . . . how's, er . . . ?

Phil Aw . . . fine . . . fine.

Spanky Great . . . great. And Lindy?

Phil She's at boarding school . . .

Spanky Managed to pass her 'qually' then?

Phil She's only eight, for God's sake. And they don't have the 'qually' now . . .

Spanky Shit . . . that's right . . . right. You lose touch don't you? Benita's four go to this free-wheelin' dive in Ipswich . . . or is it Droitwich? Anyhow, it's all finger-painting and rolling joints in the johns. Not one of the little bastards knows one end of a Cuisenaire from the other . . . Hey, tell you who we bumped into in Nassau – fuckin' Rod, man.

Phil Rodman?

Spanky Rod Stewart, man. Just split with The Faces to get his own shit together. Total headache . . . wish you could've been there. Total fuckin' headache. We had this five-a-side match on the beach . . . zonked out of our gourds, right? Listen to this . . . listen to this. . . Wee Billy the drummer broke his femur going for the coconut and never knew nothing about it till we're in the air over Boston four days later. Big stewardess was sashayin' down the aisle with a six-pack of Coors for the pilot . . . Wee Billy sticks out the leg . . .

Phil What were you asking us how she is for?

Spanky Eh?

Phil You're just after asking how she is.

Spanky Who . . . your maw?

Phil Lucille. Thought she told you where to find me on the phone? Could you not've . . .?

Spanky Don't be stupid . . . I got Chico to talk to her. She would've blown me out . . . you know that . . .

Phil What are you doing here?

Spanky Huh?

Phil Eh?

Spanky I came to see you, man . . . what is is this? Hey, come on . . . it's cool . . . yeah? Shit . . . where's it at if you don't know where the fuck it's at . . . right? (*Slight pause.*) Hey, listen . . . did Lindy get that gear I sent across?

Phil What gear's this?

Spanky From LA. Don't tell me it never got here? Roller skates . . . Mr Nudie-shirt . . . what else did they put in?

Aw, yeah . . . kiddy's lunchpail with a rattlesnake handle and a picture of Alice Cooper spewing his ring up on the side . . . No? Aw, shit . . . I told them. Her birthday was what . . . last Wednesday?

Phil Tuesday . . . she got a cake.

Spanky Shit. She would really've gotten into this lunchpail.

Phil That big, was it?

Spanky They had other ones . . . Dracula's Skull . . . Ali's Boxing Trunks . . . aw, yeh, and a Headless Chicken where you put your playpiece down its throat and your hard-boiled egg up its . . .

Phil D'you mind? I'm not long after my breakfast.

Spanky Yeh, it's an off-the-wall town, LA. Really wacko. You could really get off on it, Phil . . . no, seriously. Fuckin' weird, man. The last night we were there the guy in the next room blew his beans off with a rivet gun . . . bled to death in the lobby before anybody sussed he wasn't joking. I thought, right . . . you're not taking any of these son. (*Looks down into palm of hand.*) It was him that sold us them. Who needs horse tranqs when you've got all that sunshine? Hey, and you want to see the art over there . . . Sixty straight miles of low-rise adobes on the road to the airport absolutely blootered in these trippy wall murals . . . Hey, was I telling you we're getting a billboard on the Strip for the new album? Which, by the way, I'd really love you to do the sleeve for . . . yeah? That's part of the reason I dropped by . . . The artwork's got to be in by January Ten . . . what d'you say? C'mon . . . say it's cool . . . yeah? I've had a word with Eddie. The new label's ready to sink some real bread into launching it.

Phil How come you're only asking us now? You've had three out in the last couple of years . . .

Spanky Four. I would've loved to . . . you know that. First bunch were real shit . . . no, really. . . This one's going to be different. What d'you say?

Phil 'Much are you paying?

Spanky I told you . . . no problem. 'Much are you asking?

Phil Twelve hundred.

Spanky What!

Phil Thought you said you wanted me to do it? What's it going to be called anyhow?

Spanky At that price a non-fuckin'-starter. Look, when I said . . . no, no . . . forget it . . . I'll speak to Eddie, okay? No, no . . . twelve hundred it is.

Phil If it's going to be a problem . . .

Spanky What's the problem? Okay, so nobody gets a grand-two for artwork . . . so? Fuck it, I'd really love you to do it . . . right? It means a lot to me . . . yeah? Right . . . that's settled. I'll get Eddie to give you a buzz when he gets back from Jamaica . . .

Phil I don't care . . . honest . . .

Spanky No sweat . . . right? (*Slight pause.*) 'Much are your pictures going for now?

Phil Depends who's asking.

Spanky No . . . it's just that I was talking to this guy on La Cienega about you . . . reckons he could shift a lot of your sort of stuff over there . . . a whole lot. Showed him that wedding present you done for us . . . know the one I mean?

Phil Thanks, pal . . .

Spanky I really love that painting . . . take it everywhere with us . . .

Phil Eh? Christ, it's this size (*Spreads his arms wide.*)

Spanky Was that size. Got this head in Marin County to saw it up into six bits . . . put hinges on it. Fits into a pouch this big. Never go on the road without it.

Phil Bloody hell . . .

Spanky You want to get some of your artwork over to the States . . .

Phil They're paintings . . . not artwork.

Spanky You're a mug if you don't. The way this dealer was talking you could really make yourself a whole mess of money . . .

Phil They don't all have to fit inside wee pokes, do they?

Spanky This guy knows what he's talking about . . . a whole mess of money. The entire rock industry's out there now . . . then there's your movie-makers . . .

Phil What makes you think I'm not making a whole mess of money here?

Spanky The sole's coming off your shoe . . .

Phil Where? Aw, bugger it. And what're you smirking at? They're still better than those efforts you've got on.

Spanky Eh? These are genuine cowboy boots . . .

Phil Ah . . . the 'genuine' cowboys going in for plastic now, are they?

Spanky What?

Phil (*examining sole of Spanky's boot*) 'Cobbled in Taiwan' . . .

Spanky Where? Where does it say that? Show me . . .

Phil D'you get the snaps I sent?

Spanky What? (*trying to look at sole of boot without taking it off*)

Phil Snapshots. I posted them to Eddie's office . . .

Spanky Aw, it was you that sent them? I thought it might've been Lu . . . yeh, yeh, he slipped them to me in Chicago . . . they wiped me out, man . . . (*trying to get boot off*) Well, don't just stand there . . . give us a hand.

Phil (*heaving at boot*) That's the last time you're going to a Gene Autrey picture . . .

Spanky (*taking out wallet of snapshots*) I was so broken up when I seen these . . . couldn't find the wah-wah pedal all night. Isn't she just the most adorable kid you ever seen in your life . . . ?

Phil (*still heaving*) Hold on . . . what am I doing here?

Spanky Same golden curls . . .

Phil Here . . . (*Hands over boot.*)

Spanky Same sooty eyelashes. God . . . (*Gazes at snap.*)

Phil God . . . (*Goes to top of rise.*) Wonder when this guy's going to get here with the monolith?

Spanky I used to bury my face in them curls every night before she went to bed . . .

Phil You didn't pass a boy with a bogie-load of cenotaphs on your way here, did you?

Spanky (*still gazing at snap*) Coming from the Kelvin Hall Carnival . . . right?

Phil No . . . Nitshill Monumental Sculptors . . .

Spanky These, I'm talking about . . . she's carrying this gonk . . .

Phil This what? Give us a look . . .

Spanky Green hair and buck teeth . . . she's got it by the seat of the pantaloons . . .

Phil (*looking over his shoulder*) That's your old dear, ya clown.

Spanky Aw, Christ . . . (*Buries head in hands.*)

Phil What's up with you now? You've said far worse about my maw.

Spanky Aw, Jeesus . . . (*Sobs.*)

Phil Okay, okay . . . it is a gonk. I'm sorry . . .

   More sobs.

Och, come on, son . . . One guy's maw is another guy's gonk . . .

Spanky I can smell her hair right now . . . aw, God . . .

Phil Aaaaahhh . . . It's the kid you're upset about? C'mon . . . (*Puts a hand on Spanky's shoulders.*)

Spanky You've tried talking to her . . . yeah?

Phil Lucille? Yeah . . . C'mon, quit bubbling, kiddo.

Spanky What did she do it for? What did she go and say all that stuff for? Eh? I never done any of the lousy things she told the guy . . . I never.

Phil Sure . . . sure . . . C'mon . . . put your bootee back on . . .

Spanky I loved that baby, Phil . . .

Phil Buck up, son. There's always . . . whadyoucaller . . .
Benita's squad . . . Get the boot on . . .

Spanky 'S not the same . . . 'S not like your own flesh
and blood . . . Besides, they hate me. They go into
my pockets and take money and dope and stuff . . .
Suffering Jeesus . . .

Phil Pull yourself together. What d'you think your fans
would say if they could see you now . . . eh? 'The Wild
Man of Rock'? C'mon . . . (*Holds boot out.*)

Spanky (*ignoring it*) I always wanted a wee lassie . . .

Phil Yeh, I remember . . . (*Chucks boot aside.*)

Spanky I never done any of them things she said I done.
How could I? I loved the pair of them. It was the drink,
Phil . . .

Phil Yeh . . .

Spanky But I've chucked all that . . . I'm clean . . . I don't
even smoke now, for Christ's sake . . . (*Lights up.*) Look
at that . . . (*Indicates face.*) You look at that and tell me,
is this the face of a man that's doing a heavy number . . .
So how come I don't get to see my only daughter . . . eh?
How come that order's still in force? You tell me. Jesus
God, I only want to see the kid . . . talk to her . . . is that
asking too much?

Phil Listen . . . why don't you drop her a line?

Spanky I've done that . . . sent her stuff . . . cowboy
shirts. . . lunchpails . . . Her mother wouldn't let her get
any of my letters. They've always finished up back on
Eddie's desk marked 'Return to Sender'. . .

Phil Good number that, wasn't it? No, listen . . . Drop
her a note at the school . . .

Spanky School?

Phil Boarding school. She can write back to you, right?

Spanky She can write now? God, that's wonderful . . .

Phil That's not all she can do. Quite the little swot, getting. Sits for hours with the *Broons Book* drawing skelly eyes on the Bairn . . .

Spanky God . . .

Phil Tell her all about the States . . . How you met up with Andy Stewart and Kris Kris – whatd'you cry him . . . I've got the address somewhere . . .

Spanky Maybe I could even . . . ?

Phil No, I don't think that would be too smart, do you, kiddo? You know what the boy said in court. No . . . best stick to sending a note . . . a card, even. Wish her a very late but very happy birthday.

Spanky Yeh, I'll do that . . .

Phil Good man.

Spanky Does she ever, you know . . . ask her mum . . . ?

Phil About her pa? Never stops, son . . . (*Finds scrap of paper with address.*) Ah . . .

Spanky And what does she tell her? Thanks . . . (*Takes scrap of paper.*)

Phil Aw . . . you know . . . that one day you're going to turn up on the doorstep . . . cut their throats. She's not long started at that place . . . First term . . . loves it . . .

Spanky (*reads*) 'Tweedsmuir Castle' . . . ? This is going to be costing me . . .

Phil 'S not really a castle . . . just a big house with castellated turrets, a moat and drawbridge . . .

Spanky Aw . . . Where's Kilkenneth? It says, 'Near Kilkenneth'. . .

Phil I'm not very sure. Somewhere out Loch Lomond direction. It was her mum made all the arrangements . . . dropped her off. You know what mothers are like . . .

Spanky I know what mines was like . . . she wouldn't've done that for us. Took her all her time to warm our underpants at the gas fire in the mornings . . .

Phil You were lucky you had underpants. Me and our Jim used to go to school with a sawn-off jumper under our trousers. You try explaining that when you're changing for PT . . . 'Haw, luk at him . . . he's goat his claes oan upside doon. Where's yur dickie . . . under yur oaxter?' Mothers? They should all've been strangled at birth.

Spanky I think mine was . . . stopped the oxygen getting to her brain. Know what she used to put in the mince every Saturday? Every Saturday without fail . . .

Phil What?

Spanky A silver thruppenny.

Phil Eh?

Spanky No kidding. And every Saturday without fail one of us swallowed it. What d'you make of that for stupidity . . . eh? Her, I mean. She seen this article in her *Red Star Weekly* about 'Giving Your Kiddies a Treat'. Some treat. Monday morning there's a big queue outside the toilet doo r . . . 'Fur Christ's sake, don't pull the plug . . . wuv nae bus fares!' It was always our Joseph too. He was her favourite. 'Ah'm daein' ma best . . . it'll no come oot!' Ahyah!

Phil Yeh . . . they've got a lot to answer for. I wouldn't have kids for love nor money . . . Eh? Not me . . .

Spanky No?

Phil Not on your life. You bring them up, they spit in your eye. Isn't that right, Ma?

Spanky Is she still talking to you?

Phil Who asks to come into this world? I certainly didn't . . . did you?

Spanky I never got to sign a form or nothing . . . no.

Phil Then you're hardly in it till you're out of it . . .

Spanky Have you been reading Patience Strong again?

Phil Well, Christ, look at it . . . what is there? You scab away for three score year and ten . . . What is there at the end of it? What d'you leave behind . . . eh?

Spanky (*sings*) I leave the sunshine to the flowers . . . I leave my dentures to the blind . . . and to the old folks I leave a young lad's dreams . . . when I leave the world behind . . .

Phil Jack it in . . .

Spanky Ha, ha . . . Ha, ha, ha, ha . . . Ha, ha . . .

Phil What's up with you now?

Spanky I've just seen it . . . ha, ha . . . ha, ha, ha, ha.

Phil An apparition? Where . . . ?

Spanky I knew there was something different about you . . . just couldn't put my finger on it . . . ha, ha. . . what is it?

Phil What's what?

Spanky That.

Phil What??

Spanky Have you been nosing about in oozey Hoover bags of late? Aw, my God . . . ha, ha, ha . . . ha. Lucille like it, does she?

Phil It's my face . . . okay?

Spanky She never cared much for the one I had either – got us to shave it off straight after thon *Juke Box Jury* the Casuals done. Christ, remember thon? What a shambles, eh? Pissed to the gills, we were.

Phil I don't know . . . you were kind of . . . you know . . . sort of . . .

Spanky Hopeless?

Phil No, no . . . chronic . . . yeah, that's it . . . bloody chronic.

Spanky That bad? Yeh, those were days, eh?

Phil You said it, Spanks . . .

Spanky Bloody hell, it's just coming back to me . . .

Phil What is?

Spanky Jacky Boy Hogg turning up at the TV studios with this hamper-load of blazers. No kidding . . . a bloody hamper-load! One with a big gusset let into the back . . . Christ knows who that was for. What a prat! And expecting us to wear them on the show! That's what got me!

Phil What're you talking about? You did wear them.

Spanky Your bloody arse! Maybe the other tools wore them . . . not me . . . your're joking!

Phil You did so wear one. Your maw's still got the photograph on top of the cocktail cabinet. Come on . . .

don't act like you don't remember it. Vents up to here and four patch pockets?

Spanky No . . . I've no recollection of my maw ever having a cocktail cabinet of that description . . .

Phil The bloody blazer! You wore it on transmission.

Spanky I bloody never! I might just've wore it for the run-through but I definitely did not wear it on transmission, right?

Phil I sat there in your living room and watched you. Kept riding up under the skiffle sash and choking you. You looked a right haddy. Even your maw thought so. Aw, yeah, you wore it all right.

Spanky I fuckin' never!

Phil (*indicating his mother's grave*) D'you mind?

Spanky Sorry . . . (*sotto voce*) I fuckin' never!

Phil Ya liar!

   Sound of motor horn off.

Spanky (*loudly*) Shut up with that, I'll be there in a minute! I'm talking to my pal! (*to Phil*) Who're you calling a liar, ya shitbag! I never wore a blazer in my natural and fine well you know it. Not this kid, kiddo. I wouldn't be seen dead in a fuckin' blazer. Pardon me, Mrs McCann, but I wouldn't. (*to Phil*) Right? I might've been a tube but I was never that big a tube.

Phil You still are a tube.

Spanky What was that?

Phil I said, your memory's playing you tricks, Spanky boy . . .

Spanky There's nothing up with my memory.

Phil No?

Spanky (*looking at him uncomprehendingly*) Sorry, I know the face, but . . .

Phil Right . . . who was it sellotaped the lump of keech to the bottom of Miss Walkinshaw's Scotch pie on the morning of September 4th, 1957, then told her that her shades were off?

Spanky Hold on . . . hold on . . .

Phil D'you give in?

Spanky No! Hold on . . . Billy Sproul!

Phil Billy Sproul was in Australia.

Spanky Your koalas! Billy Sproul was sitting next to me and Jimmy Robertson in the canteen that morning . . . I remember it distinctly. He had a crab roll and a Milk-maid bar. He never went to Australia till the afternoon.

Phil So how come there's a signed postcard with a picture of a kangaroo with a roll of lobby carpet in its pouch dated September the second and postmarked New South Wales stuck up next to the hot-water geyser in the Slab Room?

Spanky What hot-water geyser?

Phil God Almighty . . . the one you could never get bloody hot water out of for the gumpot, ya moron. Next to the Jimmy Dean poster!

Spanky Which belonged to me, by the way . . .

Phil What did . . . the Jimmy Dean poster? Your beans! It was either me or Jack Hogg that brought that in.

Spanky I got that off the big checkie at the Alex . . . What're you giving us? I'll even tell you his name . . . er, Danny Something, Danny . . . Danny . . .

Phil Danny Cosgrove?

Spanky That was him!

Phil Danny Cosgrove was the wee guy from the Dye House that fell into the vats that Christmas and lost an eye.

Spanky Aw, yeh . . . so it was. Who'm I thinking of? Danny . . . Danny . . .? (*Snaps fingers.*) Frankie Sheridan!

Phil Eh?

Spanky Frankie Sheridan. Stayed up the next close to us in Beltrees Crescent. I used to get guitar lessons off him on a Gibson Kalamazoo that once belonged to Cowboy McCormick, the boxer . . . which is why he gave us the poster.

Phil That does not make sense, Farrell. If he was giving you the lessons . . .

Spanky There was only two strings on the guitar. D'you not remember Frankie Sheridan?

Phil Should I?

Spanky You must. He never missed a go-as-you-please in the Town Hall. Used to get up there every Monday night and give it laldy. Christ, he backed your Jim on 'Hey, Joe' thon time. Remember him now? Always wore this light-green suit with missing teeth . . . no?

Phil I should be able to place that outfit . . .

Spanky You and me were there the night he got his head kicked in for . . . hey, it's just dawned on me . . .

Phil What?

Spanky Is this not the very place that you and me . . .

Phil You and me what?

Spanky You know . . . the boy?

Phil Boy?

Spanky I thought it looked familiar, but . . . Jesus, so it is. I remember that cherub with the kilt and the fly swat. God . . .

Phil Suddenly you don't feel so good . . . yeah?

Spanky 'Many years ago is that now?

Phil (*shrugs*) Four or five . . .

Spanky (*going to top of rise*) Yeh . . . you can just see the top of the lum from here . . . Real bummer that day, wasn't it? Yeah . . . a real bummer . . . Took me about six weeks to get over it . . .

Phil But you did eventually? That's good . . .

Spanky I remember hitting the motorway and having to pull into the first lay-by . . . couldn't see a fuckin' thing.

Phil Foggy, was it?

Spanky Tears were streaming down my cheeks . . . never even realised. Thought it was the windscreen at first . . . started wiping it with a pair of rompers . . . And you know the funniest thing . . .? I had the radio on . . . know what was playing?

Phil Don't tell me . . .

Spanky No kidding, man . . .

Phil You're kidding.

Spanky I'm not. It was weird, Phil . . . really weird. Go on . . . you start it.

Phil It wasn't . . . was it?

Spanky Start it.

Phil (*sings*) Your eyes are the eyes . . . of a woman in love . . .

Spanky No, no . . . 'Sergeant Pepper's Lonely Hearts Club Band' . . . got us right here.

Sound of horn off.

All right, all right, I'll be there in a minute, I said! Knock it off, will you!

Phil You can go now if you like.

Spanky In the middle of a rap?

Phil A what . . . sorry?

Spanky We're talking, aren't we?

More horns.

Knock it on the head, baby! (*to Phil*) Yeh, that's what we were, you know that? You, me and Heck . . . 'The Lonely Hearts Club Band' . . .

Phil (*loudly*) He's just coming, Chico!

Spanky No . . . seriously . . . it's something that struck me at the time . . .

Phil It was nineteen fifty-seven, stupid . . . the Beatles were still surrendering to Anne Shelton.

Spanky No, no, no . . . listen. There we were . . . nineteen years of age . . . right?

Phil That much is reasonably accurate. Go on . . .

Spanky Scabbing away in this shithouse of a Slab Room grinding up paint for a bunch of baboons that peered through the clatty windows like one of us had shat in their shades . . .

Phil We did sometimes.

Spanky You know what I mean.

More horns.

Shut your face!

Phil Anyway, you were saying?

Spanky What? Aw, yeh. There we were . . . you've got your maw . . . I've got my problems . . . and Hector's got just about everything you can think of up with him. 'The Lonely Hearts Club Band' . . . yeah?

Phil Eh?

Spanky You know when you're on the road . . . right?

Phil No, I don't.

Spanky You get to turning stuff round in your box . . . think back to when you were that age . . . the worst thing that happened to you . . . how you reacted . . .

Phil Do you?

Spanky Know the worst thing that happened to me?

Phil Is this getting recorded for the *Reader's Digest*?

Spanky Remember that morning you told us your maw got lifted the night before . . . papped back in the asylum . . . ?

Phil Vaguely. You're not going to tell us that bothered you?

Spanky You sat down on this drum of Persian yellow . . . and this stupid label was sticking out the back of your jersey . . . I kept staring at it. Just staring at it . . .

Phil And?

Spanky I just kept staring at this stupid label . . .

Phil And that's the worst thing that's ever happened to you?

Spanky Up till then . . . yeah. I kept staring at this label. Weird, eh?

Phil Well, you'd certainly have to flesh it out a bit if you wanted to peddle it as a motion-picture treatment.

Spanky Then there was that freaky stuff in the lay-by after the boy copped his lot. In fact, I was rapping to Kristofferson about that very thing . . . and you know something? He got exactly the same.

Phil Maudlin? Yeh . . .

Spanky He had these two chinas got wasted in Vietnam and he's driving down to Santa Monica for a gig . . . just heard about it that morning . . . zap! Smacks him right between the eyes . . . doesn't know what the fuck's going down. Pulls the motor off the highway into this kerbside taco joint . . . staggers in for a couple of shots. Guy asks him what he's shivering for . . . it's about a hundred and forty in the shade . . . Real spooky . . . no?

Phil Not particularly.

Spanky What would you call it then?

Phil Romantic, kiddo . . . totally and utterly romantic. You like this picture of yourself as the working-class 'sensitive' stunned into mute but nevertheless deeply felt pair-bonding with a clown that cannae put his bloody pullover on right . . . or slumped over the wheel of an Austin A40 sobbing your dinner up over an undersized tool you didn't give a monkey's about while he was alive. 'S this how it tells you to behave in the *NME*?

Spanky When your maw's stone arrives do me a favour – crawl under it!

Exit, minus one boot.

Phil How d'you think I felt! (*to his mother's grave*) This is all your fault! (*Looks up.*) And yours!

Enter Workman. He is dressed in dungarees, muffler, cap, heavy boots. He carries a spade and a delivery sheet.

Workman Plot One-Two-Three!

Phil Hello!

Workman You'll be . . . (*Consults delivery note.*) 'Mrs McCunn', will you?

Phil McCann! Yeh. What kept you?

Workman McCann? (*Looks at sheet.*) Aye . . . well, keep your fingers crossed it says that on the stane, son. (*loudly*) That's us, Alec . . . get her aff the lorry! (*to Phil*) Now . . . ?

Phil That's her there . . .

Workman Fine. Your mother, is it? Aye . . . she'll be pleased to get her stane up . . .

Phil I'll be pleased to get her 'stane' up . . .

Workman Gives the departed a little dignity, I always think . . .

Phil Yeh . . .

Workman (*loudly*) You'll need to put her on the barra with the blaw-up tyres, Alec . . . the grun's like saft shite up here!

Phil Thank you . . . What's been the hold-up? I've been standing here for about two hours . . . it's bitter.

Workman Och, I've seen worse winters than this, son. Nineteen forty-seven . . . now, there was a humdinger for you. Couldn't get a spade into the likes of this . . . (*Starts cutting turfs.*) There was about fifty of the buggers lying under a groundsheet over there . . . all waiting for a thaw . . .

Phil Yeh, very interesting. Headstones we talking about?

Workman Stiffs. The finish-up they had to get the Sappers in with a mechanical digger . . . bumped the lot into the one big pit. Thank Christ they never asked us to supply a stane for that bunch. It would've been the height of the Blackpool Tower. (*loudly*) How're we doing, Alec son! (*to Phil*) You don't have to hang about on my account, you know . . .

Phil I want to get a photograph . . .

Workman Aw . . . (*Straightens up, lifts cap and runs a hand through his hair.*) D'you want me to give Alec a shout?

Gets a look from Phil.

Ahhhh . . . the stane . . .? Aye . . . (*Carries on digging.*)

Phil How long d'you reckon you'll be?

Workman Well, I've yet to come across a stane that'll stroll up that hill and dig a trench for itself . . .

Phil Yeh . . . very droll. Just get on with it, eh?

Workman digs.

Workman Aha . . . getting a bit of seepage here, son . . .

Phil Bit of what?

Workman It's with your mother's resting place being on the breest o' the brae . . . 'Granny's Hielan' Hame' sort of style. You're getting all the moisture draining off the slope into her lair. No . . . I'm not too happy about this. You'll not get a stane to stand upright in this glabber . . .

Phil Aw, that's brilliant, that is.

Workman Nup . . . there's not a stane hewn that'll stand up in this mulch . . .

Phil Yeh, yeh . . . we heard you the first time . . . what're you going to do about it?

Workman Not a lot you can do . . .

Phil You not got any pumping gear with you?

Workman Pumping gear?

Phil Pumping gear . . . like they have in the bilges of boats . . . You know . . . 'Man the pumps!'. . .

Workman Was she a seafaring wumman?

Phil Suffering God . . .

Workman You know the best thing you could do, son?

Phil No . . . but you're going to tell me. What?

Workman Have them shifted.

Phil Have 'them' shifted?

Workman Her remains . . . have them shifted. She's just sooking it up here. Look . . . it's like a soggy sponge . . . (*Squelches boot in ground.*) Course, you know what this used to be, don't you? Before the British Army used it as a target range, I mean . . .

Phil Eh?

Workman A bloody marsh, that's what it used to be . . . a bloody marsh . . . all marshlands about here . . .

Phil I'm that glad you came . . .

Workman If she was mines I'd have her shifted . . . Still, we'll do our best, eh?

Phil Yeh, thanks . . .

Workman Not that it'll do much good, mind . . . There isn't a stane made that'll keep its feet in this for more than six month . . .

Phil Six months is fine . . . just get on with it and cut the cackle . . . okay? (*Goes to top of rise to watch the unloading.*)

Workman Nup . . . not a stane that's made . . .

Phil (*watching Alec unloading*) Is he always as devil-me-care as this? I've seen three-toed sloths move quicker in a coma.

Workman He goes at his own pace, does Alec . . .

Looks around for something to bale water out of hole with.

Phil (*loudly*) Come on . . . get bloody on with it!

Workman I wouldn't do that, son . . . you'll only antagonise him. (*Finds Spanky's discarded boot.*)

Phil Antagonise him? You mean get his goat like creatures with a nervous system? Christ, if he goes any slower he'll be back in forty-seven with the frozen cadavers. (*loudly*) Going to hurry up, pal? There's some of us don't want to end our days in here just yet!

Workman (*shaking his head*) Tch, tch, tch, tch . . .

Phil What's he stopping for?

Workman I told you not to annoy him . . . (*Chucks sodden boot aside. Climbs out of trench.*) Tch, tch, tch, tch . . .

Phil What did I do?

Workman Tch, tch, tch, tch . . . (*Exits.*)

Phil Suffering God on the Cross . . . (*Slumps to ground.*) Sorry about this, Ma . . . I know how much you've got your heart set on this neo-granolithic monstrosity. Ha . . . nice to see you haven't moved, Tommy son. Just having a natter with your next-door neighbour there . . . Annie McCann . . . Tommy Quick. Me and wee Tom's old chums. Right, kid? Met each other the last time I was up this way. Last but one time I was up . . . For the wee guy's send-off . . . the one that got banjoed with the · breeze block in the Baths, remember? I pointed him out to you that time you, me, and my Auntie Fay were strolling across to the EC Tea and Coffee Bar . . . He was the short chap hanging out the window of the Top Security Wing with his flies unbuttoned . . . gave us a lend of his belt . . . mind? That's right. You flung a whole box of New Berry Fruits at him, as I recall. It was springtime . . . crocuses were coming up in fistfulls . . . went nice with that blue smock effort you were wearing with 'Ward Four' stencilled on the yoke . . . You ever seen these things, Tommy? No, of course, what am I talking about? You can also get them with 'Brain of Britain' across here in big white letters . . . (*Indicates chest.*)

Enter Spanky.

Spanky (*loudly*) Come out, ya little bastard!

Phil Stay where you are, Tommy son.

Spanky See, when I get a hold of you I'm going to kick your arse from here to Puerto Rico and back, d'you hear me?

Phil This'll be the lovely wee Spanish American guy? Scabbed off in the motor, has he?

Spanky He's left the bloody motor . . . scabbed off with a full bottle of tequila. (*loudly*) If I ever catch you you're going to wish your *madre* had flushed you down el lavvy pan when you were delivered! Honest to Christ . . . you do your best for these people . . . what d'you get? Ripped off and shat upon from a great height!

Phil No . . . don't tell me . . . Stout Cortez . . . 'Upon a peak in Darien' . . . right?

Spanky You can laugh . . . I'll need to get a taxi now.

Phil He might've left you the keys . . .

Spanky He did. Where's my other boot?

Phil What's the big problem then? Or is driving yourself about beneath your dignity these days?

Spanky Lend us a coupla quid for a taxi, will you? (*Hunts around for boot.*)

Phil I haven't got a couple of quid. What're you looking for?

Spanky My missing boot. C'mon, don't be lousy, Phil . . . I've got to get to Luss to get changed . . . I'm doing a TV show at seven . . . c'mon . . .

Phil You've got a bloody motor sitting there . . . that'll get you to Luss.

Spanky And what happens if I get stopped? Eh?

Phil Anticipating a road block of your fans, are you?

Spanky By the filth, dummy.

Phil Ah . . . the engine's clogged up? Thought you said it was new?

Spanky The fuzz . . . I don't get my licence back till seventy-eight, do I? And don't tell me she never told you that one . . . where is that bloody boot of mines?

Phil Do my grimy old ears deceive me or is this the man that traded riffs with Frankie Sheridan talking? You're feart you get stopped?

Spanky I've got stuff in the motor, stupid. Lend us a few quid for a taxi . . . come on.

Phil A few? It was two a minute ago.

Spanky Two quid's not going to get us to Luss, is it? Make it four, okay?

Phil I don't have four . . . I don't even have two . . . and what is this? You're a successful rock star . . . what about all them ballparks you laid waste . . . you must be rolling in it . . .

Spanky You don't suppose I carry it about with us, do you? Eddie sees to all that . . .

Phil Let Eddie see to lending you four quid then . . .

Spanky He's not here, is he!

Phil Phone him . . . there's a box at the corner.

Spanky He's in Jamaica, for Christ's sake! (*Finds boot.*)

Phil Phone the bloody Samaritans then!

Spanky I've no fuckin' money!

Phil Explain that when you get through . . .

Spanky Aw, shit! (*He has just put his foot in boot.*)

 Enter Workman.

Workman (*to Phil*) Just as well for you I had a Mars bar handy. He's back on the job. (*to Spanky*) Is that your wagon down there, cowboy?

Spanky Uh?

Workman I don't want to put the wind up you but there's a wee dark-headed fulla circling round it with an empty meths bottle . . .

Spanky What?

Workman . . . I told Alec to have a word with him but by the time he's got the paper off that Mars bar . . .

Spanky Ho, ya dago shithead! (*Exits.*)

Workman Now, where did I put that . . .? You haven't seen a wumman's wellington lying about, have you?

Phil has moved to top of rise.

Workman Tch, tch, tch, tch . . . (*Surveys trench.*) Unless we lay some pipework . . . put in a stank about here . . . No, you don't want to go exhuming anybody's relatives if you can avoid it . . .

Phil (*loudly*) No, no . . . creep up on him, Spanks! Take him by surprise! Ach, you've blown it, ya balloon! After him, son!

Workman D'you think you could tone it down a shade? You're on consecrated soil, remember . . .

Phil (*loudly*) No, no . . . he's away in the bushes, ya mug!

Workman Tch, tch, tch, tch . . .

Phil (*turning away*) He'll never catch him . . . not in them high heels. How's it going, pops?

Workman I just wish you'd put us wise to this when you placed your order. I'm pretty sure we'd've advised a cairn,

Phil Stop moaning and dig, will you? As long as the bit with the writing on it's visible . . .

Workman I wouldn't even be too sure about that . . . I'm down a good eighteen inches as it is . . .

Phil Lean it against a coupla bricks then . . . just as long as I get a snap to show the old man . . .

Workman You did say this was your mother, didn't you?

Phil What's that remark supposed to mean?

Workman Well, I know this much . . . if you were anybody belonging to me and I was in there I'd be face down in my box right now. (*loudly*) I don't suppose you thought to chuck some clinkers onto the lorry, Alec son? (*to Phil*) You'll still be here when I get back, Mr McCunn?

Phil McCann!

Workman Aye, you'll still be here when I get back though? (*Exits. Off*) Are you there, Alec?

Phil What did you go and die for!

Enter Lucille.

Lucille Are you still here?

Phil Ahyah! Don't do that! What're you doing here?

Lucille Is he away?

Phil Is who away?

Lucille Aw . . . he never found you then? After me coming over the back way . . . look at my good shoes . . .

The heel has broken off one.

Phil Your hair's a right mess and all . . .

Lucille That's from juking under about four acres of barbed wire . . .

Phil Course he found me . . . somebody told him where I was, didn't they?

Lucille (*alarmed*) Where is he?

Phil He's away. What did you come here for?

Lucille I couldn't sit at home, could I?

Phil You could this morning when I asked you.

Lucille That was different. And take the cellophane off the vocal chords . . . I can't stand it. I was frightened you were going to bring him back to the house . . . you know what you're like.

Phil What did you tell him where to find me for then?

Lucille I didn't know it was him, did I? It was some guy with a funny voice that phoned . . .

Phil Ahhh . . . so you only tell guys with 'funny' voices where I am, is that it?

Lucille Cut it out. I thought it might've been that bloke that's got the chip shop in Orchard Street you keep telling me's going to pay you a hundred quid for a mural . . .

Phil What would he be wanting coming to see me in a cemetery, for God's sake?

Lucille How the hell should I know? He's Italian.

Phil Eh?

Lucille We could be doing with the money. If you'd been in darkest Borneo I'd've sent him out on the first cleft stick!

Phil Keep your voice down, will you?? You want the entire world to know that I'm doing murals in bloody chip shops! And don't keep going on about money. You should've thought about that before you left hubby . . .

or at least made better financial arrangements with the bastard. He's just back from the States absolutely manky with the stuff . . .

Lucille Yeh, that would've suited you fine, wouldn't it? He was ordered to pay Child Support for Lindy . . . that was the arrangement. I didn't want any of his lousy money! Not that he ever had any. You don't exactly need to hire a Pickford's pantechnicon to lug home your wages from a bottom-of-the-bill spot at a St Vincent de Paul record hop!

Phil Well, he sure ain't short of a few dollars now, doll.

Lucille And it's the one thing I don't go on at you about! What the bloody hell d'you think Lindy's away at school for? So that I can get out and earn some money so that you can get on with this 'work' you're always on about and give me peace . . . and I don't mean crappy murals in bloody chip shops either!

Phil Then what did you tell the guy where to find me for?

Lucille What guy?

Phil The Tally guy!

Lucille It wasn't the bloody Tally guy, ya clown . . . it was him!

Phil I know that! But it could've been the Tally guy! Aw . . . I give up!

Lucille So do I! You twist everything, you!

Phil I twist everything! I twist everything! You're just after telling every bastard within a radius of ten miles that 'We could be doing with the money' for some stupid mural and now you're saying your child's at boarding school so you can go out and work so I don't have to do it! Make up your bloody mind, sweetheart!

Lucille You call me 'sweetheart' one more time and you're joining your mother down there . . . right!

Phil You leave my mother out of this . . . I'm warning you, Lucille . . . just leave her out. We know you never liked her.

Lucille I didn't care one way or the other about her, ya stupid pig. It was you that never liked her . . . don't lam that onto me!

Phil What're you talking about? That woman was a saint! Me . . . never liked her! I worshipped my mother!

Lucille She embarrassed you . . . you said it yourself!

Phil When? When did I say that?

Lucille Like I embarrass you!

Phil That's right . . . change the subject! What're we getting now? What's this 'Like I embarrass you' nonsense, eh? Come on . . .

Lucille You know exactly what I mean. Yes . . . embarrass you! You can't make up your bloody mind how to behave in front of other people when you're with me . . . God, you can't even make up your mind when the pair of us are by ourselves! One minute it's all abject apologies . . . the next thing it's threatening to punch me in the mouth. And over what? Over what? Christ alone knows! If you were that desperate to do 'something' you'd do it and quit blaming everybody else. Well, not this mug, buster. I learnt my lesson from that other shit.

Phil Maybe you should've stuck to that other shit!

Lucille Maybe I should at that. At least he was consistent. We all knew he was rotten. What is up with you?

Phil What's up with me! Me! Look, I'm sorry . . . right!

Lucille Don't come near me!

Phil I said I was sorry! What d'you want me to do . . . go down on my knees? You're not on, sister!

Lucille Aaaaaargh!

Phil What've I said now?

Lucille Leave me alone!

Phil Ach, bugger off . . .

Lucille You bugger off!

Phil How can I bugger off? I'm waiting to take a snapshot! (*Pause.*) And how come you twigged it was him anyhow?

Lucille What?

Phil See, if you're lying to me, I'll kill you . . .

Lucille What're you on about now, ya lunatic?

Phil Don't call me that! The guy with the funny voice – how come you knew it was George . . . eh?

Lucille He was phoning for George . . . get it right!

Phil Phoning for him then!

Lucille It was something he said . . .

Phil Speak up, for God's sake.

Lucille It was something he said! I only tumbled to it later . . .

Phil What?

Lucille 'The boss said to thank you for the photos . . . her hair's just how he remembers it.' I thought it was the Tally guy talking about those stupid sketches you showed me . . .

Phil What stupid sketches!

Lucille For the mural . . . Lady Godiva sitting side-saddle on the black pudding!

Phil Aw, yeh . . . right.

Lucille Then when I was looking through the wardrobe to send off Lindy's gymshoes I saw the photographs were away . . .

Phil What're you looking at me like that for? He's her father, isn't he?

Lucille That doesn't mean you can send him snaps of her without telling me. His mother's got copies . . . he could've got them off her, ya idiot.

Phil Where's the harm in sending the guy some snapshots?

Lucille What has he been asking you? Are you listening? I said, what've you been telling him about Lindy?

Phil I never told him anything. We were just rapping . . .

Lucille Wrapping what? What else were you giving him?

Phil The same as you're giving me right now, Lucille . . . a royal pain!

Lucille Well, you deserve it! I've never come across such a stupid individual in all my born life. Is this the Dux of St Saviour's Huts I'm talking to? The six-year-old that won a ten-shilling Windsor and Newton voucher for a pastel rendering of 'Mother and Son' in nineteen forty-four? Take it from me, pal . . . you grew up into a right dough-heid. You were so telling him stuff . . . I can see by your face!

Phil Look, will you get it into your thick skull I did not tell him anything . . . now, shut up, will you! (*Pause.*) What am I supposed to say to the guy, for God's sake? That she never got a cake for her birthday? That she never went to the Kelvin Hall Shows with her granny? That she never . . .

Lucille That is quite a bloody lot, you know!

Phil It's hardly the story of her life, is it?

Lucille And how would you know? You never take the slightest interest, do you? Well, do you?

Phil She's his! Not mine! Yours and his!

Silence.

Listen . . . I didn't mean. . .

Lucille You never do, do you!

Phil I didn't mean it . . . okay?

Silence.

D'you hear me? I didn't mean it . . . I'm sorry.

Lucille You're always sorry . . . I'm sick to bloody death of it.

Phil What was that?

Lucille I said, it could've been worse . . . you could've blabbed about her new sch . . . aw, God, you never, ya lunkhead! Aaaaaaaargh! See you, Phil McCann!

Phil Calm down . . . calm down . . .

Lucille How could you be so dumb, ya stupid bastard?!

Phil Will you please calm down!

Lucille Calm down! You don't know what he's like. He'll stop at nothing now to find out where that school is!

Phil Get a grip of yourself . . .

Lucille You know fine well he got me outside that Sheriff Court and said if I ever let Lindy out of my sight for one second . . .

Phil He's only going to drop her a note . . .

Lucille You don't mean you gave him the address!? Aw, Jesus God in heaven! (*Puts heel-less shoe on and makes to leave.*)

Phil Hold on . . . hold on . . . (*Stops her.*)

Lucille Let me go, you swine! Let me go . . . I'm warning you!

Phil (*holding her*) He's only away seeing to his stupid motor . . .

Lucille He's got a car!?

Phil No, no, a Kellogg's cut-out of the John Cobb Special with a rubber band and a wind-up key . . . Course he's got a car.

Lucille Let me go! Aaaaargh . . . I hate you!

Phil Will you shut your face and listen for a second! He's away seeing to the car 'cos the lovely wee Hispanic roadie he picked up in downtown LA got severely narked at having to hang about for His Highness, so he took off into the bush with a bottle of tequila . . . only to return a short time later stoned out of his noddle and looking to 'customise' the boss's transport with the now apparently empty container . . . namely, one glass beaker bearing the legend 'Not To Be Taken Internally', right?

Lucille What??

Phil You're not going to make me say all that again. Just get it into your head he's not going anywhere at the

moment . . . he's stymied. Look, here's old Carnalachie.
He'll set the record straight.

Lucille I still hate you! Aaaaaaaa . . . my arm!

Enter Workman.

Phil Tell the lady . . . Buffalo Bill's at your back . . . right?

Workman Is he? (*Peers over shoulder.*)

Phil The guy in the strange boots . . .

Workman Alec, you mean?

Phil The guy with the hairdo and the Cyril Lord 'designer'
jeans!

Workman Aye, Alec . . . what about him?

Lucille Did somebody drive off in a motor's what he's
asking?

Workman Aye, but . . .

Lucille See that!

Phil It's not my bloody fault! Where're you off to?

Lucille To phone the school, ya cretin! Ahyah! (*She
starts to limp off but cockles.*)

Phil I'll go! Give her a hand up, will you! What'll I tell
them?

Lucille On no account to let him see her . . . He does
not have access. Ow . . . He's liable to cram her into his
boot and blow . . .

Phil Right. (*Exits.*)

Lucille Hell, shit, and fornication!

Workman You'll be one of the family up to pay their
respects, like?

Lucille (*clasping ankle*) Ohyah ohyah . . .

Workman (*at trench*) Of course, you could always apply a waterproof membrane and hope for the best . . .

Lucille Eh?

Workman Still no guarantee she'd ever stand completely upright under her own steam . . .

Lucille Are you talking to the doctor down there?

Workman Aw . . . she was a medical man, was she? I got the impression she might've been a matelot . . .

Re-enter Phil out of breath.

Lucille Did you get through!

Phil Give us a chance . . . I only got as far as the gravel path . . . I need change!

Lucille See you! Ask him for some . . .

Phil (*to Workman*) Any change, pal?

Workman No . . . In fact, it's getting more and more like the Okeyfenoky Swamp every minute . . .

Phil Jeesus . . .

Lucille Reverse the charges . . . only hurry up!

Phil I'm going! I'm going! Here . . . (*Hands her the camera.*)

Lucille What's this??

Phil The memorial tablet . . . if he gets it up while I'm away snap it quick before it sinks . . . you're a doll! (*Exits.*)

Workman Then again, you could think of introducing some concrete piles down there . . . tie them onto the

base. Mind you, there's no saying that would do it. The
Army tried that with their tank targets during the war . . .
first spit of rain the bloody lot of them shot into the air
like clay pigeons. They'd've been better using the buggers
for ack-ack practice. . . (*loudly*) Isn't that right, Alec? I'm
telling the chap, McCunn here, about . . . (*Turns to see
Lucille.*) Oh . . . Aw, aye . . . about this being an aquatic
shooting gallery!

Lucille Going to keep your voice down . . . it's going
right through my ankle.

Workman Alec was one of the first conscripts, you
know.

Lucille How fascinating.

Workman By the time they got him into uniform the
Yanks were doing the boogie-woogie doon the Shams
Aleesey . . .

Lucille Are you going to be much longer getting this
stupid stone up?

Workman We're doing our best, hen.

Lucille That's fine. Only it'll be pitch-dark soon . . .
(*Examines camera. Notices absence of flash.*) What're
we going to do about lighting it?

Workman Ah . . . you're thinking of having the 'Eternal
Flame' burning, sort of style? Aye, that's proving quite
popular across the water, I hear. Mark you, I never seen
nothing on the delivery sheet about that. Might be a
good few days before we can lay on the gas supply . . .
(*There is a metallic clang as his spade hits object in
trench.*) Hello . . . you might be in luck . . .

Lucille The photographs . . . for sending to his late
mother's sister-in-law . . .

Workman No . . . I thought we might've struck a gas main there, hen. (*Examines trench.*) Of course, there's always your paraffin model . . . that comes in an awful lot cheaper . . . Burns with a deep-blue flame.

Lucille You not got anything in green? She was a Catholic.

Workman (*hits object, another clang*) What the bloody hell is this?

Lucille If it's a box of Spanish doubloons you and me'll go halvers . . . don't let on to his mother . . . right?

Enter Spanky suddenly. He is mud-spattered, dishevelled, his jacket torn.

Spanky Aha!

Lucille Aaaaaaaaaaaaayah!

Together What're you doing here!?

Spanky Good God . . .

Lucille Good grief . . .

Workman (*staring down hole*) Good Christ . . .

Spanky I thought you were my roadie there . . .

Lucille Thanks a million!

Spanky No . . . you've got exactly the same hairstyle from the back . . . Good grief . . .

Lucille Good Christ . . .

Workman (*still staring down hole*) Good God . . .

Lucille I thought you were away in your motor?

Spanky Eh?

Lucille (*to Workman*) Hoi . . . I asked you if he went
away in his car and you said . . .

Workman No, no . . . you asked me if 'somebody' went
away in a car . . . it was the other fulla . . . the meths
drinker in the technicolour troosers . . .

Spanky What?? (*Races to top of rise.*) Shiiiiiiiiiiit!

Lucille You had me worried sick, George Farrell!

Spanky If he trashes that limo blood will be spilt!

Lucille Are you listening to me?

Workman (*peering into trench*) She's a bad-looking
bugger all right . . .

Spanky It's not even insured or nothing. What am
I talking about! It's not even paid for . . . aw, shit!

Lucille I said, you really had me upset, ya pig!

Spanky Huh!?

Lucille I still am upset . . . look at me . . .

Spanky What?

Lucille Look at me!

Spanky I am looking at you. God, you're still one good-
looking doll, Lucille . . .

Lucille Shut up! You realise you had me climbing the
walls with your capers!

Spanky Aw, God . . . don't tell us it's hit the music press
over here already!? Shit! Eddie said he was going to take
care of it. Hey, listen . . . no, listen . . . I'm absolutely
swore off the hard stuff now. No, seriously . . . I mean it,
for keeps this time . . . honest. Anyhow, it wasn't that

big a disaster. Who needs that kinda bread? Look at the Stones when they done their first Stateside tour . . .

Lucille I'm talking about our daughter!

Spanky Yeh . . . how is she? Phil was saying something about a new school somewhere . . .

Lucille Yeh . . . he even gave you the address!

Spanky Shit, so he did . . . (*Puts hand to pocket, which is now hanging off.*) Don't tell us I've lost it . . . aw, stroll on . . . look at the bloody jacket . . . six hundred bucks down the toilet . . . (*Takes it off.*) I'll kill that wee kid-on Yankee fucker when I get a hold of him. Chased him through a turnip field for about seven miles . . . know what he done? No, seriously . . . Sat down on a pile of neeps and smoked a whole joint while I'm hanging from the barbed wire . . . are you into that? Never even offered us a toke. (*Flings jacket over tombstone.*) Hey, is that a camera?

Lucille Eh?

Spanky Let's see it . . . (*Grabs camera.*) No, no . . . stay where you are, doll . . . (*Squints through viewfinder.*) I've got a Pentax in the motor but it's knackered . . . wee bastard's been using it for a bottle-opener . . .

Lucille What're you doing, ya creep?

Spanky Aw, come on, sweetheart . . . you can do better than that . . . big smile for Georgie . . . (*Snaps.*) Yeah . . . (*Snaps.*)

Lucille Give me that back!

Spanky God, you're still a good-looking doll, Lucille . . . (*Snaps.*) Anybody ever tell you that? No . . . don't move. (*Snaps.*)

Lucille Will you stop giving us a showing-up, George Farrell? See if it wasn't for this ankle . . .

Spanky Hey . . . d'you know how you look? Stay right where you are. (*Snaps.*) No . . . listen . . . seriously . . . (*Snaps.*) Remember you and me went on that . . . picnic? (*Snaps.*)

Lucille This is ridiculous . . .

Workman Does any of yous belong to this tarpaulin . . . no? (*Lifts Spanky's jacket.*)

Lucille What picnic?

Spanky To Inverbeg . . . (*Snaps.*) Just before we got married. (*Snaps.*) D'you not remember? We drove down in the old heap . . . (*Snaps.*) You looked sensational that day . . . (*Snaps.*) C'mon, doll . . . don't tell us you don't recall . . . (*Snaps.*) We fought like cat and dog. (*Snaps.*) You were six weeks pregnant . . . (*Stops dead.*) Hey . . . shit! Don't tell me!

Lucille You dare say a word to him and I'll murder you!

Spanky Shiiit! Wait till I tell Benita. (*Snaps.*)

Lucille Who's Benita?

Spanky Chico's young sister . . . (*Snaps.*)

Lucille Who's Chico?

Spanky Benita's big bree . . . (*Snaps.*)

Workman No . . . we'll need a bit more wadding round her yet . . .

Spanky (*coming to end of spool*) Shit . . .

Lucille You wouldn't like to quit saying that, would you? Only I'm feeling slightly queasy right now . . .

Spanky Yeh . . . shit . . . sorry. You used to be sick as a pig when you were carrying Lindy . . . right? (*Unloads camera.*)

Lucille Thanks . . .

Spanky Where did I fling that jacket? (*Sticks spool in jeans pocket.*) I'm sure I had a jacket with us . . . hey, listen . . . I was going to send her a Christmas present. Lindy . . . yeah?

Lucille What?

Spanky What kind of stuff is she into right now? I'll get Eddie to pick her out something special . . . you can send it on to her . . . yeah? Hey . . . did Phil tell you I was shipping a whole mess of gear over from the States for her?

Lucille Gear?

Spanky Bunch of cowboy shirts . . . coupla pairs of roller-skating boots . . . aw, and a honey of a lunchpail. You want to get a load of this . . . really tasteful. You wouldn't be a pal and send them on to this school of hers, would you, gorgeous?

Lucille Me . . . ? Send them on . . . ?

Spanky Once they arrive. That's not asking too much, is it?

Lucille No, no . . . only . . .

Spanky Only what? They are allowed to get parcels from their folks, aren't they?

Lucille Yeh, yeh . . . but . . .

Spanky Alcatraz, yeh . . . you can see them drawing the line at . . . ah . . . I see what you're getting at. Soon as one of the staff claps eyes on this lunchpail . . . zap . . . it's straight into the old doompher . . . right?

Lucille moves across.

Shit . . . you can't trust any of these bastards, can you?

Lucille moves closer.

Don't worry, doll, if anything goes missing I can always get Eddie to . . .

She puts her arms around his neck.

Hey . . . what is this?

Lucille This is for being an even bigger balloon than I ever remembered . . .

Spanky Eh?

She kisses him.

I don't get it . . .

Lucille Good . . . let's keep it that way . . . And this is from Lindy . . . (*Kisses him again.*)

Spanky It's only a seventeen-dollar-fifty lunchpail . . .

Enter Phil.

Phil I managed to get through to the janitor eventually but he said . . . heh, what the bloody hell's going on here?

Workman (*passing him on way out*) I'm going to get a pail of cold watter to chuck over her . . . (*Exits.*)

Lucille Hi . . .

Phil What is this! You're supposed to be off cramming an innocent child into the boot of a Daimler Sovereign, ya bastard! Get your manky paws off my wife!

Sound of motor horn.

Spanky (*loudly*) I'm there, Chico baby! (*Tries to disentangle himself.*) I'm there already!

Lucille (*to Phil*) You want to see your face . . . it's a picture . . .

Phil And yours is going to be a masterpiece when I get you home! (*to Spanky*) Right, you!

Spanky Listen . . . great seeing you again, man . . . sorry, I've really got to zap off . . .

Phil You're not going anywhere just yet, pal! Get them up!

Lucille Don't you dare, George. (*to Phil*) Will you behave like an adult, please?

Phil Why should I? You don't. You heard, Farrell . . . get them up!

Spanky Listen . . . I'll have a word with Eddie . . . see if he can get them to go to three hundred on the sleeve, yeah? (*to Lucille*) Hey . . . I never told you. I've just bought a rabbit hutch in the Trossachs. You and the boy here must come over . . . I'll get Eddie to arrange it . . .

Phil dunts him on the back of the head.

Ohyah!

Lucille Stop that, you!

Spanky Ahyah!

Sound of horn.

You pump that horn once more and you're getting offed, ya gaucho scumbag! Hey . . . that's not a bad title for the album . . . Spanky Farrell's 'Gaucho Scumbag'. (*to Phil*) D'you want a pencil to take that down?

Phil Are you going to defend yourself or do I have to thrash you first!

Lucille Och, give us peace . . . and quit dancing about like that . . . it looks really stupid in those trousers. (*to Spanky*) When're we going to see you again?

Phil Stay out of this, Lucille . . . this is between him and me . . . I'll deal with you later. C'mon . . . (*Threatens Spanky.*)

Lucille I give up . . .

Phil (*tripping over on shoe with flapping sole*) Ahyah . . .

Spanky Look, man . . . cool it . . . just cool it . . . yeah? Things are very seldom how they appear to the outsider. Tell him, Lucille . . .

Phil What were you kissing her for?

Spanky How should I know! I've got a motor waiting!

More horns.

Phil What were you up to with him!

Lucille We were going to elope. I think I prefer waking up in the mornings with a black eye and a vomit-covered corpse with the D'Ts. Don't be any more stupid than you can help.

Spanky We'll send you an invite this time – okay?

More horns.

Look . . . I really will have to go. . . If you're serious about wanting a fight I'll get Eddie to arrange something when he gets back . . .

Phil Ya bastard! (*Trips and falls to ground.*)

Spanky (*to Lucille*) So long, doll . . . you look terrific. See and take care now. (*to Phil*) Bye . . . Dad . . . take it easy, d'you hear?

More horns.

I'm coming! (*Exits. Sings, off.*) Twenty tiny fingers . . . twenty tiny toes . . .

Phil (*loudly*) You might've given us a hand!

Spanky (*off*) On the baby's knuckle or the baby's knee. . . where will the baby's dimple be? Baby's cheek or baby's chin . . .

Phil (*to Lucille*) What's been going on here!

Spanky (*off*) Seems to me it'll be a sin . . . if it's always covered by a safety pin . . .

Enter Workman, carrying a pail and blankets.

Workman Now, there's nothing to go getting yourself into a lather about, son . . . she's not due to pop off just yet . . .

Phil Eh?

Spanky (*off*) Where will the dimple be . . . caramba!

Workman I've sent Alec to phone . . . they should be here within the hour . . .

Phil (*to Lucille*) I don't see what there is to smile about! Could you not've mended these for us?

Points at shoe.

Workman He's promised to sprint at least a part of the way . . .

Lucille I've got something to tell you . . .

Phil Eh?

Workman Excuse me, hen . . . (*Crosses to trench.*)

Phil Who should be here within the hour? (*to Lucille*) What's he raving about?

Lucille I've got something to tell you, I said.

Workman These boys'll soon have the screens round her . . .

Lucille It's happened at last . . .

Phil What has?

Lucille What you've been waiting ages for, ya dummy . . .

Phil Aw . . . (*Crosses to trench.*) Where is it . . . has it sunk?

Lucille I'm going to have a baby!

Workman Twenty-five-pounder if I'm any judge . . .

Phil What?

Lucille A baby . . .

Workman Right ugly brute . . .

Phil I don't believe it! You mean . . .? C'mere . . .

Lucille Mind my hair! (*They embrace.*)

Workman I wouldn't stand too close if I was you, son . . . unpredictable, these buggers . . .

Phil You can say that again, gramps . . .

Workman There's not much likelihood of you getting any snapshots today . . .

Phil How d'you feel?

Lucille How do you feel?

Phil Like somebody just put a bomb under us . . .

They kiss.

Workman I said, I don't reckon you'll be getting too snap-happy today, son . . .

Phil (*examining camera*) You're not going to believe this, Daddyo, but I forgot to put a spool in . . .

Lucille We can always come back . . .

Phil You're getting partial to this joint, aren't you?

Lucille Yeh . . . about as partial as I'm getting to you. Let's go and break the news to Uncle Jack . . . eh?

Phil Put in our order for a blazer . . . right? You are going to have a boy, aren't you?

Lucille God forbid . . .

Phil You're asking for a punch in the mouth.

They kiss.

Workman (*peering into trench*) Och, in the name of Christ . . .

Lucille God, it's chittering . . . (*Shivers.*)

Phil Here . . . (*Takes off coat and drapes it round her shoulders.*) Never let it be said the McCanns are ungallant . . . (*He is wearing a blazer with a gusset let into the back.*) You can work right up till your eighth month, you know . . .

Workman You wouldn't credit that, would you?

Lucille Thanks a million . . .

Phil Goodnight, Ma . . . Goodnight, Tommy . . .

Lucille D'you not mean Hector?

Phil Yeh . . . Goodnight, Hector! See you sometime, eh?

Workman Ay. Goodnight, Mr McCunn . . . goodnight, lassie . . . (*Straightens up holding a tin helmet from the trench.*) And if you pass Alec on your travels don't go and drop a brick about the bloody 'bomb' . . . I'll never hear the end of it. Mum's the word . . . okay?

Phil (*taking Lucille in his arms*) Mum's the word, pops.

Lights fade. Curtain.

Viewforth High School